West Indies in England

The Great Post-War Tours

West Indies in England

The Great Post-War Tours

JOHN J. FIGUEROA

THE KINGSWOOD PRESS

First published in Great Britain in 1991
by The Kingswood Press
an imprint of Methuen London
Michelin House, 81 Fulham Road, London SW3 6RB

A CIP catalogue record for this book
is available from the British Library
ISBN 0 413 64390 5
Typeset by Deltatype Ltd, Ellesmere Port
Printed in Great Britain
by Clays Ltd, St. Ives Plc

Contents

Acknowledgements

Many people, over the years, have been exceptionally helpful to me as I collected the facts about West Indies Test cricket, watched the games, and met the cricketers and fans. I can thank only some of them publicly.

The old Caribbean Service of the BBC comes first. Then the Gleaner Company of Jamaica and especially Hector Wynter when editor; Dr Colin Hope of *Caribbean Contact*, and Tony Cozier of the *West Indies Cricket Annual*. By allowing me to cover cricket in England, they made it easier for me to write this book. As did Mr Alva Clarke, an old BBC colleague, now Head of Commonwealth Broadcasting, and Professor G.E. Mills of the Jamaica Cricket Board.

Dr C. B. (Bertie) Clarke, of the West Indies and Northamptonshire and Essex, deserves special mention. I learned a great deal about cricket (and West Indies tours) from him when we played together for the BBC, under Leo Bennett, and for the West Indian Wanderers, which Bertie himself captained. He and Learie Constantine and Kenneth Ablack used to persuade such stalwarts as Everton Weekes and Frank Worrell to play for our team. One could not help but learn from such company, which often included also Allan Rae and visitors like Snuffie Browne.

I am most grateful both to my editor, Tony Pocock, and to my wife, Dorothy Alexander. They have not only helped to weed out infelicities of style, but also provided the necessary help, motivation and pressure. Tony is an old hand at editing, and most persuasive. My wife was a sports mistress and coach, and is a member of a prominent sporting family.

With such help, I trust that I have not gone too far wrong, and will both inform and please my readers – as the old rhetoricians were wont to recommend all writers to do!

Finally, I must thank the following for their kind permission to reproduce these photographs: Patrick Eagar (9, 14, 15, 16, 18, 19, 20, 21), Hulton Picture Company (1, 2, 3, 4, 5, 6, 7, 10, 17), and the Press Association (11, 13).

J.J.F.

A Game of Cricket

'Capital game – well played – some strokes admirable,' said the stranger, as both sides crowded into the tent at the conclusion of the game.

'You have played it, sir?' inquired Mr Wardle, who had been much amused by his loquacity.

'Played it! Think I have – thousands of times – not here – West Indies – exciting thing – hot work – very.'

'It must be rather a warm pursuit in such a climate,' observed Mr Pickwick.

'Warm! – red hot – scorching – glowing. Played a match once – single wicket – friend the Colonel – Sir Thomas Blazo – who should get the greatest number of runs – Won the toss – first innings – seven o'clock a.m. – six natives to look out – went in; kept in – heat intense – natives all fainted – taken away – fresh half-dozen ordered – fainted also – Blazo bowling – supported by two natives –couldn't bowl me out – fainted too – cleared away the Colonel – wouldn't give in – faithful attendant – Quanko Samba – last man left – sun so hot, bat in blisters, ball scorched brown – five hundred and seventy runs – rather exhausted – Quanko mustered up last remaining strength – bowled me out – had a bath, and went out to dinner.'

'And what became of what's-his-name, sir?' inquired an old gentleman.

'Blazo?'

'No – the other gentleman.'

'Quanko Samba?'

'Yes, sir.'

'Poor Quanko – never recovered it – bowled on, on my account – bowled off, on his own – died, sir.'

Charles Dickens, *Pickwick Papers*

1

A Beginning and an End

1950 and 1988

On a sunny morning in August 1950 as I settled into my seat at the Oval, at the pavilion end, Allan Rae took up his position at third man on the boundary. He shouted across to me, 'Hi John, just like Sabina Park'. For he and I, in different ways, had grown up at Sabina, which looks up to the mountains, the Blue Mountains, in our native island, Jamaica. He waved as he settled down to watch Hutton taking strike. Exclaimed a lively post-war blonde, as ever taking advantage of the sun, 'Oh, he speaks English.'

Allan was in fine form. He had scored 109 in the first and only innings of the West Indies in that game. At Lord's, in the first Test which West Indies had won in England, he had scored 106. The young lady was also in excellent form, showing that difficult-to-understand English ignorance of people from 'overseas' even when they were colonials, as we were in those days. But she had an eye, bless her, for a lively-looking young man much in the public eye. In 1950 England was still struggling to recover from its splendid war effort. Things were dull, and excitement a rarity. Now excitement is not so rare, but the attitude to overseas people has changed little.

I must admit to a special interest in that 1950 tour. I was then doing a great deal of work for the BBC's Overseas Service, and the first game that I helped to cover was the first victory at Lord's. The press was housed where the Warner stand now is, but at no great height above the field. C. B. (Bertie) Clarke, who had won a place in the 1939 West Indies touring team and later played for Northamptonshire and Essex, and Learie Constantine, later to be Lord Constantine and an outstanding Trinidadian politician, helped with the broadcasting of the games. I sat beside Jimmy Cozier, the father of the present West Indian journalist, and had to run to the public telephone booth from which we telephoned our copy to Cable & Wireless, to warn him that John Goddard had taken a magnificent catch to dismiss Parkhouse off Valentine. It was towards the end of play, and Jimmy had gone off to the booth, which was near to where the present Lord's cricket museum stands, to inform Barbados of the doings of Washbrook and Parkhouse, and Ramadhin and Valentine. I caught him just in time for him to change the end of his cable.

Things moved at an easier pace then, and I remember how gently R. C. Robertson-Glasgow ('Crusoe'), the highly literate cricket writer, leaned over the tea table to enquire of 'C. B.' (Bertie Clarke) what his exact opinion of the game was. We were taking our tea in the big marquee pitched in the Rose Garden. But much of the English press was then, as it is now, mostly trivial and uninformed, and prone to 'stirring it up'. One remembers their querying the fact that an *Indian*, Ramadhin, was playing for the West Indies. And one paper wrote of Everton Weekes as an off-spinner because he loosened up at the first Lord's net by indulging himself with off-spinners, none too convincingly.

The press too were so busy – *à la* present day *Sunday Times* – trying to find brutal fast bowlers among the touring party, that Ram and Val, and C. B. ('Boogles') Williams, a not inconsiderable googly bowler, missed their attention for a while.

That first net was something to behold – not only Ram fooling all and sundry, his cap firmly raked on his head, his white shirt buttoned down to his wrists; but also E. W. Swanton, of the *Telegraph*, not yet dubbed 'The Bishop of Barbados', balancing on a shooting stick, black bowler perched above a tweed jacket of wide cut and wider squares.

I shall be expressing my high opinion of the 1950 team quite often. Beyond a doubt some readers will wonder how I can compare them so favourably with the 1988 side – in fact even with that of 1963. So it should be of interest to look over the touring party which came to England in 1950 and so surprised English players and critics alike.

First of all note the date: 1950. The West Indies had last been in England in 1939, just before the outbreak of the Second World War. Indeed, during the third and final Test of that series at the Oval, England's captain, Walter Hammond, made loudspeaker appeals for recruits for the armed services, and within hours of the game finishing the team was on the way home before, as the English like to say, the balloon went up.

Constantine stayed, and did distinguished war service. And the youthful C. B. Clarke wanted to stay on to read medicine at university, but the manager, Jack Kidney, would have none of it without permission from Bertie's father. Cables were not quick enough what with the institution of near censorship, and Bertie was carefully returned to his father in Barbados, via Toronto and New York. But in nine days he was on a boat back to England, war or no war, to become a doctor, and to play county cricket with distinction. Many of us thought he should have been selected for India in 1948–49, as were his other young colleagues of 1939, J. B. Stollmeyer and Gerry Gomez.

These two, after the long stretch of eleven years, were all that remained of the 1939 team. During the war years, as was to be expected, there was little inter-territorial cricket in the West Indies – and that mainly between Barbados and Trinidad. Jamaica particularly suffered from lack of outside competition. Players such as the fast bowlers Hines Johnson and Dickie Fuller, and opening batsmen J. K. Holt Jnr and L. V. Dujon, the father of the present wicket-keeper, were much handicapped by this lack. Nor should one forget the left-handed bowler G. H. Mudie who had played his part in the famous Sabina Park victory over England by an innings and 161 runs in 1935 – the game in which the deft and utterly dependable George Alphonso Headley scored 270 not out, in a total of 535 for 7 declared.

The 1950 West Indies touring party, then, contained only two players who had played in a Test in England before: J. B. Stollmeyer, whose brother Victor had unfortunately given up cricket, and Gerry Gomez. Both were well known in the West Indies where they helped to form the mainstay of the Trinidad team. Gomez's Test scores in England in 1939 were 0, 11 and 11. Stollmeyer had scored 59, 0, 5, 10 and 59. Stollmeyer had once been expected to be a troublesome leg-spinner, but in the end he concentrated on being an opener. Beyond a doubt the partnership he built with the left-handed Allan Rae contributed greatly to the shock which the English public, and cricketers, received in 1950. Gomez was a considerable all-rounder, a fast-medium swing bowler, who also bowled good off-breaks. He was a sharp fielder, a fighter, and after a shaky start a more than useful bat.

When we make comparisons later on between the 1988 and 1950 teams, more extensive statistics will be brought forward. But as we shall see, what was forgotten about this team was not only how well individuals had done at home, but also how brilliantly West Indies teams had recently performed in India and at home.

The 1950 team which lost the first Test to England by 202 runs was: Rae, Stollmeyer, Worrell, Everton Weekes, Walcott, Christiani, Gomez, Goddard, Johnson, Ramadhin, Valentine. We of course now know what power and run-scoring ability was packed into those 'three Ws'. But even in 1950 commentators should have recalled that during the 1947–48 England tour of the West Indies Worrell and Weekes had clearly signalled what was to come. (Worrell 97 at Queen's Park and 131 not out at Georgetown; Weekes 141 at Sabina Park). Later on we shall enjoy their performances in India in the 1948–49 series.

Allan Rae, except that he had done well in India, was a bit of an unknown quantity when the series began. He had not been originally an opening batsman, but rather a very hard hitting no. 5 or no. 6 – until he and the so-underrated Arthur MacKenzie opened the innings for Jamaica against Barbados at Sabina Park in 1947. They put on 76, of which MacKenzie made 35; Rae eventually fell for 111. The interesting thing is that the former, an excellent wicket-keeper, had been no. 10, in the previous game, and Rae was no. 6.

Rae, a law student in London at the time of the 1950 tour, had played good club cricket in England for Winchmore Hill and the BBC, just before going to India. (His father, who failed on the 1928 tour despite the fact that his batting was much admired by Bill Bowes, had also played for Winchmore Hill.)

Of the rest of the 1950 first Test team, only Ramadhin and Valentine were really unknown – yet they were to give the tour the name by which it will always be remembered. They both played at Queen's Park, Port of Spain, when Jamaica visited Trinidad for only the second time ever, in 1950. Jamaica had visited Barbados a few times, but was always somewhat isolated from the rest of the then British West Indies. True enough, 1,200 miles of sea separated Jamaica and Trinidad, and travel in those days was by schooner or steamer, but Jamaica, in any case, has always tended to look towards New York rather than south to the other islands.

In that 1950 Trinidad game, Valentine (not yet 20 years old) did not take a wicket for Jamaica and conceded 111 runs in 39 overs. The Trinidad batsmen had a run feast of some opulence: Ganteaume 147, J. B. Stollmeyer 261, and K. B. Trestrail 161 not out! But Ramadhin (three months short of 21) made his mark with 5 for 39 in 16 overs for Trinidad. It is said he so comprehensively bowled Ken Rickards when set on 40 in the first innings, and on 57 in the second, that all the *cognoscenti* present were willing to book his passage to England, even though this must have been his first first-class game!

Rickards was one of Jamaica's best, who lacked only the killer instinct that would have made him a world batsman. In the second 1950 game against Trinidad he got 71 and 83, both top scores. But he once again fell to Ram, when he was on 71; of the rest, only his captain J. M. Groves (with 38) scored over 25! With hindsight one can now understand the wealth of West Indian cricket in 1950 when Rickards could not earn selection on the party touring England, and Trestrail, having done so, could not make a single Test appearance – except as a substitute at the Oval when he took two catches.

John Goddard, captain of that 1950 first Test team, was a stubborn but not strokeless left-hander who had some huge scores to his credit in inter-*colonial* cricket, as it was then called. His most remarkable was when he and F. M. Worrell scored 526 runs between them for Barbados against Trinidad at Kensington Oval in 1944; he scored 218 and Frank 308, both not out. In the same year Goddard scored 179 against British Guiana. He was fifth in the Test averages in India in 1948–49 with 47.50, behind Weekes, Stollmeyer, Walcott and Rae. He was also a brilliant field, and a more than useful bowler.

Robert Christiani (British Guiana) was next in the Test averages in India with 42.00, scoring 107 in the first Test, and 74 in the second. He was a remarkable all-rounder, not in the usual sense, for he bowled and kept wicket as well as batted. His brother, Cyril, who was an outstanding keeper, died tragically in British Guiana. Robert had scored 126 and 54 in 1944, in the first game of the series against Trinidad at Queen's Park. And he scored 128 later that year against Barbados at Georgetown. And at the same ground, in 1946, he scored 149 against the same team.

Hines Johnson was an outstanding fast bowler for Jamaica and was inexplicably left out of the team going to India, only to be picked for England at the advanced age of 40. He was what might be called a fitness freak; a tall man, he had a truly beautiful action, and great control. In the first Test in 1950 he bowled 10 overs for 18 runs in the first innings, injured himself and could not bowl in the second. But in the third Test his steadiness and speed were most useful. He bowled, in the match, 55.4 overs for 3 wickets at the cost of 124 runs.

In the second and fourth Tests Prior Jones (Trinidad) took Johnson's place. He had taken the highest number of wickets in Tests on the India 1948–49 tour, 17 at an average of 28.17, Gomez being his nearest rival with 16 at 28.37. Jones led the first-class averages in India, taking 51 wickets at an average of 18.54 per wicket; next to him was Gomez who took 71 at 18.70 per wicket.

There was much talent in that group of players. It was not by chance that they won a series for the first time in England, and paved the way for the great feats that were to come. This feeling of their strength is increased when we think of those who could not get a Test place: Roy Marshall, Kenny Trestrail, 'Boogles' Williams, Lance Pierre. Just to list them is enough to make the point. And remember the feats of Roy Marshall: three centuries on the tour, and later those which were to come to Hampshire!

Lance Pierre, who swung the ball about, was fourth in the first-class bowling averages of the tour: 24 wickets at an average of 23.20 runs. His problem was that he was not quite consistent enough. On his day he was perhaps the best of the quick bowlers. It is worth noting, however, that over the whole tour the three quick men took 91 first-class wickets between them – while Ramadhin and Valentine took a total of 258.

Of the Tests themselves, England won only the first, at Old Trafford on a dustbowl. Old Trafford was the venue for the *first* Test. The wicket caused much concern, and was described by some of the players as being something like a second-class dirt road. The England spin bowlers, Berry and Hollies, did rather well: the former 9–116, and the latter 8–133. The 'explanation' for the state of the wicket, believe it or not, was that rain had been so scarce that the wicket was much drier than the ground staff had expected. Whatever the reason, at the end of the game the wicket was quickly watered before any of us could get a good look at it. Things were rather more authoritarian and secretive in those days, and in any case England had scored a resounding victory by 202 runs! In the first innings Godfrey Evans, coming in at no. 8, had scored 104, Trevor Bailey, at no. 7, 82 not out. Their sixth-wicket stand of 161 has been bettered for England, in England–West Indies Tests, only by Greig and Knott (163) at Bridgetown, Barbados, in 1973–74. Of the West Indies batsmen only Weekes and Stollmeyer did anything; the former got 52 and 1; the latter, 43 and 78. Although Alf Valentine got 8 for 104 in the first innings, in the second his 3 wickets cost him 100 runs. Ramadhin got 4 wickets in the game for 167 runs. England had batted first.

The second Test, as we shall see in the next chapter, provided an historic victory for West Indies who confirmed their form three weeks later at Trent Bridge. This game was illuminated by 261 first-innings runs from Frank Worrell that would have shone out on the brightest of days. It was his highest Test score and helped to set up a 10-wicket win.

Hutton had to withdraw just before play began through lumbago, so Simpson, on his home ground, opened with Washbrook. They did not prosper, being parted with but 6 on the board. England actually sank to 75 for 5, but eventually managed 223. Top scorer was the bowler Derek Shackleton with 42, another bowler, Roly Jenkins, being just behind him with 39.

By contrast, West Indies did not lose their fifth wicket until 535. It was an innings in direct reverse to England's, for the collapse came in its second half, the last 5 wickets going for 23. Apart from Worrell, Weekes made 129, with Rae's 68 the next highest. Bedser, by now well established as England's dependable workhorse, was true to form with 48 brisk overs (more than anybody in the first innings) and 5 wickets for 127, astonishing figures in face of the onslaught from two of the Ws (the third, Walcott, rested from his Lord's century with a mere 8).

In their second innings England, in another startling contrast, kicked off with an opening partnership of 212 (Simpson 94 run out, Washbrook 102). Then Parkhouse, Dewes and Evans all got into the 60s, and England were all out for 436, leaving WI 102 to win, which they arrived at without loss. Look at the bowling in England's second innings: Ramadhin 81.2 overs (5–135), Valentine 92 overs (3–140): 173 between them, four other bowlers contributing a total of 72.

The fourth (and final) Test at the Oval was another WI victory, detailed in chapter 7, so that they had pretty convincingly won their first series in England, and against some pretty good opposition too.

So much, then, for the strength of the 1950 party; but, of course, 1988 was not exactly a pushover. By that time Allan Rae had served nobly for a number of years as President of the West Indies Board, and was just handing over to another 1950 success, Clyde Walcott, who along with Worrell and Weekes made up the formidable three Ws as they became bracketed. Allan caused annoyance to the anti-apartheid lobby in England and elsewhere. He declined to be declared 'an honorary white' in order to visit South Africa and 'see for himself' the 'great changes' which cricket was making to the racist regime there.

The question being asked in 1988 at the beginning of the tour, as much by the casual ladies and gentlemen in the sun as by the *aficionados*, was 'Can the West Indies ever be defeated?' It was an odd question. No team is ever invincible; and no country, or group of countries, can *always* win at any sport. One country might have its run of successes. But in the end all of us who play or watch or write are but humans, participating in what is a great and fascinating game – but, heaven help us, still a *game* – despite all the money now to be earned from it, and all the perks such as splendid cars advertising some company or the other, and all the nationalist jingoism regularly introduced by people who should know better.

In fact, I would say that the 1988 West Indies team, at the beginning of the tour when speculation was taking place, was not as balanced or as good as the 1950 team. That earlier side really had an all-round strength not noticed fully at that time. The bowling of Ramadhin and Valentine and the batting of the three Ws tended to overshadow all else. But the opening pair in 1950 were outstanding, combining the solidity of Rae with the elegance and stroke-play of Stollmeyer, who in 1939 had shared second-wicket stands with George Headley of 118 at Lord's and 113 at the Oval. The captain, John Goddard, who was to be criticised later for his captaincy on other tours, was a formidable all-rounder. His close-to-the-wicket fielding was as good as that of A. P. F. Chapman in the 1920s or of Logie today; and he had behind him that remarkable unbroken 526 partnership with Frank Worrell against Trinidad in 1944. His bowling can be judged from the Oval Test: in the first innings, 17.4–6–25–4, in the second, 9–4–11–1. Five wickets at the cost of 36 runs is not bad against any Test team, especially for a quickish off-break bowler.

West Indies also had in Gerry Gomez another outstanding all-rounder, who could bowl medium-pace swing or off-spin, and who scored 74 in that Oval Test and 70 in the second innings at Lord's. Clyde Walcott (168 not out at Lord's) was the wicket-keeper who could also open the bowling as he did at Old Trafford, when Hines Johnson, the splendid fast bowler from Jamaica, had injured himself.

It is important to take note of all of this – *and* the consistent brilliance of the three Ws – in looking at the 1988 team; and in assessing the recent reputation of the West Indies, and especially in taking with a grain of salt the present conventional wisdom that West Indies cricket began with the inestimable Frank Worrell's team.

There is another consideration: the relative strength (or weakness) of the 1988 England team, compared with that of 1950. It is amazing how statistical and other comparisons are often made without any reference to the quality of the opposition. Admittedly the England 1950 team had suffered throughout the war and after, not least of all because of the general devastation of the country. One is likely to forget, for instance, or not to know, that at the 1948 Olympics, held at London's Wembley stadium, the athletes had to be helped over the then rationing of food in Great Britain with a supplementary allowance. Further, England had been defeated by Bradman's 1948 Australians in no uncertain manner. But then again, that Australian team must have been one of the strongest ever put together: one need only name the first five batsmen to make the point – Morris, Barnes, Bradman, Hassett,

Miller. The bowlers were not too bad either – Lindwall, Miller, Johnson, Johnston, with Toshack to seal up an end hermetically.

The 1988 England team was not a distinguished one. It was often difficult to name more than four players who, one felt, must be in the side. And even then one's selection was likely to be controversial. My four were Gooch, Dilley, Gower and Lamb – plus, I suppose, Small when he was really fit. But a discussion of the English weakness must be left until later. At present we should just remember that outstanding as the performance of the 1988 West Indies team was, it did not meet with the most spirited or capable opposition. On the other hand the 1950 team faced, among others, Hutton, Washbrook, Compton, Simpson, Yardley, Bedser, Hollies and Evans.

The most encouraging and interesting thing about West Indies performance in 1988 was the way in which the team came together and blossomed in the face of early defeat, and despite the inexperience of some of its players. It must not be forgotten that one of its most promising batsmen, Simmons, was felled in the opening days of the tour. It was his first (and, as it turned out, only) innings, against Gloucestershire. On a lively wicket and not wearing a helmet, he had scored a good 53 when he was hit by a fast rising ball from Lawrence. A blood clot developed, and an emergency operation carried out almost immediately. In fact many say that Simmons is lucky to be alive; and one is glad of that. But it would have been wonderful to see him grow and mature even as it has been delightful to see Logie at last really make it with the bat, and Hooper improve with every appearance.

It has been a pleasure – in fact an education – to cover West Indies–England confrontations since 1950. And I invite you now to join me on that 1988 tour, the last one I am likely to cover, and to glance across the West Indies cricketing years in England from 1950 to 1988.

2

To Full Strength

Lord's, 1950 and 1988

It is appropriate to single out the Lord's Test of 1950 and to couple it with that of 1988. First, because the earlier match was the first Test that West Indies won in England; and the shock for the home fans must have been the greater when you remember the outcome of the previous Test just twelve days before. Second, because the 1988 win really set the English fans (and, one suspects, the English cricket establishment) thinking, 'Can we ever beat these people?' England had been whitewashed ('blackwashed', the press called it) in the Caribbean in 1985–86 as well as at home in 1984; in this Lord's Test it looked briefly as if at last WI were on the rack – but humiliatingly for England they wriggled off it.

The atmosphere at Lord's between 24–29 June 1950 increased in excitement as play went on, as if there was a mass sixth sense that something out of the ordinary was boiling up. Maybe too a West Indies team had never had quite so much support. New immigrants were establishing themselves socially and economically in this strange and cold land . . . and this was the first opportunity for these new Londoners to take time out at Lord's to encourage their compatriots.

The win was comprehensive, by 326 runs – no mere sneaking past the post but a thumping, unarguable victory. By coincidence it was by the same number of runs that West Indies scored in the first innings. Rae made a cultured, almost thoughtful 106, Weekes 63 and Worrell 52, leg-spinner Roly Jenkins taking 5 for 116 and Bedser 3 for 60 off 40 overs. England began their reply in no seeming trouble, getting to 62 before the first wicket fell. Then they ran into what was rapidly to become spin trouble, and in the end no one made more than Washbrook's 36. Ram took 5 for 66 (43 overs) and Val 4 for 48 (45 overs) in their meagre 151.

The lead of 175 seemed to release something in the WI second outing. Weekes was run out for a second 63 and Walcott, refusing to be outdone by his fellow Ws, scored 168 to be not out when the declaration came at 425 for 6 – Gomez chipping in with 70. This left England with a massive 601 to win; the only real question was, could they last out for a draw? The West Indians in the packed ground began a buzz of expectant excitement when the great Hutton was out for 10, bowled middle stump shouldering arms to Valentine. The score then was just 28. Edrich was patently ill at ease whilst 29 runs were added, contributing only 8 before Ramadhin had him caught. They got to 218 for 4, then the slide set in, the next 6 wickets falling, amid increasing noise, for 56 runs and the innings ending at 274. Washbrook had batted beautifully for 114, Parkhouse well for 48 before being brilliantly held by Goddard. This time, Ramadhin took 6 for 86 (giving him 11 for 152 from 115 overs), Valentine 3 for 79 and 7 for 127 in 116 overs for the match. Goddard had achieved the remarkable figures, in his only spell of the match, of 6–6–0–0.

All during that last day, as maiden followed maiden, the runs were squeezed out, the wickets fell, every single person in the ground was utterly absorbed. That is not to say quiet – the emotion was too great for that. At the end, the victory completed, it all got too much and the West Indian supporters exploded from their seats, ran on to the sacred turf and gathered, a grinning, cheering, dancing crowd, in front of the pavilion demanding to salute their heroes up on the balcony. The officials were horrified at first, but then – just a little patronisingly, perhaps? – stood back and enjoyed it with everyone else.

An occasion – a match – to remember and relish. And some of the radio commentators, exactly like their present-day colleagues, found the whole thing rather boring! *Not enough variety in the bowling, so much spin; where were the speedsters* à la *Constantine and Herman Griffith?*

All things considered the whole thing came as a bit of a surprise to many pundits, English and West Indian. It should not have. Leaving aside the West Indies defeat of the Gubby Allen team of 1947–48 – when Len Hutton had to be flown out to strengthen a really weak side – the true situation had been written large in the Indian subcontinent in 1948–49.

To take England's tour first. The first Test, played at

Kensington in Bridgetown, Barbados, ended in a draw. But in a low-scoring game Stollmeyer made 78, and Gomez 86. This game, incidentally, was the gentle Jim Laker's first Test, and he took 7 for 103 in the first innings. In the West Indies second innings R. J. Christiani got 99, and leg-spin bowlers E. A. V. Williams and 'double ugly' Ferguson scored 72 and 56 not out respectively. Ferguson did not make the 1950 team to England. But of course Gomez and Stollmeyer did. The second Test (Queen's Park Oval, Port-of- Spain, Trinidad) was also a draw. But future events were already casting their shadows before them: not only did the West Indies openers, Ganteaume and Carew, who were not to make the 1950 tour, make centuries, but Worrell and Gomez scored 97 and 62 respectively.

The third Test, at Georgetown, British Guiana West Indies won by 7 wickets, Worrell scoring 131 not out. And the final Test, at Sabina Park, Jamaica, was also won by WI, Everton Weekes getting his maiden Test century with 141 and Ken Rickards, one of the best Jamaican batsmen ever but not included in the 1950 touring party, got 67. England lost despite 107 from Winston Place, and 60 from Len Hutton. West Indies had done well even though Headley was injured in the first Test and took no further part in the series. West Indies had won the series 2–0, with two games drawn.

All this took place in the first post-war England tour to the Caribbean. Perhaps it was not properly understood as a foretaste of West Indies strength because the England team was not the best that could have been chosen, and the war years were still taking their toll in England.

But more and better, from the point of view of the West Indies, was to come during the 1948–49 tour to that home of the ancestors of many West Indians, the subcontinent of India. It was a high-scoring series, with the bat so dominating the ball that four Tests were drawn, the West Indies winning the other. At New Delhi, in the first Test, WI made their highest Test score up to then, 631. This was the more remarkable inasmuch as they lost Rae (8), Stollmeyer (13) and Headley (2) quickly. But – dire pointers to 1950! – Walcott was run out for 152; Gomez stumped on 101; Weekes was caught Hazare for 128, and Christiani caught Hazare for 107. Goddard scored 44, and Denis Atkinson 45. For

India only Ibrahim (85 in the first innings) and Adhikari, 114 and 29, both not out, really compared.

The second Test, at Bombay, was again a draw. West Indies, batting first, declared on the third day with 629 for 6. Rae and Stollmeyer opened with a partnership of 134, Rae getting his maiden Test century (104, c and b Phadkar). Weekes scored 194, Christiani 74, while F. J. Cameron (75 not out) and Atkinson (23 not out) laid on the bat until captain Goddard, who did not bat, declared. West Indies bowling made little impression in the second innings, and India, after following-on, lost but 3 wickets in saving the game. The redoubtable Hazare made 134 not out, and Modi 112.

In fact what was becoming clear to those watching the games closely was that West Indies bowling was somewhat below par. As *Wisden* was to put it: 'Both sides lacked fast bowlers up to international standard.'

The third Test, at Calcutta, was likewise a draw but had a lesson, for those who could read it, about the growing strength of the West Indies. Everton Weekes made 162 in the first innings, and by getting 101 in the second became the first batsman to score five successive Test centuries. (Oddly enough he was caught and bowled in both innings by Ghulam Ahmed.) Walcott scored 108 in the second innings in 175 minutes even though he was not fit! Unfortunately West Indies slip fielding was just not up to scratch. But on the other hand the following bowling figures (first innings) are worth quoting:

	O	M	R	W
Gomez	32	10	65	3
Ferguson	29	8	66	3
Goddard	13	3	34	3

Gomez bowled both medium-pace swing and off-breaks around the wicket. Ferguson, as was noted above, did not make the 1950 team.

The fourth Test, at Madras, was the one which West Indies won – by an innings and 193 runs! Rae (109) and Stollmeyer (160) set a West Indies opening record of 239. (The now well-known firm of Greenidge and Haynes raised that to 296 against India at St John's, Antigua in 1983.) It was Stollmeyer's first Test century and completely justified Clarence Passailaigue's diktat to us youngsters at Jamaica's Melbourne CC: 'Never miss a Jeffrey Stollmeyer innings; that is pure music.'

Everton Weekes, well on his way to a sixth successive Test century, was run out backing up when 90. Gomez (50) and Cameron (48) added spice lower down the order. They were both dismissed by Phadkar who took 7 wickets for 159 by often bowling – as *Wisden* put it – 'considerably short of a length to make the ball lift at an alarming angle.' The article went on, 'Trim and Jones, West Indies pace bowlers, emulated Phadkar's methods with much success.' West Indies only innings yielded 582. India: first innings, 245; second innings, 144. In that second innings the relevant WI bowling figures are again well worth quoting:

	O	M	R	W
Jones	10	3	30	4
Gomez	20.3	12	35	3
Trim	16	5	28	3

Trim, of course, did not make the 1950 tour to England.

The fifth Test, the second at Bombay's Brabourne Stadium, was drawn. The result was much in the balance until the end. But as the injured Sen was unlikely to bat when India started the last over needing 11 runs to win, they in fact were down to their last pair. They managed to get 5 of the needed runs. There must have been some weakness in the West Indies tactics which allowed India to get quite so close; but maybe WI had decided to go for the win although they were one up. In the first innings, Goddard having won the toss for the fifth time in a row, Stollmeyer (85), although suffering from muscle trouble, and Weekes (56) added 110 for the third wicket. And although Christiani scored 40 and Goddard 41, West Indies could get only 286. In the second innings they fared worse – 267, of which Rae scored 97 and Weekes 48, with Goddard 33 not out. India were able to get 355 for 8 in their second innings, having been set 361 to win in 395 minutes.

It had been a long and gruelling tour but West Indies showed to all who could see that they were really growing as a cricket power. Their batting had been much more remarkable than their bowling. Rae and Weekes scored six first-class centuries,

Walcott five, Stollmeyer two. Christiani, Gomez and Carew scored one each; Carew, remember, did not make the 1950 tour.

What West Indies needed was a world-class bowler or two. While many were looking for such a find in the speed department, who should fall from the heavens – or from the guango tree from which even the great George Headley had watched Tyldesley bat – who but 'those two little pals of mine/Ramadhin and Valentine'? Gentle slow bowlers, but deadly, especially in 1950 in England.

Little changes, and it is important for all cricket lovers, West Indians particularly, not to forget that we did have world-class players even before the teams of Worrell and Lloyd. And perhaps English selectors should bear in mind that at Lord's in 1950 both Ram and Val were playing in only their second Test match, the one being 21 years of age, the other 20! It would also be nice to know – perhaps some PhD student could be set to find out – when last the English media found a game boring when England were either winning or refusing to take singles, or any other runs, so as to save a game by a glorious draw!

Just before the second day of the second – the Lord's – Test of 1988 I had written: 'Today will decide the tour, I think. WI batting is brittle, and England are trying to get back . . . So if WI lose this one they will be skidding on the downward slope. For one thing Gatting will be coming back after his "indiscretion" [allegedly with a barmaid during and after his birthday celebrations] and the England team will be stronger.'

At that stage, it must be remembered, England had won the three one-day internationals; the first Test at Trent Bridge had been drawn, and accepted as drawn as soon as it was clear that Marshall, suffering from a rib-muscle injury, would not be called upon to bowl, except briefly, in the second innings. And at Lord's, where I was making my jottings, England were 20 for 1, in reply to WI's 209 all out, Dujon having been bowled for 53 by Emburey, and Logie being caught by Emburey, at backward point, off Small, for 81. So these two had scored 134 out of a total of 209. Dujon had been out of form for a long time, and Logie's promise with the bat was beginning to look deceitful before both of them had defied the English bowling here and saved the West Indies from embarrassment.

So the second day of the second Test was about to set the tone and outcome for the rest of the series. On that day England performed really inconsistently. It is true that the climatic conditions were not exactly Caribbean, or even English 'in flaming June'. But England's performance foreshadowed much that was to come.

They started the day in fairly dark conditions and by 1:45, just after lunch, they were 100 for 2 with Gower on 36, and Gooch 35. These two batsmen have held up the West Indies from time to time – the former most memorably at Sabina Park in 1980–81, and the latter at Lord's in 1980. But by the time Pringle had been caught by Dujon off Walsh the total had declined to 134 for 5, and 6 runs later, when Marshall trapped Lamb lbw for 10, 6 wickets had fallen for 140! After the eighth wicket had fallen for 157, Jarvis decided on attack, and hit his first ball for 4 through the vacant mid-off position. He did not last long, even though the English crowd had started to cheer loudly every run that was scored – always a bad sign! And soon enough the team was out, 44 runs behind the small West Indies score of 209. At first the West Indies bowling had not been on the spot, although Ambrose seemed to improve all the while, and was pitching up and forcing the batsmen to play. But – and this also was prophetic of what was to come – Marshall's second spell made all the difference, and he ended up with 6 wickets for 32 runs in 18 overs, 5 of which were maidens. Mainly because of his efforts England had failed to build on their more than fair beginning.

But whereas in recent years it has tended to be the bowling which carried the West Indies, now in the second innings the batting looked not only better but much more balanced. No longer was the main burden left on captain Richards's shoulders. Greenidge, liking Lord's as usual, scored 103 off 192 balls in 242 minutes, and hit fourteen 4s. Logie was not out 95, unfortunately not getting his century which one or two of his more impatient partners should have helped him to achieve simply by staying with him. Dujon, as elegant as ever, but now with a surer touch than recently, contributed 52, getting out to Jarvis – in-swinger, inside edge of the bat and on to the leg stump. The ball was no doubt a good one, but he helped it on to his wicket.

Viv Richards carried on from his Trent Bridge performance rather than from his quick demise in the first innings. He scored a lively 72, without the brutal directness of Trent Bridge, but lively none the less, getting to 51 in 60 balls, with eight 4s and one 6. He went from 51 to 55 with a lovely drive to square leg, from 55 to 59 with perfect timing wide of mid-off, from 60 to 64 with a similar shot but more towards extra cover, from 64 to 67 with a cut, and from 67 to 71 with a delicate leg-glance. He was bowled by Pringle as he tried, once too often, a one-day, 'no-slip', off-side tickle, which really should not be elevated to the status of a cut.

England in their second innings managed 307. The weather had been quite gloomy, and so had been much of the cricket. One had the impression of two mighty Titans, both wounded, but with England more severely so. There were some remarkable flashes amidst the incursions of gloom: Greenidge and Richards in the second innings, Lamb's defiant 113 for England, Marshall's bowling. There was, too, the run-out which ended Lamb. Hooper swooped on the ball, picked up and threw with one lovely continuous action to Walsh, who had covered the wicket quickly and had no trouble in taking the return and breaking the stumps. Lamb's valuable contribution was made off 213 balls in 338 minutes, and contained fifteen 4s.

Marshall's 6 wickets in the first innings included 5 for 13 in a spell of 10 overs. Walsh also turned in a fine performance. These two together with really excellent fielding meant that England lost by 134 runs in the fourth over after lunch on the fifth day. Marshall's bag for the game was 10 for 92 in 43 overs, a wicket in every 25.8 balls. Dilley had taken 9 wickets for England in 50 overs for 128 runs – a wicket in every 33.3 balls, at one and a half times the cost of Marshall's wickets.

West Indies had passed the test of Lord's, and any doubts about the team were starting to fade. Not that they were the greatest, but that, with any care and fighting spirit, they should always, in 1988, be greater than England.

One of the comparatively new Test institutions not in evidence in 1950, and still not accepted, nor considered important, by some 'up-market' journalists, is the after-the-match press conference. After the Lord's Test, for instance, the England manager, Micky Stewart, said some extraordinary things. One was that the England team had planned to make 250 runs a day in order to surpass the 441 by which the West Indies led before England started their second innings. If that was really their plan then their team was even weaker than it appeared to be. For it failed by 135, more than half of a day's allotted ration. And Lamb really seemed, after a long dry spell, to be the only batsman who was not overawed. Stewart then went on to say that 'West Indies deserved their victory, but we feel that they were not that much ahead . . . next game England have an even-money chance' – to win, presumably!

There was also much talk of England having the worst of the weather and of the conditions. There is no doubt that the weather and the differing conditions of cloud cover, and of light, make cricket in England not quite the same game it is elsewhere. But in general this fact must favour the 'home-town' players. The whole of this question will constantly arise, especially the way in which some batsmen seem unable to adjust to English conditions. For example, up to the second Test and in fact after, Richardson, a gifted player if ever there was one, was just not performing with the bat.

But perhaps Stewart's most interesting statement – he is not exactly unwilling to make pronouncements – was, 'Marshall is a fine bowler, but he is just a bowler'; a statement which is palpably true, but which reflects on the subsequent performance of English batsmen who often could not be characterised either as fine batsmen, or even as 'just batsmen'.

Perhaps had he been 'cricket manager' at the Lord's Test in 1950 he might have been tempted to say that Ramadhin and Valentine were fine bowlers, but 'just bowlers'. Fortunately, or unfortunately, there were no 'cricket managers' then – and no press conferences.

3

Some Old and New Aspects of Cricket

The Run-up to Lord's, 1988

Much had happened before the second Test at Lord's. For one thing, despite the change of attitudes to cricket and to games in general, the tour started, on 5 May, with a fun, charity match at Uxbridge. This gala event between the WI team and an international XI under the leadership of Clive Lloyd set things off in the right direction. Lloyd's team included Imran Khan, Joel Garner and Farouk Kirmani, captain of Canada.

The game caught some of the old spirit of touring, when the Tests were not considered to be the only cricket to be played, and when meeting new people and broadening one's experience were all a part of playing and winning. There was a whiff of the times before grounds became mass-advertising hoardings, and helmets were something worn by firemen.

The extensive Uxbridge ground had a bit of the country fair about it, with colourful marquees selling special West Indian food and drinks which even hardened press men were happy to sample. The event was promoted by the Commonwealth Society for the Deaf, and very much supported by Sir John Stowe, who had been Colonial Secretary in Jamaica and then Governor-General of Barbados. Many of us were delighted to know that the West Indies cricket authorities and the players had agreed to help this excellent cause. Sir John had been a person much concerned with the community and was of great help to the University of the West Indies when I was Professor of Education there.

The game also gave a chance to the younger players to meet the new and difficult English conditions in a relaxed atmosphere. One of the problems which all touring teams now face is a dreadfully rushed schedule with a minimum of games before the Tests and the one-day internationals. New players have little opportunity to stake a claim to a place on the Test team. So the tendency to stick with the older and proven players is encouraged.

Young Arthurton played for Lloyd's team and took the opportunity to knock Viv Richards, his touring captain, all over the place – much to the pleasure and amusement of the crowd of Caribbean heritage people who had gathered for their first view of this new West Indies team. Clive Lloyd scored 37 not out for the international team; Kirmani 53; Arthurton 86. The West Indies got the 229 set them in 46.1 overs, with the loss of but 1 wicket; Greenidge retired at 90, and Haynes at 50.

The West Indies having disappointed in the World Cup, and just managing to draw the recent Pakistan tour in the Caribbean, there was much knowing talk and shaking of heads about this new lot, and not least of all about the new captain, Viv Richards. It is quite amazing, it seems to me, how captains are judged. Little note ever seems to be taken of the quality of the team they lead. They are praised when they win with an outstanding team, blamed if they lead ten half-blind men who find it difficult not to lose. But there is nothing like winning as far as the average fan is concerned. And all is soon forgiven a captain as soon as the team wins a few games in a row, even if they are lucky enough to be playing against a really inferior side.

One of the matters we shall constantly consider is the real strength of the English Test teams in 1988, and of course the captaincy of Viv Richards. We must also take a look at the whole question of the banning of players who continue active links with South Africa. It is not the only political question around. There is, for instance, the constant idea, once again raised by the chairman of selectors, Peter May, and strongly supported by his predecessor, Alec Bedser, that foreign players should be severely limited in English county cricket. In fact some time ago there was a move to have at least one competition from which they were to be wholly banned.

Cricket cannot be detached from the social and political context in which it is played, even if it should, like art, insist on *not* being used in ways totally against the spirit of games in general and of cricket in particular. But to assert that the game does take place in a social context, which necessarily implies moral as well as aesthetic values, is unfortunately to annoy some people who like to mouth rather thoughtlessly, 'Sport is sport, and politics, politics.' As if any serious event which grows and takes place within a country can really be hermetically sealed off from the culture and values of that country! In this matter we have the difficult task of walking a tightrope stretched between totally irresponsible demands for freedom, and equally authoritarian demands that all people of good will must bow to every boycott made in the name of 'solidarity'.

The first first-class game of the tour was on 7 May at Hove, by the sea, against Sussex who were celebrating their 150th year. The walk from the station to the ground was cooler than the weather forecasts had promised, and the sea mist was not far away. In fact the sun did not shine until Richards came in to bat. All were waiting to see him, and he did not disappoint.

Impatient West Indies fans have wished, from time to time, not so much to drop the pilot as to shoot the captain – 'Captain, the ship is sinking', they forget, was sung to a famous *politician*, and would have been out of place at Hove during that first game of the tour.

Hove is the ground which had seen the sparkle of Ranji and Dexter, and the pontifical authority of David Sheppard. But the West Indies started in a manner suitable to the threatening mist, coolly and carefully: the first hour yielded 49 runs, Greenidge having departed for 15 with the score on 22, immediately after striking two promising 4s. Sussex supporters, *habitués* of the ground, assured us that the sun was just behind the clouds. They were much more correct than they realised, for with the score at 94 for 5 Richards was joined by Harper, and things brightened up all around.

The trouble with great batsmen like Richards is that they make it look so easy. They leave us little to describe. He got to 50 in 93 minutes, having faced 73 balls and hit six 4s and two 6s. One of the latter did the ball serious injury as it broke through a window some twenty feet above the straight long-off boundary. But many of his strokes were more subtle, a deft push to leg or a slowly rolling ball to backward mid-off. He had added 68 to the partnership when it yielded 100 in 25 overs, the total being 194 for 5. The sun continued to shine brightly through a steady sea breeze, and the leg-spinner Clarke came in for some warm treatment as Richards approached his 98th first-class hundred. This he achieved, as the total got to 261 for 5, with a deft paddle around the corner. His hundred had taken 163 minutes and 128 balls. He had then hit ten 4s and four 6s, and had moved, with Harper, to a stand of 169.

He was eventually out caught on the deep square-leg boundary by Alan Wells off the South African Merrick Pringle for 128, the total being 321. His off-driving, from wide of mid-off to extra cover, was clean and authoritative, giving the fielders no chance. Even his 6s were effortless. His only danger seemed to be that very fine cut – or perhaps more accurately called a tickle to the off – which one supposes he developed for use in the one-day, no-slip-fielder game. It could give him trouble whenever he meets the very best of bowlers. But there seemed little doubt then that he would soon join that special small band of non-English players, who have scored 100 centuries: Bradman (117), Turner (103), Zaheer Abbas (108).

Neither Logie nor Hooper lasted for very long, but the latter looked good, if a bit airy and iffish when playing back, on the leg-side particularly.

On the whole the first-class games throughout this tour offered little excitement. The recent tendency is to treat only the Tests and one-day internationals seriously, and to think of everything else as preparation. This attitude caused criticism in the press of the captain and manager of the West Indies. And it is undoubtedly hard on the paying spectators when first-class games are treated mostly as practice matches, and no real attempt is made to win them or to make a real contest out of them. The West Indies were blamed for taking this kind of attitude to the Northamptonshire game, when they seemed intent on practice rather than 'making a game of it'. The Worcestershire game, which could have been exciting because of Hick's phenomenal batting, was marred by rain. And one county at least was much criticised for fielding a non-first- class side against the tourists.

So the most important things that happened before the Lord's Test were: one, the clean sweep England made of the Texaco one-day series; and two, the way in which the opening Cornhill Test at Trent Bridge was drawn. To these two matters we must turn our attention, with emphasis on the first Test and the role of Marshall.

The one-day games, so well supported by both Texaco and the fans, seem to have left little lasting impression. England made a clean sweep: they won the first game, at Edgbaston, by 6 wickets; the second, at Headingley, by 47 runs; and the third and last, at Lord's, by 7 wickets. England could hardly have done better in this, their chosen type of game. It is unlikely that at the time of their victory England realised how much of a choice they had made in that direction. They still don't seem to realise that that choice must affect their performance in the more prestigious Tests.

There seems to be a general expectation that English teams should do excellently in both forms of the game. It is not so much having to play some one-day games but rather the great emphasis put on them in England where there are three one-day competitions intertwined with regular county cricket, and where supporters tend to take the one-day game more seriously than the first-class game. One of the things at stake is the development of the degree of concentration needed for Tests. According to Don Wilson, then the head MCC coach, writing in *Wisden*, today young players 'get in, get their 30 or 40, and their concentration goes'. And he blames this on the fact that their minds and attitudes seem to be formed by the one-day game in which only the openers, and perhaps nos. 3 and 4, can afford to build up an innings. He contrasts this attitude with that of the 'great players – when they got to 25, they got 50, and when they got 50, they went on to 100.'

He makes a further point about all this which is well worth quoting: 'I realise that one-day cricket is a big money-maker, but as things stand at the moment, without being a Test player a young cricketer won't get to play in the big one-day internationals . . . I think as coaches we have to concentrate on [the county game] and say that our aim is to produce good three-day county cricketers and Test cricketers. Then we might also have better cricket.'

From the point of view of the West Indies, that 1988 mini-series was really a disaster. On one or two occasions it showed up some real weaknesses in Richards's captaincy, and made it quite clear that the team was new and inexperienced, and had not yet gelled. In fact when after the final one-day game at Lord's, Richards said that they had come for the Test series and intended to win that, it sounded a little like whistling in the dark to keep the *duppies* away. Later in the season he did not hesitate to remind press conferences of this claim. Whatever they had come for they could have done better in the one-day games. The weakness of the WI overall performance rather flattered the home team – a fact that neither the home team nor its supporters seemed to realise.

The awards of Men of the Series, and of each Man of the Match, are most interesting in the light of what happened during the rest of the tour. Men of the Series were Gatting and Marshall. And without a doubt, when these were in form their teams performed well. Gatting became a 'faller' during the Trent Bridge Test at the birthday party fence; Marshall nursed his injured rib, and used his experience to make all the difference to the West Indies. Gatting, though indiscreet and stubborn, could have had more help from his management, but it is hard to think that more could have been done for Marshall than Richards and his manager Hendriks did.

Gladstone Small was man-of-the-match for the first game, played at Edgbaston on 19 May. His statutory 11 overs cost him only 31 runs, and he took 4 wickets. Dilley, on the other hand, yielded 64 runs for his 11 overs, taking but 1 wicket. Pringle showed that parsimony for which he is famous, allowing but 26 runs for his 11 overs and 1 wicket. The trouble is that in Test matches against good batsmen, one has to bowl many more than 11 overs and also do more than keep the score in check! Walsh, having previously taken for the West Indies in international one-day matches 63 wickets at an average of 27.40 runs each, was not yet in control and yielded up 50 runs in his 11 overs. 'New boy' Ambrose, with but three international matches to his credit, allowed 39 runs in his 11 overs, and accounted for Gooch.

West Indies batted first, and scored a modest 217 in 225 minutes. Logie and Hooper both scored 51, each of them having received 96 balls. It took England 53 overs, in 206 minutes, to score 219 for 4 wickets. Captain Gatting was in form: off 125 balls he scored 82 not out, reaching 50 off 86 balls. The openers Gooch and Broad gave England a good start, and were not separated until they had put on 70.

In the second match, at Headingley on 21 May, Pringle was named man-of-the-match: his 11 overs cost him 30 runs for 3 wickets; he also top-scored with 39 runs. The nearest of the West Indians to his bowling figures were: Bishop, 11 overs for 32 runs and 2 wickets; and Ambrose, 7 overs for 19 runs and 1 wicket. (Ambrose was also second top-scorer for his side with 23.) Considering that England batted first and won by 47 runs, although they made only 186, one is likely to blame WI batting. But it is quite clear that Richards did not handle his bowling well. He bowled himself for 8 overs in which he gave up 33 runs. But Ambrose and Marshall were underbowled: Marshall 9 overs, 29 runs for 2 wickets; Ambrose, as we have seen, 7 overs only.

Richards might have been saving Marshall, but he would have got much closer to keeping the English total even smaller by a more astute handling of the bowling. It was not his fault that there were 13 no-balls, and 3 wides. Perhaps he, and others, felt that England were not scoring much, anyway! And perhaps England were too easily satisfied to have won after scoring only 186! West Indies had played only 46.3 overs of the 55 allowed them when they were all out.

If all those 13 no-balls had not been wasted, and had the 'new hopes', Simmons and Richardson, managed a little more than 2 runs between them, the game would have been thrillingly close. Not to mention that a batsman of Richards's quality and reputation should not have found himself unnecessarily, and rather carelessly, bowled when set on 31 – even if the ball did keep a bit low. Further, it should not have been too difficult for him and two others simply to have grafted for a little longer. Then the series might have been even when the big game at Lord's arrived. The game certainly gave the impression that the West Indies effort had been rather unplanned and somewhat casual. The problem might have been lack of 'in the middle' practice. Nowadays there are so few county games, so little time between getting off the plane and facing international opposition! The one-day series started just twelve days after the opening of the first county game.

So England were unexpectedly two up when we all went to Headquarters, amidst some of the worst weather of the tour.

England continued their winning streak, claiming the game by 7 wickets. Once again the West Indies bowlers managed to allow the opposition 21 extra balls by way of no-balls and wides. It is quite amazing that a team which likes to call itself 'professional' and 'champion' constantly finds it so difficult to limit the no-balls – not only in the one-day games but even under the less rigorous rules in the Tests and county games. At one stage there were suggestions that the team should impose fines on those who continued to give away runs, and the opportunity for more runs, by this amazing and careless practice.

Man-of-the-match at Lord's was England's Dominican-born DeFreitas: 11 overs for 20 runs and 1 wicket. He also fielded brilliantly. West Indies managed to lose 3 wickets by the run-out method, including Logie for 0, but certainly not through his fault. Hooper was out trying an impossible second run. West Indies, except for Greenidge, Dujon and Marshall, gave a pretty lacklustre performance. Walsh, however, did produce his 11 overs for 11 runs only. But the bowling was not cleverly handled: Hooper had 10 overs for 54 runs, and Marshall and Benjamin had but 9 overs each. Richards did not bowl at all. It was very difficult to read what was going on. In fact Richards's captaincy and frame of mind, inasmuch as they could be judged from his performance, were causing some concern. For it was not difficult for West Indians to remember that good teams had fallen apart from time to time – especially when the captain could be seen, fairly or unfairly, to be not doing well either as leader, tactician or in his own playing performance.

The England players who were declared man-of-the-match, in this mini-series, did not really shine in the Tests; whereas Marshall did. And Harper, played only in the first one-day game, proved his worth in the Test series. But, without a doubt, England dominated this Texaco tournament.

Just as in baseball one tends to think of the pitchers as being the people who win or lose games, so in one-day cricket one tends to think mainly of the bowlers. But batsmen also can make the difference, and in this series England had two batsmen who scored a total of over 100: Gooch (103) and Gatting (140); West Indies had none. Their highest individual total came from Greenidge (78), followed by Hooper (75), and Dujon (69). Each of these scored less than Broad of England on 82.

Even allowing for the fact that one-day cricket is not Test cricket, the West Indies real achievement on this tour was to recover from such a disappointing start. They themselves worked hard to gain their final victory, but they were not unhelped by the Gatting incident and subsequent sacking, and the lack of concentration by some of the English players in the Tests, especially when facing the constantly improving Ambrose and Bishop and a recovered old hand like Marshall.

As England did so well in the one-day games, and so badly in the Tests, one has to raise a few questions about the organisation and administration of the game in England: should selectors choose two different squads for England? Should they reorganise the home game so as to lessen the importance given to one-day matches? What would be the financial implications of such a change of emphasis? The crowds are not exactly flocking to the regular county games – nor to Tests against Sri Lanka.

In fact one of the more amusing and comical situations in present-day English cricket, and its press coverage, is the orchestrated complaints about the West Indies 'slow' over rate, and their 'boring' fast bowlers. Yet the seats were sold out for the Texaco series and more than well occupied during the 1988 Cornhill Tests – and not mainly by Caribbean heritage people, who perhaps found the higher entrance fees a little beyond them, and the regulations about banners, drums, and so on, at Tests and one-day internationals, not a little culturally biased against them.

But it is absolutely amazing how many real honest-to-goodness English people will pay lots of money to see the West Indies play 'boring' cricket. Admittedly 'boring' is a word used by English culture in a very special way not likely to be understood correctly except by those brought up with it. I suspect the word is meant to convey the speaker's unquestioning disapproval, rather than anything the ordinary person could easily discover outside the disapprover's consciousness. I suspect also that people who do rather too well too regularly are likely to be considered *boring*.

In which case, once the one-day series ended, the West Indies team did tend to become *rather boring!*

4

The Weather and Marshall

The First Test, Trent Bridge, 1988

After the defeats suffered by the touring team in the one-day series, and considering the not outstanding performances in the county games, even avid West Indies supporters were beginning to wonder what would happen in the first Test. The weather had been none too good: players had had little chance to play themselves in. Richardson, from whom much was expected, hardly seemed to warrant his Deloitte's standing of no. 7 in the world. Benjamin was injured, and one felt that, despite assurances to the contrary, Marshall's ribcage problem might easily recur.

What made uncertainty even greater, as one drove north up a fairly sunny M1 from Woburn, was the statement which Viv Richards had made that the West Indies had really come for the Tests rather than the one-day games. If, then, West Indies were to falter in the first Test the effect on the rest of the tour could be calamitous. And the rumblings in the Caribbean against captain Richards would intensify.

The weather, as one steered gingerly into the car park close to Trent Bridge on the first morning, was none too promising. By 10:24 one was looking down from the highly perched press box into a misty morning, the sun having totally disappeared. But one felt that when the West Indies batted, if Greenidge and Haynes could give the team a good start and Richards could get real support from some of the youngsters, then they should score enough to give their bowlers a chance.

In the event England won the toss and went in to bat. Marshall opened to Gooch, using three slips, a gully, and a silly mid-on. The first over yielded 9 runs, including a no-ball. Patterson started the second over of the game with a wide. The wicket seemed slow and not really of even bounce. The bowling was not particularly wicket-taking stuff. After Marshall had bowled five overs (5–0–18–0) he was replaced by Ambrose, who bowled well. But after 10 overs in the first hour's play England's total was 44, Gooch 25, Broad 15.

At 12:25, after the light had thickened from time to time, the sun seemed to win out and brightly illuminated the English batsmen who appeared to be on top – Gooch 29, Broad 25, and the total 60 for 0 in 19 overs. For the 20th over Richards called on Hooper's off-spin. The young man responded well, as did Walsh from the Radcliffe Road end. When Gooch scored 29 he had achieved 4,000 runs in Tests. He seemed set for a big score and was on 45 when lunch was taken (after 27 overs) with the total on 80–0. Broad was on 28. West Indies did not seem to be in a particularly good position. Gooch was in form: the wicket did not favour really fast bowling, and even though he had been unsuccessful before lunch Marshall was the only bowler with a touch of class.

Lunch is sometimes a wicket-taker: on this occasion it emphasised Marshall's skill and enterprise: he cut down his pace a bit, and coming in from the pavilion end swung the ball at will. He soon beat Gooch with three successive balls, the second one of which went straight from the bat to Greenidge at second slip. Gooch, on 69, started to walk: but the catch had not been held. Marshall's bowling became so outstanding that the usual theories about cloud cover and general changes in atmospheric conditions started to pour out from broadcasters and experts in the press box. No doubt these things make a difference, but some bowlers seem to be able to take over while others complain about flat pitches and doctored wickets. And this wicket gave the impression, from afar at least, of being prepared for seamers rather than genuine pace men. So Marshall seamed and swung. And Gooch soldiered on. But when he had scored 73 Marshall hit his leg stump. Gooch, in form, had driven towards extra-cover, was beaten by the swing and movement off the pitch and apparently edged the ball on to his wicket. He had batted for 175 minutes, received 131 balls, and hit eight 4s.

Marshall had bowled 12 overs and given up 33 runs. He was not having much support from the other bowlers. Walsh was yielding up no-balls, one of which pointlessly bowled Broad when he was on 41 and the total at 132 for 1. The England team with Gatting and Gower yet to come was accumulating runs in a way that, together with the cold weather, discomforted the West Indian fans present – especially a group of ardent 'fanaticos' from Antigua.

But in the event only the English fans need have worried. For after the opening stand of 125, Gatting went at 141, having scored but 5 runs, and Lamb was lbw to Marshall for 0. Even at 161 for 2 England had seemed to be doing well. But both Broad and Lamb went at that score and at 186 Gower became Ambrose's first Test wicket in England when he was on 18, caught by Dujon off a good ball. Pringle, not considered by many to be really an England no. 6, was looking good when bad light interrupted play at 5:50 with England on 202 for 5. They returned soon after, but there was not much play left.

At the end of the first day things still seemed evenly poised. England had squandered the chance which a solid opening had given them, but Pringle was looking better than expected, and Downton, who was with him at the close of play, was known to be a stubborn and able bat. Further, with the weather and the forecast gloomy, England had exactly 220 on the board. Another 50 or so would, especially if conditions got worse, test the new West Indies side, always bearing in mind that they might have to bat last.

The day's play had illustrated the difference between one-day cricket and the 'real thing'. Thank heavens we had had more than 11 overs from Marshall, but we also had time and the pace of events that allow the tension and drama to develop; the field placing was always attacking, so one's attention was riveted not on the negative tactic of saving runs but on the bowling and the close-to-the-wicket fielding, and of course on how the batsmen would cope with these. There was much 'slowness', and some boredom, but these, like the narrative passages in an epic poem, were always building up to exciting moments and memorable performances.

Marshall's first spell from the Radcliffe Road end was fast but not as effective as we might have hoped. He probably had not then fully assessed the wicket and the conditions, but two other factors, I think, also had some bearing. He had not been perfectly fit before and had not had enough work. The other factor was umpire Bird. I do not mean in any way to question this gentleman's honesty or ability. But he constantly calls attention to himself: whenever the bowler delivers he walks up to where his front foot has landed, and to where he has followed through, and he makes an exhibition of himself as he marks off and assesses what has happened. It must be most off-putting to a bowler who is having trouble either with no-balls or running on to the pitch. The latter was bothering Marshall very much, he was in danger of being warned and he certainly did not wish to be warned off from bowling. In any case he was pitching a bit short – not in the sense that he was bowling what the English press like to call bouncers – but he was not constantly forcing the batsman to play, nor giving the ball enough chance to swing.

When after lunch he came on from the pavilion end, where umpire Birkenshaw was standing with quiet authority, he cut his speed down slightly, kept the ball up and swung it both ways in a remarkable way. He had shortened his run but this helped his control rather than slowed him down. It was only when one studied the TV playbacks at night that one could really see just how much he was moving the ball. Richards was wise to nurse him. It was good that Ambrose turned up trumps: clearly bowlers do better in tandem – Hall and Griffiths; Lindwall and Miller; Ram and Val; Lock and Laker, and (dare we mention them?) Larwood and Voce, the latter's name being emblazoned on one of the stands at Nottingham.

The second day's play was characterised by dreadful weather, a dreadful English performance, and more excellent bowling from Marshall backed up by Ambrose.

After one ball the players were driven from the field by rain, which fortunately did not last. Nor did Pringle whom Marshall bowled, at 11:23, for 39 with an excellent in-swinger which hit the leg stump. Emburey lasted four balls but did not score – caught Dujon, bowled Marshall, with the total at 223 for 7.

As Marshall walked back to his place in the field at fine-leg the English crowd generously and loudly applauded him. No doubt the overcast conditions suited him and made it difficult for the batsmen, but his control was remarkable especially as he was swinging in and out. With the departure of Emburey his figures were: 26–4–56–6. It was the sixteenth time he had taken over 5 wickets in a Test innings.

A good indication of the state of the weather was that at 12:00 Viv Richards called for his long-sleeved sweater. The state of the England team was equally uncomfortable: 245 all out, having lost 5 wickets in less than an hour's play for 25 runs.

Ambrose did well with figures of 26–10–53–4 in the first innings including a spell of 3 for 2 in eighteen balls towards the end of the innings when he bowled most sensibly at 'nine, ten, Jack'. Hooper had turned the ball and bowled well on the first day. His analysis was 8–1–20–0.

So unpredictable was the weather that although it was cold, dark and raining before West Indies went in to bat at 12:19, by 12:35 the sun was shining. But, as the saying has it, it flattered to deceive, for the good light lasted only until lunch, when West Indies had scored 8. After a boring delay play was resumed at 4:15.

The 50 came up during the twenty-second over. Greenidge, who had been going well, seemed to lose concentration and did not take advantage of being dropped by Emburey in the slips off the luckless Jarvis. He almost immediately swished at a ball outside the off stump giving Jarvis his first wicket in the series. West Indies were 54 for 1, and enter Richardson, wearing a white sun hat!

It is worth mentioning that Richardson fanned at the first ball, because he is fancied by many to be a promising opening bat. He was lucky to escape. He and Haynes went on steadily, the latter off-driving beautifully from time to time. But with the total at 84 for 2 after 30 overs, Emburey came on and had Richardson caught at silly mid-on by Gatting. It was the sixth time in seven meetings that Emburey had defeated Richardson. It was his first wicket in a Test in England since 1986!

West Indies were on 126 for 2 at close of play. It looked as if it was up to the experience of Greenidge and Richards.

The morning was at first bright and shiny, a day for a deck chair on a cruiser. But the clouds were near enough. And only 5 runs were added when heavy black rain started to pour down on us. It was decided that there would be an inspection at 1:30. Unexpectedly, by 2:00 play was resumed. But the light was never very good, and at Haynes's dismissal for 60 Hooper came out amidst the encircling gloom. Jarvis was bowling well – 2 for 28 in his first hour's spell. Richards was playing carefully and encouraging Hooper at every step. The captain reached his 50 after eighty minutes of batting and nine 4s. But even after the sun returned to cast shadows at about 3:00 he was playing defensively.

After one of those committee meetings which England Test teams seem to like, Emburey came on to a widely spread field. Richards immediately straight-drove him for a 4 which was not all that far from Lamb at long-on, then late-cut him beautifully for 3. Hooper then scored two 4s, bringing the total to 204 for 3. Richards, when on 72, was painfully hit on the little finger by DeFreitas, and went from 73 to 79 with a mighty drive well over a widish mid-on off Emburey whom he was treating very roughly. At 3:35 the light was just too bad: the score was 230 for 3, with Hooper scoring an excellent and elegant 32. Early tea was taken, and at 4:00 play was resumed.

At the close West Indies, on 264 for 4, were 19 ahead of England, with 6 wickets in hand, including those of Logie and Hooper – and Marshall!

Monday was beautifully clear and sunny, with a quite cool but gentle breeze. Trent Bridge kept up its reputation for not having crowds as large as one expects. Even allowing for the fact that it was Monday, the stands seemed rather empty for a first Test against the West Indies. Those who were there were to see England being – slowly at first, and then quite briskly – pushed out of the game.

Hooper and Logie were the overnight batsmen. Hooper got to 52 with a lovely straight-drive off Dilley. He had received seventy-two balls in 115 minutes and hit five 4s. He had been deft and elegant, and always in charge. And he immediately moved on to 55 and then to 59 with a lovely square-drive. Dujon, who had taken Logie's place when the total was 271 for 5 in the 77th over, looked as if he too were going to be in excellent form, and the first hour's play yielded 48 runs.

The odd ball was popping, and of a sudden the light started to fade. With the score on 309 for 5 Dujon played a really bad shot and was caught and bowled by Dilley for 16. From the moment that Marshall, his replacement, played his first ball it was clear that he was about to reassert his claims as an all-rounder. And he had scored 12 when lunch was taken; Hooper was on 84, and the total 334 for 6, a lead of 89. As this was a third of the way through the fourth day, and with the weather not in a stable mode, the shadow of deadlock seemed to be spreading over the game.

But at least it looked as if after lunch Hooper would gain a well deserved century and Marshall show us most clearly that he knew how to handle a bat as well as a ball.

Half an hour after lunch West Indies led by 101 but they had lost Hooper. Ambrose decided to add his name to those fast bowlers who are more than wielders of the long handle. His height and the fact that he is left-handed added to the discomfort of Emburey *et al*. And Marshall decided to step up the pace. He used a clever mix of quietly placing the ball, together with one or two enormous hits. He got to 51 with two 6s off the targeted Emburey to bring the total to 403 for 7, a lead of 158. He had already hit five 4s. It seemed remarkable that Gooch was not called into the attack as West Indies seemed to be on the way to leaving England at least as many to get as they had scored in the first innings.

Marshall went from 52 to 65 in the following manner: 6, 1, 4, 2. But just as he looked set for a quick century with the score on 425 for 7 he was bowled pulling away from a straight ball in an attempt to cut. He had done very well but it was an unfortunate way to go after hitting three 6s and six 4s in two hours and eighteen minutes off eighty-eight balls. Ambrose batted intelligently for 43 runs before more or less running himself out even though Gooch hit the wicket smartly with his throw. When the declaration came, the English bowlers had not fared well. Jarvis was the most successful – if that is the right word to use: 18.1–1–63–2. Dilley had 101 scored off him, DeFreitas 93, and Emburey 95 in 16 overs!

So England started their second innings at 4:15, 203 runs behind the West Indies. There were then nearly four full sessions of two hours each left in the game. Unless WI made a few early breakthroughs England looked like saving the game. But there would always be Marshall to contend with.

By the time the last over of this fourth day started England had collected 67 runs for the loss of Broad's wicket, caught by Dujon off Ambrose for 16. Gooch was on 38 and was as solid as ever. He did survive a very confident appeal for lbw – never a thing easy to judge from the press box, but from looking at the TV playback, and from discussion after the game in the famous marquee, one wondered whether he had not been fortunate. But I am sure that there were other occasions when he might have felt that he had not been given the 'benefit of the doubt'.

There was some feeling about the matter because everyone knows what a solid batsman Gooch is, both a fighter and a strokeplayer. To have dismissed him as well as Broad even before the last day started would have 'made' the Test for the West Indies. Their bowling had been tight but not penetrating. This was not surprising as the wicket, although, as Richards put it, exploding from time to time, had little in it for fast bowlers, and the atmosphere had cleared up considerably. Ambrose was the only wicket taker, ending up the afternoon with 1 wicket for 13 runs in 8 overs. Marshall's 8 overs had cost him 14 runs.

Although logic stressed that the game would be a draw, and the final morning's bright sunlight promised no help to the bowlers, feeling was on the side of the West Indies: Marshall had really impressed on that first afternoon of the game! England no doubt knew that showers were expected, and so if they were careful they should be safe.

We were wondering whether Marshall was suffering from his rib injury. What at one stage was thought to be policy in holding him in reserve could have been necessity. Gooch soon got the single he needed for his 50 from a gently placed shot to short-cover, moving the total to 87 for 1. He had hit four 4s, and his partner, Gatting, was on 15. At last Marshall was recalled, and in his second over, the total being 116 for 1, he clean bowled Gatting's off stump. In the first innings the captain had scored 5; now he had managed to get 29.

By lunch England had added 72 to their overnight total, and Gooch and Gower showed no sign of getting out. It became clear after lunch that Marshall was injured and unable to bowl. Gower got his 50 shortly before tea, when the score was 241 for 2. He was looking solid and had hit six 4s. With Gooch on 128, they had added 125 so far. Immediately after tea Dujon missed a difficult chance when the ball went off the inside edge of Gooch's bat. Dujon was already moving to cover the line of the ball as it left the bowler's hand; he had to change direction, and although he managed to be at full stretch the ball shot under his hands. If only

Gooch had been removed then there might have been a chance for West Indies to win.

The bowlers were having trouble with their footholds, and it was not until Gooch was on 146 and the total 277 that he was out – caught at the wicket off Patterson. Gower was then 71. Gooch had really played well, defending and attacking as circumstances and the bowling demanded. His innings took 410 minutes and 303 balls. He hit fifteen 4s. Lamb looked none too safe, and West Indies supporters really missed Marshall. Even Gower towards the end of a saving innings looked uncertain under Patterson's peppering – he lost his helmet at one stage. But it was clear enough that there could be no decision, and at 5:30 the game ended.

During the weekend, apparently, some of the England players had 'lived it up' more than Gatting's birthday warranted, and more than the selectors (and the lively Pharisees in the community) were willing to accept. Gatting subsequently lost the captaincy because of the jape. Manager Stewart, never at a loss for a word or an excuse, came under heavy criticism, and many, with that especial attraction of the English for spicy scandal, fished in the lower reaches of the press for bits of gossip. Words such as *orgy* and *moral* and *honour* were bandied about, as were *curfew* and *discipline* and *manager*.

On the strictly cricketing side the Test, despite the rain and state of the pitch, did produce some outstanding features: the bowling of Marshall (and his batting), the batting of Gooch and Richards, and the promising performance of Hooper. Marshall was made Man of the Match.

Walsh and Patterson, however, had not quite found their feet, tending to bowl flat out, manfully plugging the ball in with speed, but not taking into account the demands of the peculiar conditions.

Richards, on the other hand, in making an awe-inspiring 80, fitted the action to the moment. When he went in Richardson had gone cheaply and somewhat airily for 17, and West Indies had started to look slightly stuck in the mire. Richards played five balls; the sixth he placed for a 2. His next five scoring shots were all 4s, suitably placed around the ground. Having put a halt to any threat of dominance from England, and in the process having brightened things up, he then showed restraint, and encouraged Hooper all along the way. The latter responded with an innings of real class in difficult conditions.

Richards's pattern of scoring after his rush to 22 was most interesting. From the pavilion end he scored mainly behind the wicket: four scoring strokes on the off-side, and two on the leg. From the Radcliffe Road end he scored mostly in front of the wicket, three times more scoring shots being made through the covers than on the leg-side, where he hit an enormous 6 off Emburey to long-on. He was a little self-indulgent to get out in the way he did. He was close to his ninety-ninth century when on 72 he was hit by a ball from DeFreitas that 'exploded'. It hurt the little finger of the left hand badly. He threw down his bat, ripped off his glove, then after attention with a pain-killing spray, continued. Bad light interrupted play. Soon after resumption the captain drove in a rather cavalier fashion at DeFreitas, and Gooch held a rocket at second slip.

Richards had made sure that Emburey had no chance to play his role of blocking up one end and deceiving flat-footed batsmen. And Hooper followed suit. This was important because from the first day Hooper had shown that the wicket would turn, even if slowly. And the one with which Emburey got Richardson *had* turned. Richards very nearly hit Emburey out of Test cricket. One wonders whether Emburey would have been selected for the Lord's Test except that in the wake of Gatting's 'indiscretion' he was called upon to lead the England side. And Emburey was not chosen for the subsequent Headingley Test.

On the other hand, Richards's treatment of him was a back-handed compliment – as if despite his not having had a Test wicket in England since 1986, he was not to be given the chance of being a problem to inexperienced West Indies batsmen.

But despite the lively efforts of the dancing girls, and the bowling of Marshall and the batting of Richards and Hooper, England had scored 301 for 3 and had broken the series of Test defeats at the hands of the West Indies by securing, with the virtual absence of Marshall in the second innings, a draw.

5

The Weather and Marshall Again

The Third Test, Old Trafford, 1988

The England dressing-room post-mortem, at the end of the third Test at Old Trafford, took so much time that I was well on the road home before Micky Stewart appeared and their press conference began. I am sure no one was so uncouth as to ask the manager whether he thought Marshall was still 'just a bowler'. And it would have been brutal to remind him of his prediction that England were an evens chance to win at Old Trafford!

The unreality of the England management was left far behind by the feeling, fairly widespread in the country, that England have some prior right to win. So that when they lost to what, on the day, was simply a better cricket team, that fact alone could never be accepted as an explanation of the defeat. The selectors, the much-maligned barmaids, the weather, the unfair use of boring fast bowlers, all of these were put forward rather than the inferiority of the team in the given context. Certainly, to have an inferior team at a given time might be connected with many factors, but need not necessarily lead to resurrecting the Romans and asking them to take over this sceptred isle once again, and to reorganise cricket along the lines of amphitheatre blood sports. Those who do not get the nod from the Emperor must die!

From the very beginning of this Test one wondered if Manchester was going to live up to its not entirely unearned reputation for rain. On the morning of the first day, Thursday 30 June, it was very overcast indeed – almost misty. The field was an emerald green, but the practice pitches, which are netted sections of the regular square, were a brownish yellow. The Test wicket was quite yellow with some grass peeping through. It did not look like a seamer's wicket. I myself was glad that Harper was playing, even though it was at the expense of Haynes who was not fit. England won the toss and decided to bat – not an easy decision, but from the long inspection which the wicket received from the English team, and from their inclusion of Childs along with Emburey (now captaining), one concluded that they expected it to take spin, and perhaps not to last too long, especially if we had a day or two of bright sun.

Marshall opened from the Stretford Road end, and Ambrose from the city end, where the new and excellently refurbished press box is perched on top of the Red Rose Suite. Gooch went through the slips off Ambrose to bring the score up to 9. Both bowlers were forcing the batsmen to play the ball, and not infrequently, to miss it. The sun came in and out, as if in imitation of the English batting. It was even bright enough to have Moxon standing on his shadow just before he played forward to Marshall in the ninth over of the game and was bowled for 0, making the total 12 for 1. Marshall's figures were then 5–3–5–1.

In the 10th over Gooch started ominously to middle the ball, but with the score on 14 for 1 his partner Gatting gave us a replay of a method by which he has from time to time lost his wicket: he padded up to a ball pitching outside his off stump, played no stroke, and was leg before wicket without scoring. The bowler was Marshall, whose figures were then 6–3–9–2! After 7 more runs Marshall was rested, and so was Ambrose. Richards was clearly not asleep, nor was he allowing anyone to snooze off.

Walsh, from the Stretford Road end, was beautifully controlled, pitching just about off stump all the while. He was soon rewarded with Gower's wicket from a slightly faster ball which got up a bit. Harper at third slip made no mistake, and England were 33 for 3 in about seventy-five minutes play. The situation was beginning to look all too familiar: were England just hopeless, or were West Indies superbly in form? But worse was to come; for even before lunch, just as one was thinking that Benjamin could be rested, he had Gooch caught by Dujon for 27, Gooch waiting quietly for the decision. England had lost 4 wickets in the morning session for all of 55 runs.

As the players went in to lunch the clouds gathered. Forty minutes later the players' shadows could be seen quite clearly darkening the grass. But the sunlight did not help the batsmen very much even though Lamb was striking the ball, for when the total reached the snow-capped peaks of 61 runs, Capel played far forward to Benjamin and was bowled, utterly beaten by an in-swinger which also cut in off the pitch. England had lost 5 wickets. Lamb was not overawed, and when the score climbed to 65 he had scored 22, coming in at no. 5. But when he was 33 he made an unwise slash at Ambrose, and was caught by Greenidge at point. Total 94 for 6. With but 3 more runs added, Downton being on 22, and Emburey on 1, at 3:07 rain and bad light stopped play. Lamb's shot might have been symptomatic of the weakness of present day 'English' batting: it seemed more related to the one-day game than to the rigours of Test cricket. Or it might simply have been that Lamb tends, on the off-side, to stand away from the pitch of the ball as he hits it – and is often quite successful while doing so!

By 3:35 a powerful shower was upon us, something like a Caribbean white squall rushing in off the sea. People scampered for shelter – there are not many covered stands at Old Trafford. Large multicoloured umbrellas were all over the place, excellent at keeping out the rain, but what, I wondered, kept out the chill? Play was somehow resumed seventy minutes later, and one wondered just how the bowlers were going to get a good grip on the ball. But Emburey was soon out, caught Dujon bowled Walsh for 1. England were still 2 runs short of 100, even though Downton was fighting hard. His was the eighth wicket to fall, caught Greenidge in the gully off Walsh for a steer rather than a stroke. He had scored 24 and the total was 113. He was one of only three batsmen to pass 20.

Despite a bit of a stir by DeFreitas (15) and Dilley (14), England were all out at 6:40 for 135. Even allowing for the conditions, and for the general excellence of the bowling, England's performance had been pathetic. The West Indies bowling figures were worth quoting:

	O	M	R	W
Marshall	12	5	19	2
Ambrose	17	5	35	2
Walsh	18.2	4	46	4
Benjamin	13	4	31	2

Play stopped at 7:00 when, as is often the case in England in midsummer, the light was at its brightest. Gooch, at slip, had managed to drop Greenidge when he was on 4, the total being 4, the score on which the day's play ended. Two hours had been lost to rain.

When I awoke next morning the sky and the trees were so heavy with water that I decided to call on old colleagues in the Manchester education authority in which I had worked for some time. So my host took me to the Greenhayes Centre, in Mosside, a West Indian enclave, where my office used to be. I was in the midst of a discussion on language teaching when I gathered from a radio, just overhead, that play would be starting at 11:00 as scheduled. A hasty taxi drive got me to the ground on time for a slightly delayed start at 11:24. I had wanted especially to see the first hour's play because, despite the way in which West Indies had been looking superior to England, the three overs which they faced at the end of the first day were not very reassuring. Greenidge had been dropped in the slips, and Richardson, although originally an opening batsman, had been far from comfortable. Emburey had put himself on just to test Richardson, and from time to time my heart was in my mouth!

On this morning, Richardson looked better, but after one or two beautifully timed shots, which took him to 23, with the score on 35, he attempted to hook Dilley and succeeded only in pulling the ball on to his wicket. I was yet to see this protégé of Viv Richards play a sensible and convincing innings in England.

At lunch time we could not believe our luck: we had enjoyed uninterrupted play since 11:24. West Indies had scored 73 for 1; more than half of the English total had been achieved with the loss of 1 wicket. When the total was 60 Greenidge had survived a boisterous appeal from DeFreitas for lbw. With the aid of the TV playback we were able to assess that the ball would have missed the leg stump. Once again an umpire, without the aid of technology, was correct in his judgement. I couldn't help recalling my amazement when playbacks were first introduced in baseball: the umpires were invariably correct, even in calling the closest 'safe on base' plays. On the occasions when umpires are shown by TV to be wrong – in run-out decisions, for instance – we should remember that, even if we expect the highest standards from them, we are the ones who have the use of technology to help us!

After lunch it did not take West Indies long to slide to 101–3.

Richards started shakily, but nonetheless in form. He dealt with one ball from Childs, who was bowling well, in a really superb fashion. It could not have been more than two inches short, he leaned back and drove it wide of mid-off for 4. But Greenidge had not been too happy, and DeFreitas had him lbw when he was on 45.

Childs, a left-arm spinner, was bowling with control and guile. The 43rd over of the innings he turned into a splendid maiden to Richards; his figures were then 10–2–25–1. The total was 121 for 3, just 14 short of the English first innings score. But with DeFreitas bowling well, and Viv Richards obviously not fit – he took painkillers from time to time for a strained wrist and had a fever –West Indies looked slightly hobbled. The strained wrist, plus some careful bowling from Emburey and Dilley, took its toll, and in the last over before tea Richards played on to Capel for 47 to make it 175 for 4. He had batted for 104 minutes, faced seventy- one balls, and hit five 4s and one 6. He and Logie had added 74 runs.

Despite continuing weather problems on the third day, Saturday, when over half the day's play was also lost, the remarkable feature of the West Indies innings was the batting right down to no. 8. Dujon (no. 6) got 67; Harper (no. 7) 74; Marshall (no. 8) 43 not out. What had been a worryingly brittle middle order had performed. Indeed, it was an all-round effort: of the eventual total, on Monday, of 384 for 7 declared, only two batsmen had scored over 50, but three had scored just below 50.

It is important to remember that on the second day the West Indies score after so many stoppings and startings was 242 for 5, Dujon 35 not out, Harper 23 not out. On Saturday, partly because of the dreadful weather, Richards felt that he did not have quite enough to declare, despite the enterprising batting of Harper, the elegance of Dujon and the forcefulness of Marshall. On Monday play could not start until 1:20. And even then it was possible only because of the splendid work of the ground staff, and the modern methods of covering extensive parts of the ground. Those water hogs are certainly among the great innovations of modern English cricket, even though the strong 'Old Time' lobby is as against covering as they were (or are?) against the wearing of helmets!

Richards eventually declared well into the day at 284 for 7, and many of us were worried that he had left it too late, that the dreadfully unsettled weather might frustrate his hopes of going two up in the series. We need not have worried. For by 12:20 on Tuesday, just before the final gigantic cloudburst, England had folded once again, defeated by an innings and 156 runs with a day to spare.

But if WI supporters need not have worried over the result, they and all lovers of cricket simply had to ask themselves what had happened to English cricket? On the fourth day, for instance, soon after the declaration and a brief interruption just after 4 o'clock, Gooch was immediately lbw to Marshall with the total at 6. The second wicket fell at 22, Gatting, who had survived a confident appeal for lbw, being caught by Richardson off Marshall for 4. Richardson then put down an easy catch off Moxon at third slip when the total was 28. And 3 runs later Gower was dropped by Marshall.

England had lost their way but West Indies were looking slightly indolent: the England cricketers found no means of exploiting this. By 6:15 Marshall had been warned twice for following through on to the wicket and Walsh replaced him from the Stretford Road end, but this also gave no ease to the England players. Walsh opened with a maiden, and Benjamin, brought on from the other end, soon had Moxon, on 15, hitting a ball straight to Viv Richards at first slip. England had sunk to 36 for 3. England managed not to lose any more wickets that evening, and at 7:08 left the field with the total at 60. But, one thought, 189 runs behind, with the weather variable to say the least, was not such an impossible situation. England could at least fight for a draw: Gower on 24 and Lamb on 6 were still there. Alas, the rest is history, as the saying has it, for England managed to get only 33 runs on Tuesday morning.

Gower, batting at no. 4, was highest scorer with 34. Nos. 5, 6, 7, 8, 9, and 10 managed to total 27. Moxon's 15 just managed to top extras at 12. No other contribution to the scoresheet achieved 10 runs. Marshall had taken 7 wickets for 22 runs, but just as significant from the West Indies point of view was that he had scored 43 not out, and Dujon at no. 6 and Harper at no. 7 had made their mark with the bat.

What had happened? Was English cricket croaking out its final death rattle? Were new bowlers like Ambrose and Benjamin just too much for them?

In any case West Indies had gone 2–0 up, with the first Test drawn. Was there any way in which England could win the fourth Test at Headingley, and thus leave themselves the prospect of evening up the series at the Oval? Many hoped – and they were not all England supporters – that they would do better. But that was not to be.

What did take place was an unreal post-mortem in which Micky Stewart flannelled like a jib in a changing wind, and people who should have known better, including the cool and much respected Peter May as chairman of the selectors, found a suitable scapegoat in the overseas players. Mr Stewart was to go so far as to say he would ban overseas players completely from county cricket, a move of which Clive Lloyd had warned when I interviewed him over a year previously. But while May was pointing the finger at overseas players, English writers were pointing the finger at him, some rather vigorously accusing him of wasting England's cricket resources; others, perhaps more reasonably, complained that there had been no overall England strategy, which could have been combined with a 'horses for courses' approach to each game and venue.

6

Was it the Drains, or were England Drowning?

The Fourth Test, Headingley, 1988

Clearly after Old Trafford England felt that drastic action was needed. A new captain, Christopher Cowdrey (following in his father Colin's footsteps), was appointed for the rest of the series. A policy of only three 'front line' bowlers was adopted; those chosen were Dilley, Foster and Pringle. Curtis became Gooch's opening partner, and Richards was made the wicket-keeper.

We now know that July 1988, in England, was one of the wettest months in recent years. We have the meteorological statistics to prove it. While the Test matches were in progress we could only feel it in our aching bones. The morning journey from Bradford to Headingley, via Pudsey of Len Hutton fame, was dangerously misty. And knowing the wintry Yorkshire wind that sweeps across the Headingley ground, one was apprehensive all the way to the press parking lot. But there the sun was bright, and the covers were off the pitch and surrounds. The umpires had announced that play would start at 11:50, and one was grateful if sceptical. Greenidge was suffering from a powerful virus, and so at last Arthurton got his chance. West Indies won the toss and asked England to bat.

At 11:47 we doubting Thomases were surprised to see umpires Bird and Shepherd making their way to the wicket. The England openers were Gooch and Curtis, Capel having been stood down. But after one over from Marshall, Ambrose opened with two wides down the off-side, and was very unhappy with his run up as he came in from the football end. It soon became clear that, although not playing beach cricket, he might at any moment have to wade through cold puddles before getting up to the wicket. He spoke to Bird. Bird pecked at the matter, then hopped over to Shepherd, both summoned head groundsman Boyce, and called for towels, the red roller, and the water hogs. The cricketers retired; Boyce and his men worked valiantly, rolling over and wringing out large towels which were rumoured to have been snatched from the players' dressing-room.

There were rumours and counter-rumours, accusations and denials, about the fresh spring that had gushed in the bowler's path, about six feet before his delivery stride. One brusque Yorkshire official brushed the whole thing aside by suggesting that modern players were always seeking 'absolutely perfect conditions' – the implication being that in his day he would have been willing to breast the foaming waves before single-handedly bowling the whole West Indies team out for less than 100. The explanation for the small sink hole which was most believed, and most strongly denied, was that Mr Boyce, much disturbed by constant criticisms of his wickets, had shifted the Test pitch somewhat towards the dressing-rooms, to get a more reliable surface. He had also, it was asserted and denied, blocked one of the drains so as to lift the water table to make sure that the new wicket did not crack or break up. But the poor man and his staff – and all of us – had had to put up with more rain than our manifold sins deserved. The result was that, to mix and dampen a metaphor, his scheme backfired.

One Yorkshire lady serving us at lunch was heard to say, by way of demystification, 'Drains were blocked to preserve the pitch, but they overcooked the goose'.

Whether a drain had been blocked, or whether some hidden Moses had struck the rock too hard, the fact of the matter is that nothing happened but lunch and blanket wringings, and the jet-like expulsion of water from the water hogs – sometimes to the detriment of the fans standing too close on the tarmac path bordering the field. Nothing happened in a cricket way until an inspection at 1:15, and a resumption of play at 2:30.

English fans are a patient lot! One hopes that on such a wet day the long absence of cricket did not cost the companies and associations entertaining customers in the hospitality boxes more than they can write off as business expenses!

Gooch went early, caught by Dujon off Marshall for 9. At the time it seemed a bad omen, for when Gooch does not get many runs neither do England. Marshall, not as effective as expected, had collected his 27th wicket in the series. Athey joined Curtis, and it was up to England's team picked for batting, with Pringle at no. 9, to build up a large score, especially as West Indies bowlers had been somewhat wayward. They had been pitching too much on the leg stump or outside, even when adopting an attacking off-side field. Benjamin, when he came on at first change, looked the best of the bowlers, and on 43 for 1, after Walsh had just failed to hold a return from Athey, Benjamin had Curtis lbw for 12.

Gower came to the wicket due some runs, which England badly needed. He almost immediately caused great excitement by being caught for 1 by Logie. But the umpire had signalled 'No-ball'!

He caused further excitement, of a different kind, by square-cutting Benjamin beautifully for 4, taking the score to 54 for 2. He then scored an elegant 2 on the leg-side. Benjamin was not holding his line as well as he needed to. So it came as a disappointment and a shock when with the total on 58, Gower was caught at the wicket by Dujon for 13. He had failed once again to build up an innings, an inexplicable lapse in so excellent and elegant a batsman with nearly 7,000 Test runs under his belt. There were immediate calls for his head.

Athey continued to play forward on the stretch for everything, as if he feared that any minute someone would play the ace and claim all the chips on the table! Walsh very nearly claimed all his stumps with a beautifully fast ball which went straight through, just missed the wicket, and rocked the wicket-keeper back on his heels. Like too many West Indian deliveries, though, it was a no-ball.

Lamb, an overseas player of the kind which apparently does not ruin English cricket, was batting beautifully, and showing up the long-standing weakness of the home grown product when it comes to launching into the driveable ball. It took Athey 109 minutes and seventy-five balls to get to 16. As he had scored one 4, he had in fact needed seventy-four balls to score 12 runs – 1 run per six balls. This was at a time when the West Indies bowlers, perhaps because of the wetness of the ball and the difficulty of getting a good footing, were not really bowling at their best.

The slippery footing no doubt also explained Logie's failure to hold a difficult leg-side catch close to the wicket off Smith when he was on 2, and the total 88 for 3. Logie struggled as he fell to the grass, trying to hold on to the ball, his thrashing legs giving the impression of a fighting fish at the end of the line, refusing to leave the water. Lamb drove off the front foot, and square-cut, with authority. With Smith he brought up the 100 by 5:28. Lamb, never getting as close to the pitch of the ball as good sense demands, hit so hard when he was driving or cutting that he made up for his lack of orthodoxy. He struck Ambrose for one particularly delightful 4 through the covers as if Ambrose were your ordinary slow-medium seamer. He and Smith also ran well-judged singles. Their 50 partnership came up in 13 overs (fifty-seven minutes).

The wicket was slower than expected for a first day at Headingley, and Smith and Lamb, who did not 'learn their cricket in England', were never afraid of taking on the bowlers. At 6:16 the total being 137 for 4, the 10,000 fans present had their second major disappointment of the day as bad light stopped play. Lamb was on 45, Smith on 23. And Benjamin's analysis was the only one worth quoting: 9–2–27–2.

The fact that Lamb and Smith did not bat in the prevalent English mode – neither did Ted Dexter in his day – should give English coaches and selectors much to think about. In a diagnosis of what is wrong with English cricket, Peter May set out a three-point plan for improvement: amending the county programme to four-day cricket, reducing counties to one overseas player each, and the preparation of better wickets. He expressed this in the acronym POW (Programme, Overseas Players and Wickets) but at the most that can be only two-thirds correct.

And so to the second day. The overnight 137 for 4 was not quite what was expected from a team selected for its batting, but Lamb and Smith were in form, and had already added 57. Cowdrey and Jack Richards – selected as much for his batting as his wicket-keeping – were still to come. And there was optimism in some quarters that the young, new and lively captain would 'make a difference'.

From the point of view of the West Indies, the day opened with little tension. The game started on time; the light was good, but the atmosphere was heavy with water, and old hands around the well-filled ground were predicting that the ball would move about a great deal and discomfort the batsmen no end. They were in fact so little troubled that by 11:47 Lamb and Smith had scored 100 together and put England on 180. Leg-byes had then contributed 18! The bowling was not impressive even though Marshall had cut down his run as he had successfully done in the first innings at Trent Bridge. The wet grass underfoot might have had something to do with the lack of real quality in the bowling. Or it simply might have been a case of the bowlers bowling as well as the batsmen allowed them to.

Then of a sudden came the break WI had been hoping for – and the blow England did not need. In taking a quick single Lamb pulled up lame. It did not at first seem serious. But the players gathered around him, and in answer to a signal physio Laurie Brown rushed on to the field. It soon became clear that his painkilling spray was really not enough, and Lamb, with his help, limped off the field. The score was 183, Lamb being 64, and Smith 38. What happened to England after that beggars description. It was unbelieveable.

Chris Cowdrey stepped forward briskly to the wicket, and immediately looked uncomfortable. And Robin Smith, who had looked so confident when batting with his fellow South African, lost his concentration, or was simply beaten by Ambrose, and was caught at the wicket at the same total on which Lamb had limped away. The score was 183 for 5; very soon it was 183 for 6, then 185 for 7, 185 for 8 and 201 all out, Lamb having retired hurt. On a team selected for its batting, nos. 7, 8, and 9 managed all of 2 runs between them, and no. 9 was Pringle, once touted in England as an all- rounder who would make the difference – who might even take the place of Botham!

England had managed to lose 5 wickets for 18 runs in forty- eight balls. They were all out about twenty minutes before the luncheon break on Friday, the second day of the Test. They had not lasted for four sessions, in a game which they simply had to go all out to win so that they could go to the Oval in a position to even up the series.

Marshall had collected his 29th wicket in the series, taking 3 wickets for 55 runs. But Ambrose was really the bowler of the innings – not that the majority of the English batsmen offered the bowlers real problems. Ambrose's figures were: 25.1–8–58–4. Note that he yielded only 2.3 runs per over, and took a wicket every thirty-eight balls or thereabouts (in fact, 37.75).

England had of course been unfortunate in the way in which they lost Lamb. But a team which is selected for batting, with Pringle, once at no. 5, now at no. 9, must score more than 201 – of which 31 had been extras! Something had gone hopelessly wrong.

Since Greenidge, an anchor man if ever there was one, was unfit and not on the team, West Indies opened with Haynes and Dujon. The latter did not last long despite his opening shot, a straight-drive for 4. He scored 13, and the opening partnership was worth only 15. Hooper came in at no. 3, and, as usual, looked good while he lasted. By 2:51 the 50 came up, and the skies poured light down on a nearly full house. West Indies went along quietly. The bowlers were not ineffectual, but playing at a total of 201 the batsmen could take their time. Hooper got to 19 with a perfectly timed off-drive through the covers for 4. But Foster, replacing Dilley, soon had him lbw while still on 19. The ball had whipped back sharply from the off, Hooper played back and was struck in front.

Richards came in to a remarkably warm reception from the usually quiet Yorkshire crowd. He let the first ball go perilously close to his off stump. But the third ball he cut very fine for 4 to the third-man boundary. He then glided beautifully for 4, drove to mid-wicket for yet another 4, turned a ball fine of square-leg for 2. He then struck the ball through Dilley at wide mid-off for 4. I wrote at the time:

'He looks as if he is going to cut loose. And there is a buzz of excitement around the ground. Foster shortens to the great man still in search of his ninety-ninth century. Richards is on to it like a tiger. He hooks the ball with vigour, turning over his wrists in the accepted fashion, as if making a two-handed cross-court drive in tennis. I look for the ball on the boundary and am surprised by the shouts all around . . .

As I glance back to the wicket I realise that Richards is as surprised as I am, for Curtis, standing fairly close at square-leg, has managed to hold on to a superb catch quite close to the grass.'

It was now 97 for 3. Richards had hit four 4s and a 2! Once again from the Test cricket point of view the game was looking a bit odd. With the West Indies facing 201, one felt that they should have been building up to something like 400 so as to win without having to return to the wicket. One wondered whether Richards, after his explosive start, might not simply have played a few quietly back to the bowler. The atmosphere was still heavy with moisture, and none of us expected uninterrupted play.

After Richards's departure West Indies seemed to be concentrating on reasserting dominance, and just after tea, when it was really getting dark again, Haynes reached 50, and the total 113 for 3. He had hit seven 4s in his 113 minutes at the wicket. Foster, at this time, was the pick of the English bowlers, but it was Pringle who dismissed Haynes just as he was looking as if he might score one of the series's rare centuries. He played across the line and was lbw for 54; the total, 137 for 4.

With Richards, Haynes, Hooper and Dujon out, this was not the kind of score the West Indies could have been looking for, but unlike their English rivals they could count on their middle and lower-order batsmen. The wickets in fact eventually fell in this manner: 156 for 5, 194 for 6, 210 for 7, 222 for 8, 245 for 9, and 275 all out. Although not dominating completely the first-innings exchanges, West Indies had established a lead of 74. This was disappointing from the WI point of view; the kind of champions they are supposed to be should have led by at least 150, and so put unnerving pressure on England.

England had done much to redeem their low first-innings score. They would have been in an even better position were it not for the sterling performance of the West Indies lower order batsmen. Harper was top scorer with 56; Arthurton in his first Test scored 27, and Logie 44. Both of these should have scored many more. Logie, for instance, just before darkness and a heavy storm stopped play at 4:49, had already hit eight 4s. But he did not heed the Caribbean proverb 'Greedy choke puppy', and hit wildly at a ball from Pringle, and spooned up – and out – to Foster. Pringle had, of course, held the ball back. A simple defensive shot would have left the whole of the third day for a century from this much improved, if still too impulsive, batsman. His 44 runs had been scored off forty-one balls.

Large umbrellas, blue, yellow and red, or quartered in blue and white, sprouted up all over the place. But there was no stopping for the rain. West Indies were 156–5 at the enforced close of play.

On Saturday morning, driving in from Halifax in the rain, I thought that we were about to lose yet another day's play. On arriving at Headingley I was surprised to hear from the public address system that the umpires would inspect the field at 11:00. This they did, and announced that there would be another inspection at noon. This was greeted with some amount of humorous disbelief because the rain was already falling. There were further inspections and promises, and at 2:40, after a wait of 185 minutes, the white-robed umpires came out of the pavilion, and play started at 2:45. But in the end the rain won the day quite comprehensively.

Four hours and nineteen minutes were lost during the day. We had 23 overs in the one hour and forty-one minutes of play allowed by the weather. Runs had been scored at the rate of 3.5 per over. The total was 238 for 8, with Harper on 31, having struck six 4s. The conditions made concentration on the part of the batsmen rather difficult. But nonetheless in the Test WI scored a remarkable number of 4s – 41 to be exact. This was not only because their batsmen see no sense in playing half-volleys and long hops defensively, but also because bowlers like Foster and Pringle, while looking dangerous from time to time, bowled entirely too many half-volleys. When the WI innings was finished Pringle would have taken 5 wickets for 95 runs, *but in 27 overs*. He was allowing some 3.5 runs an over. In the conditions (slow outfield) and remembering the low score of his team, this was simply not good enough as Test bowling. Ambrose had allowed but 2.32 runs per over in taking 4 wickets, and Benjamin but 3 runs per over in taking 2.

But we are running ahead of events. Saturday afternoon ended with the field flooded, the breezes calm, and gentle sunlight shining over everything. West Indies were 37 runs ahead with 2 wickets standing, and with forecasters saying that isobars and wind directions were 'unsettled', it still looked as if England might 'hold strain' and squeeze a draw from the damp conditions.

On Sunday the 'glorious uncertainty' of English weather was made manifest. We drove over from Halifax to Harewood – passing through Headingley – for an excellent roast beef and Yorkshire pudding meal, and then on to Harrogate to see the roses which themselves were adversely affected by the record rainfall. But on this sixty-mile spin we encountered not a single drop of rain, only very high winds sweeping enormous fluffs of cloud across a cheeringly blue sky. Yet we knew that many local friendly games, such as Press v. Personalities, had been called off because of flooded fields.

On Saturday evening we had left a flooded Headingley, quiet in the clear amber light of an after-the-storm calm. On Monday morning, despite the adverse forecasts, when play started on time the field was awash with bright sunlight. West Indies had a lead of 37 runs with 2 wickets in hand, but that did not seem much against an England team selected with the emphasis on its batting.

It did not take Benjamin long – at no. 10, but no slob with the bat – to run himself out by simply not grounding his bat. True enough the throw was accurate, the fielding sharp, but he charged in with bat in the air, and the umpire had no doubt that he was well and truly out. Walsh joined Harper, but the bowlers, especially Pringle, kept going down the leg-side. Harper took over cleverly, and was soon on 50, which he scored off ninety-six balls, hitting eight 4s. And at a minute before noon this last pair had added 25 runs. When shortly after noon Harper was eventually out, caught expertly by Gower off Foster, he and Walsh had added 30 runs, and West Indies on 275 had established a lead of 74 runs. But with general weather conditions still unsettled – even if at that moment the sun was shining brightly – and with but five sessions of play left, it still looked like a draw or a close finish. Most likely a pale draw, with England stonewalling and holding on despite Lamb being unlikely to bat; it seemed the more likely when, as the teams left the field for the luncheon break, a thunderstorm threatened. Gooch was serenely on 17, and Curtis on 4.

The light brightened considerably after lunch and England went on to 52 from a mishit by Gooch off Walsh which went through the slips. The bowling was not quite tight enough, but Curtis survived a terrific lbw appeal off Ambrose who was looking sharper than the other bowlers. In fact he soon yorked Curtis's leg stump comprehensively. The force of the ball also disarranged the middle stump. Curtis had scored 12; the total was 56.

Gooch appeared to lose concentration now and again, but continued to score, until on 50 he was caught by Hooper off Walsh to make it 80 for 2. England had now wiped off the West Indies lead and, were 6 runs ahead with 2 wickets down. Gower and Smith were yet to come. Would the especially-chosen batsmen, Cowdrey, Richards and Pringle, come good in their second innings? Could they at least save the game for England – not without the help of Dilley who had scored a Test half-century before this?

The answer is now too well known to prolong the agony. England's batting failed once again. Gower, having scored 2 for his 7,000th run (in 100 Tests), flicked Marshall down the leg-side, and Dujon took a rather good catch, moving far to his right. One could not help recalling how Gower, in better times, had saved England at Sabina Park in Jamaica with his vigorous knock of 154 not out against Marshall, Holding, Croft and Garner.

Smith scored a crisp 11, but never looked like lasting before Marshall made him his thirty-first victim of the series, lbw, when the total was 105. To the surprise of many, Lamb came in at no. 8. His pulled calf muscle clearly causing him pain and rendering him immobile, he scored, with the help of his runner, Smith, 19 runs, including three 4s. Not only was he last man out, but at one stage he had to farm the bowling in order to hide his colleagues from the attack, now scenting victory but still not as impressive as it could have been. One wondered why at one stage Lamb, who eventually lasted one hour and twenty-nine minutes, was not tested by Harper whom he could not have played without moving his injured leg. Against the fast bowlers he tended to plant himself firmly and to hit as hard as he could. *His score of 19 was more by 1 run than the total put together by Cowdrey, Richards, Pringle, Foster and Dilley!*

England's batting had again fallen apart despite the sunshine of the afternoon, and the packing of the side with 'batsmen'. One has to balance against Lamb's injury the absence of both Greenidge and Richardson from the West Indies team. I myself would have preferred Harper for Richardson from the Manchester Test on. But the captain and the excellent management would not have agreed with me.

At 6:06 on that bright Monday afternoon the umpires took up their posts. Haynes and Dujon opened, needing 65 to win. The first over yielded 4 runs, the second 4, the third 4. By close of play Dujon was on 17, Haynes on 10.

I nearly missed the final 4 to mid-wicket with which Dujon sealed the victory early on Tuesday morning and put the West Indies 3–0 up in the series. I had gone to Thirsk for the Monday night where a group of Jamaican officials and fans who had come over for this Test and the final one at the Oval had been staying at a lovely pub run by a member of the West Indian Degazon family. We had a wonderful night so I made sure to leave early. Unfortunately I have always found getting to the suburb of Headingley one thing, but finding my way into the Yorkshire CCC another. So I nearly missed the final drowning, when not a drop was falling, of England's hopes.

Much as I would have appreciated the early start home down the M1 to Woburn Sands, I attended the press conference, waving my pass at the officious, uniformed Guardian of the Gate. Viv Richards appeared first with a delicately held flute of champagne. He was immedately asked about the move to restrict further, if not to ban altogether, overseas players, and to blame them for England's poor performance. His answer was direct and pointed: he had learned from playing with and against such overseas giants as the South African Mike Procter. Why could not English players do the same?

'Some big men in the game should be honest,' he said, 'they know exactly what is wrong with cricket in England.' And he made it clear that he did not have overseas players in mind.

But he would not boast or be over-sanguine about the strength of the WI team. He was very pleased with the way in which they had come together, but he was awaiting Australia as the test in more ways than one. Viv Richards's direct attitude contrasted wonderfully with the show put on by Micky Stewart and Chris Cowdrey. The latter, even allowing for his baptism of fire, was rather pathetic: 'It was a real pity that we lost by 10 wickets. We were better than that' . . . 'We beat the bat often.'

The English are great winners – generous, unboastful, full of praise for the defeated; but what a mess they make of losing! One would never have guessed from their press conference that Ambrose (24 years old, Test debut 1987–88) had taken 7 wickets in the game for 98 runs in 45 overs, and had been made man-of-the-match by Ted Dexter! Nor that Benjamin (23 years old, Test debut 1987–88) had taken 4 wickets in 14 overs for 29 runs.

At one stage Cowdrey agreed with members of the English press that perhaps the slip fielders had been standing too close together. One wonders where he and manager Stewart were when this was happening – asleep on another planet?

But three really interesting things came out of this press conference: one, Micky Stewart's unequivocal statement that he would ban overseas players from county cricket; two, that he feels that the internal structure of cricket, as it is played in the UK, needs close examination. (He added that the same is true of football.) He spoiled this interesting point about English cricket by seeming to imply that it was too 'social' – whereas, according to him, social cricket was not played in the West Indies! The third interesting point was that both Stewart and Cowdrey complained about the doctoring of the wickets in county matches – to gain a result. (Not in favour of the visiting team, surely!) Yet those of us with memories longer than three weeks could easily recall the written denial, not to mention the spoken disapproval, when Richards had said at Old Trafford that the wicket had been so prepared as to cool down the West Indian fast bowlers. Now at Headingley, so worried about the 'underpreparation of wickets' were the manager and the captain and many of the press present, that there was quite a discussion on how to make sure that the counties provided better pitches. Fines, perhaps, for blatant 'underpreparation'? Their suggestion, not mine!

Perhaps the main point which is not getting quite enough consideration is the number and variety of one-day games being played in England, and the way in which they are mixed in with the more traditional forms of cricket. Have England not in fact chosen to be champions of the one-day game? And no less a supposed traditionalist than Len Hutton is on record as saying how much he would have enjoyed the one-day game. Has anyone seriously considered, not scrapping Tests, but reducing them to four days? Could it be that for everybody, players and fans and press alike, five days, with Sunday intervening, is just too much?

No one ever solved the problems of that so-called blocked drain. And no one has given any acceptable explanation of the fact that English Test cricket was looking, on that fine morning, so bedraggled that some felt certain that it has already sunk for the proverbial third time below the waters of international cricket.

7

The Oval Tests

1988 and 1950

Although names like Tang Choon and Achong have not recently featured in our cricket, West Indies did the Chinese thing at Kennington Oval: on the eighth day of the eighth month of 1988 they won by 8 wickets. But the victory did not come easily. The formidable West Indies reputation was somewhat tarnished by their reply to England's first-innings score of 205; they could only muster 183. The first 4 wickets fell for 57 runs. In fact, Dujon was made man-of-the-match on the strength of saving West Indies by his excellent innings of 64. Gooch, Foster, Benjamin, Harper, Greenidge and Haynes were all in contention. But Fred Trueman was absolutely correct in his award.

Once again, before going into the details of the 1988 match, let us recall the 1950 West Indies Oval performance. The direct comparison will highlight some fundamental differences in the cricket of the two eras.

There were no man-of-the-match awards in 1950, but had there been the contenders would have been: Len Hutton 202 not out and 2; Allan Rae 109; Frankie Worrell 138; and Alf Valentine 10 wickets for 160 in the game (6 for 39 in the second innings). I suspect that Valentine might well have been given the nod.

West Indies came into the match determined to show that there was no fluke in their wins at Lord's or at Trent Bridge in the preceding Test. On the other hand, England, having won at Manchester, intended at least to even up the series and hold in check these new upstarts.

West Indies batted first for a commanding 503, of which Rae made 109 – solidly, in his manner – and Worrell a delightful 138; these two were backed up by 74 from Gomez and 58 not out from skipper Goddard. The most successful of England's bowlers was the quickish leg-spinner, Douglas Wright, with 5 for 141 off 54

England's first innings was odd beyond understanding. Hutton took out his bat for 202, Simpson made 30, Compton was run out for 44; five of the others did not get into double figures. All out for 344, having been 310 for 5. In the follow-on they collapsed for 103 with David Sheppard, now the respected Bishop of Liverpool, top-scoring on 29. The point, one feels, was established.

Hutton's first innings of 202 was remarkable even in this remarkable game, for not only did he carry his bat but he made nearly two thirds of his team's total. It was not the first, or indeed the only, time this astonishing man proved himself such a worthy and honoured opponent. One remembers his pre-war performances; and he was to prove himself again in 1954 at Sabina Park in an innings that few who saw it will ever forget. He saved the series for England by a feat of total concentration, scoring 205 out of 414 in reply to a West Indies total of 139.

Late on the first afternoon of the innings he fended off King's remarkable spell. It was a piece of fast, hostile bowling which impressed even those who had seen Lindwall, Miller and Voce, and were later to thrill at Hall, Roberts and Holding. At one stage, late on that first day, in evading one of the thunderbolts, he lost his cap and was very nearly out hit wicket! He was very much captain and Yorkshire on that occasion, remonstrating with Trevor Bailey, opening with him, for 'taking risks' when all of thirty-five minutes of play remained! In fact, the strokeless wonder was left to face quite a bit of Frank King's concentrated speed, and Len survived not only King but nine bowlers including Ramadhin, Sobers (4 for 75), Gomez and Atkinson, to score the saving 205. (WI went on to make 346 in their second innings; England won by 9 wickets.)

Only one of his team-mates scored over 31, Wardle with 66; in 1950, as we have noted, the next highest score to his 202 not out was 44 by Denis Compton. It is amazing that a man whom Frank Worrell, on occasion, dubbed the greatest defensive bat to play the game, also had to be, as he was at the Oval in 1950, England's highest scorer by far.

Hutton represents an aspect of selection which England's selectors today are said to have forgotten: a good man is good however young he may be. I first saw Hutton, in Jamaica on a Yorkshire pre-season tour, when he was 19 and already a full county player for two years; he played his first Test when he was just turned 21. (Another instance was Denis Compton, only 19 at his first Test.) Hutton often told me that he felt that early trip with Yorkshire had taught him a great deal. He was always grateful to his county for their foresight in taking him on at such an early age, and he recalled with pleasure the hospitality which he received. George Headley told how he had to interpret between him and the young Jamaican Johnny Groves when the latter, in his marked Jamaican accent, tried to communicate with Len about the bat he was using, and Len found himself bewildered – just as did Johnny when Len tried to reply in the broad Yorkshire of his youth!

He died, as Sir Leonard, in 1990, still held in great affection throughout the cricketing world. But nothing is simple in life or cricket, and I fear that his great quality as a Test batsman lessened his contribution when he became captain. Certainly it left its mark on present-day English cricket: how often in the Caribbean – where he is much respected – did we see him pull down the shutters and 'shut up shop' a good forty-five minutes before close of play!

In that 1950 Test the bowling Hutton was playing against was not exactly weak. In fact there were some stunning performances. In the first innings Worrell bowled 20 overs for 30 runs, without taking a wicket. In the game Goddard took 5 for 36. (In the first innings he managed 4 for 25 in 17.4 overs.) Ramadhin took 4 for 101 in the game, and Valentine had that 10 for 160 including 6 for 39 in 26.3 overs in the second innings.

And so West Indies wound up the wonderful 1950 Test series 3–1 by an Oval victory. They won by an innings and 56 runs against an England side whose first six batsmen were: Hutton, Simpson, Sheppard, Compton, Dewes and Bailey. Yet the 1988 West Indian team has so often been felt by English commentators to be some sort of invincible behemoth.

A glance at the overall performance of the West Indian batsmen in the 1988 first innings – on the best wicket of the series – will question this judgement: first of all they lost 4 wickets for 57. Then recovered to 126 for 5, faltered again at 155 for 6, 156 for 7, 167 for 8, and 168 for 9. *Dujon's 64, and Logie's 47 were the only scores above 20!* Hooper, having come in at no. 3 with the total on 9, and having shown that he has lots of time to play the ball, was absurdly out, following a ball outside the off stump.

It is not too much to say that Hooper and Richardson disappointed during this tour: Hooper's batting average was 32.89; Richardson's, 19.92. Compare these with Marshall's at 32.11. In 1950 the person who equally disappointed was the now forgotten Ken Trestrail. He never did make the Test team, not for lack of talent, nor because the competition was so hot, but because he really lacked the right temperament, and was very stubborn. This he showed in a remarkable way early in the season when he had his chance against MCC at Lord's. Just before tea he laid the bat on the leg-spin and googly bowler, Jim Sims. He square-cut him for 4, then drove him through the covers for 4. I think that he also late-cut him. Over tea Trestrail was advised by some of the more experienced players that he should be careful about playing back and cutting Sims, who had an excellent googly. The very first ball after tea Trestrail decided to show that he could deal with Sims, went back to cut a leg-break, and was clean bowled by a googly!

In 1988 we could see that West Indies would soon need a new opening pair, and I have been assured by people who should know that Richardson is a good opener. Manager Jackie Hendriks referred to his 'excellent hard-wicket record'. But the overall West Indies batting still looked a bit brittle in England: the leader of the tour averages was Harper (77.75), and Dujon was third (50.08). The 'new boy' who did well was Arthurton (av: 49.90), and this promises well for the future, as does the maturing Logie (av: 41.85).

Will Arthurton and Logie produce the real temperament for Test batting? This business of temperament, raised about Trestrail above, and the question of a certain kind of cussedness, is central but difficult to assess.

However, to return to the Oval in 1988: the real point for West Indies cricket was that in a difficult position, having a deficit of 22 in the first innings, and being set 225 to win on a turning wicket, Haynes and Greenidge decided to leave nothing to chance, got their noses over the ball, and put on 131. They knew what many in the well-filled Oval did not know, namely that Richards was in hospital, in great pain, and could not bat. And they simply and finally shattered the old stereotype, which even some West Indies fans seemed to like, of being calypso cricketers. Haynes for a long time scored very little; he had obviously decided to take on Childs, the left-hander who looked as if at any minute he could prove dangerous.

Clearly, for this performance, credit must be given to Gordon Greenidge who took over the captaincy, and to Jackie Hendriks, the manager. Hendriks really did a splendid job, having to build up morale not only over the one-day losses, but also in dealing with the near-death of Simmons. He also skilfully protected his young, inexperienced players from some of the wolves in sheep's clothing who still graze around the perimeters of the English press 'seeking whom they may devour'. It is to be hoped that his experience will not be permanently folded away in mothballs.

From the point of view of English cricket the failure of the batsmen in the second innings is frankly inexplicable. Let us grant that Benjamin, a newcomer, was bowling well above form, and that Harper had the magic figures of 6 overs, 3 maidens, 9 runs, 2 wickets. But how can one explain that Foster, the no. 9 batsman, was the second highest English scorer with 34, and that even with extras at 33, England could still score only 202?

Of this total Gooch scored 84! Six batsmen between them scored all of 14 runs. One wonders, really, whether the selectors can be blamed for such a low-grade virus of a performance.

That West Indian calypso reputation referred to above had been based partly on the unknown ability of people like Learie Constantine to entertain, and bring 'a little life and colour' into the game. Learie had scored a vigorous 79 at the Oval in the last Test before war settled down on the world in 1939. And Ken (Bam-Bam) Weekes, in making 137, had displayed left-handed shots hardly ever seen before. And those who know about the game never tired of referring to Victor Stollmeyer's 96. He had run out George Headley, and that seemed to concentrate his mind. He had been ill for most of the tour, and in the only Test of his career played quite the opposite of calypso cricket. No doubt the calypso reputation had also been partly reinforced by the Kitchener calypso, composed after the 1950 Lord's victory, about 'Those two little pals of mine/Ramadhin and Valentine.'

It cannot be by chance that only people like Lamb and Robin Smith, and at a different level, DeFreitas, all non-native English players, will consistently strike the ball in Test matches. Even when the bowlers are those supposed murderous fast bowlers!

But in 1950 it took more than the often proffered image of wild vigour, and unfair fast bowling, to defeat the England team at the Oval by an innings and 56 runs. Fast bowlers Prior Jones and Worrell bowled 43 overs between them of the first innings 179 for 4. No fast bowler at all was used in the second. Goddard, slow-medium, bowled 9 overs for 11 runs and 1 wicket; and Gomez, medium, 8 overs for 6 runs. Ram & Val did it all alone (52.3 overs between them out of 69.3), and there were few complaints against them, except that, according to some BBC broadcasters they got through their overs *too quickly! Put too much pressure on the batsmen* – not to mention the gentlemen commentators.

For the 1988 Oval game I forsook the press box – which has been 'improved': it now perches on the top of steep interminable steps, and is not too easy to see from. When one is seated at one's desk one discovers that the railing around its balcony has been cunningly set at eye level. The ceiling is suitably low so that standing up to watch is none too easy, nor is writing from the upright position. The oddest thing is that its total inconvenience is explained on grounds of safety. Apparently since the dreadful fire at the Bradford Football stadium and the many spectator deaths, local authorities have been insisting on high standards of safety. An excellent idea, but it should not be beyond the ability of even bureaucrats to design a safe press box from which one can actually see the game. So I watched from the members' end, just a few rows above ground level. The cricket seemed and felt less remote, and one was in close touch with the reactions of the fans.

I was not greeted this time by any old friend fielding at third man; mainly because the modern game uses that position infrequently. But from fine-leg – employed even when a bowler has four slips and a gully – Courtney Walsh gave me a quiet nod after one of his excellently economic overs.

One could not help noticing one enormous difference (compared with 1950) in the fans around one – there were so many West Indian faces of so many different kinds, with slightly differing accents from Barbados and Jamaica and Antigua and St Vincent. Sometimes the noise level was rather high, despite the quite childish banning of trumpets, drums, conch shells, banners 'in the interest of the safety of all'. (Lethal weapons, drums and banners!)

One rather large chap, in a red baseball cap, who, despite the ban on the 'importation of excessive amounts of alcohol into the Oval' – of course the money-making bars were not closed – had imbibed not wisely but too well. He kept giving umpire Bird a hard time until a comrade shouted that if 'the big mouth' did not behave better he would have to be reported to his wife! One much quieter protester shouted 'No-ball' after almost every delivery; he was seated at a very fine fine-leg position! And a gentleman, of Indian heritage, from Trinidad (shades of dear old Ram), kept complaining very quietly in the second innings that Gooch (84) was not scoring fast enough. 'People pay to see you make strokes, man', he kept muttering.

Despite the strong support from West Indian heritage people in that 1988 Oval crowd, it was not really fan support, nor magic, nor reliance on Chinese lucky numbers, nor 'brutal fast bowling', that created the victory, but the maturing of a new side, and the concentration of old hands. The game was much more closely contested than some of the figures tend to show; it was probably the best of the series. England actually led on the first innings, and had an opening stand of 50 in the second. Their overall batting let them down throughout, most remarkably so in their second innings. But the game was not clearly lost or won even after it became obvious, in the second innings, that the West Indies opening pair were taking things very seriously.

England would do better to note that South Africans Lamb and Smith at times nearly collared the West Indies bowling, and that some English players were being bowled while playing forward defensively! Some things are really wrong with English cricket: a too-frequent loss of technique and of concentration; too many changes in selection and selection policy; a certain lack, on the part of the management, of a creative realism; undue emphasis on one-day cricket; underprepared pitches; absurd home schedules, and far too much cricket at home and abroad, leading to a staleness and an inability to concentrate in Tests.

The truth of the matter is that things move very slowly in England, and it has taken a long time, despite the success of West Indies in England as long ago as 1950 – and of that wonderful

Australian team of 1948 – for it to sink into the English consciousness that winning is not the prerogative of England at cricket.

Winning can never be by right. Any more than it can be the only thing that matters. But if you wish to win, by fair means only, then choices have to be made – between, for instance, the enormous emphasis on the one-day game all through the season and a return to the better aspects of the traditional game. And opportunities must be given immediately to any brilliant young player who may suddenly grace the counties.

Nothing more significantly symbolises the reactionary attitude of too much of English culture, and therefore of their cricket, than the facilities and food offered to the paying public – as contrasted with the invitees to sponsors' tents, and even there the drink is always better than the food. It does not really help to say that things have improved, for then one wonders how anyone, 'in the old days', ever put up with attending the games.

Perhaps more symbolic and significant, however, is the constant bleating from certain quarters about batsmen wearing helmets. 'Hobbs wouldn't have worn one, would he?' some high-pitched public school voice will put forward, as if proving Euclid's *pons asinorum* theorem for the first time. Who knows? In any case plastics were not invented in his day! And didn't he, as I once heard a liberated lady ask about a modern player, wear a box? Or, as she further commented, are brains simply less important in the average male's outlook on cricket and on life?

8

Highs and Lows

1963 and 1957

I have often argued that the best West Indies team, all things considered, to tour England was that trail-blazing side of 1950. During the four Tests the same opening pair was always used; as were the next eight in the order. The eleventh player was either H. H. Johnson when he was fit, or Prior Jones. Players of the quality of Ken Trestrail and 'Boogles' Williams just could not compete with the three Ws and Ram and Val *et al* for a place on the Test sides.

But Tom Graveney argues that the 1963 team was one of the best of all sides that ever visited England, including the 1948 Bradman team. If we stop to think of that team for a moment we shall see what kind of claim Graveney is making. For older readers it is probably enough just to name the first five in the batting order to begin to appreciate the powerhouse that the Australian team represented: Morris (8 career centuries v. England), Barnes (2 v. England), Bradman (19 v. England), Hassett (4 v. England) and Miller (3 v. England).

If we note the no. 3 in the line-up – the agreed greatest modern batsman, with a career average of just over 95 – we start to get the picture. But the left-handed Morris, who was to score 111 v. West Indies at Queen's Park Oval, and Keith Miller (147 at Sabina followed by 137 at Bridgetown and 109, again at Kingston), all on the 1954–55 tour, were not exactly sluggards. In fact a friend whose first big game was the last Bradman Test at Lord's confessed that whilst he remembers being impressed with the great man, he could not remember exactly what he did; he had no difficulty, however, in recalling the 6 off a full toss that Miller, batting at the Nursery end, hoisted way up into the stands just behind square-leg.

The rest of that Australian team, incidentally, was Harvey (6 centuries v. England), Johnson, Lindwall (1 century v. England),

Tallon, Johnston, Toshack. Toshack, a slow-medium left-hander, was one of the meanest bowlers imaginable, pushing the ball into middle and leg, and bringing it back a bit. Miller formed with his partner Lindwall one of the most hostile opening attacks known up to their time. Lindwall's forte was the ability to bowl a much faster ball without apparent change of action. His late, ducking in-swinger was one of the most difficult balls to play, and he and Miller, in Australia, upset the one-time successful West Indian openers, Stollmeyer and Rae, with sharp bouncers. Johnson was a good off-breaker, who later captained Australia and who was good enough to open the batting when at Old Trafford Barnes was severely injured standing at a suicidal silly mid-on position. Bill Johnston was really two bowlers in one: a left-handed medium pacer with excellent control, and a slow left-handed, back-of-the-hand spinner. What a team!

So let us look at the 1963 WI Team which Tom Graveney feels was a match for that Australian powerhouse. Much has been made of the fact that the same ten men played in all the Tests, but that also happened in 1950. In 1963 Hunte opened with three different partners in Carew, McMorris, and then, finally, Rodriguez was brought in. The old firm of the three Ws was no longer a going concern, but Frank Worrell was with us as captain. The rest of the unchangeable ten were Hunte, Kanhai, Butcher, Solomon, Sobers, Hall, Griffith, Lance Gibbs and D. L. Murray. Notice the balance and the variety. In fact it is of this team that Garfield Sobers says, 'The best team I ever played on'.

The team won three Tests, lost one, and drew one. Of their number Hunte, Kanhai, Sobers and Griffith were named among *Wisden*'s five cricketers of the year. Yet in the Tests the batting was dependable rather than prolific: four centuries only were scored, two by Hunte, one by Sobers and one by Butcher. In the Oval Test, second innings, Hunte scored an unbeaten 108 (out of 255 for 2), having defied the English attack for five hours including a solid first-wicket stand of 78 with Rodriguez. In this way he contributed greatly to the 8-wicket win, with a day to spare. But it would be ridiculous to forget Kanhai's lively 77, and Butcher's 31 not out. The Test batting averages, against Trueman, Shackleton, Titmus, Lock, and Dexter, tell the same story of balance:

Hunte	58.87
Kanhai	55.22
Butcher	47.87
Sobers	40.25

Even in the fielding the same contribution on all sides is shown by the interesting figures that David Allan, behind the stumps, who did not play a Test, caught 46 and stumped 9; whereas D. L. Murray, the Test wicket-keeper, caught 42 and stumped 7.

No England player was allowed to score a century in the whole Test series! Their batsmen included: Barrington, Dexter, Cowdrey, Close, and Richardson, but, oddly enough, not Graveney who was suffering a strange ignoring by the selectors.

Again in the whole series, WI's main bowlers were Hall, Griffith, Sobers, and Gibbs. In the dramatic drawn second Test at Lord's, 'Hall, in particular, and Griffith showed remarkable stamina', *Wisden* declared. Hall bowled for the whole of play on the last day: for three hours and twenty minutes. Except for five overs Griffith shared that spell with him. On the other hand, in the Birmingham Test, which followed Lord's, Sobers took 7 for 140, and Gibbs 5 for 77.

West Indies put their stamp on the series right from the start. On a slow and true wicket they opened the first Test at Trent Bridge with 501 for 6 declared, Hunte getting 182 and Kanhai 90 (run out). England replied with 205 (Dexter, the captain, 73) and, in the follow-on, 296, towards which Micky Stewart, now his country's manager but then a Surrey opener, made 87 before becoming one of Gibbs's 6–98 victims to be added to his 5–59 of the first innings.

This left West Indies needing 1 run to win with a day-plus to get it in. In cricket's full solemnity the rites were duly completed off the first ball, and everyone prepared to gather again at Lord's.

The Lord's Test, affected by rain, was the famous one in which fortunes swayed back to a schoolboy-fiction finish, wounded hero and all. McMorris failed as an opener, and although West Indies managed 127 for 3, Sobers and Kanhai having put on a lively third-wicket stand of 63 in sixty-five minutes, they were all out for 301. The highest scorer was Kanhai on 73. His fellow Guianese, Joe Solomon, made 56.

England's reply fell 4 runs short, Dexter making a buccaneering 70, standing up to the pace and banging off some thrilling shots. Griffith was awkward to play though, taking 5 for 91 in 26 overs. (Trueman had taken 6 for 100 in 44 overs.) In their second innings, West Indies found Trueman just as difficult to play; and they fared no better against the recalled Shackleton. The former took 5 for 52; the latter 4 for 72. West Indies lost 5 for 104, but when Butcher, whom Sobers calls 'a vastly underrated player', had made 129 and Worrell 33, and bad light stopped play on Saturday afternoon, all seemed set fair for West Indies. But they managed to lose 5 wickets on Monday morning for 15 runs in all of 6 overs. Apart from Butcher and Worrell only Kanhai reached double figures.

So when England took their stations, even though rain was interfering, they needed but 234 runs to win and even up the series at one victory each. Unfortunately for them Cowdrey was injured, had a bone just above the left hand broken, and would enter the final lists only in the direst of circumstances. Despite Barrington's 60, including two 6s off Gibbs in one over, and Close's 70, he did have to take his position in the centre. Wickets had started to fall ominously: 203 for 6, 203 for 7, 219 for 8, 228 for 9 . . .

When Hall started his last knife-edge over 8 runs were needed, with 2 wickets standing. Singles came off the second and third balls but Shackleton was run out off the fourth ball by Worrell who, grasping the ball, beat him to the opposite wicket.

Enter Cowdrey, prepared to bat using his right arm only; two balls to be bowled; 6 runs needed. Fortunately for him, and perhaps all concerned, he was at the bowler's end. Two wild deliveries by a hyped-up Hall – he was in his fortieth over, unchanged since play had restarted, and had taken 4 wickets – and England would have won. One accurate yorker and D. A. Allen might have been castled. In the event he played out the two balls, leaving all to argue about whether Close was right to come down the wicket to the quickies, whether Trueman, who was to bat well on occasion, should not have achieved more than a duck, whether West Indies second innings need really have been so undersubscribed by so many batsmen. Never mind: in every respect it had truly been a game to remember.

England squared the series in the murk and rain of Edgbaston through which Fred Trueman stirred the embers of gathering age to maybe his last great performance: 12 for 119 off 40.3 overs in the match – 9.91 each and a wicket every three and a half overs. Dexter won a toss he would probably rather have lost and took first innings on a wicket that was wet underneath. Hall could find no bounce, but Sobers curved the ball in the damp to take 5 for 60; England 216. West Indies reached 110 for 4 – and the next morning were all out for 186 in eighty minutes, Trueman cutting his run and speed to make the ball move late for 5–75.

England then pressed on as fast as they could amid the showers and poor light and declared at 278 for 9, leaving WI to get 309 in 280 minutes. At lunch they were 55 for 3; less than one hour later, in another rout, they were all out for 91, leaving England victors by 217 runs. Trueman this time had taken 6 of the remaining wickets to finish with 7 for 44 off only 14.3 overs.

The sun shone again at Leeds, and on a firm wicket Sobers led the way to 397 (after they were 71 for 3), Kanhai again falling in the 90s. England met Griffith in rampaging mood; he took 6 for 36 in their 174. Only the bowler Tony Lock topped 50. Adding to their lead of 223, WI arrived – not without early hiccups – at 229, Butcher scoring 78 and Sobers adding a 52 to his first-innings century. A target of 453 was never a reality, and despite 50s from Close and wicket-keeper Parks England fell 221 short. It had been a workmanlike team performance by West Indies, who, as we shall see in chapter 12, continued in that vein at the Oval.

One of the remarkable things about the whole of the series was that neither Valentine nor Allan nor Lester King nor Seymour Nurse played in a Test. Moreover skipper Worrell and manager Berkeley Gaskin had eighteen men in their squad fairly early on. Rodriguez had injured his knee, and the very promising Barbadian all-rounder, Tony White, was sent to take his place, but Willy soon recovered.

The team was a balanced one; but the great thing was that they all pulled together in a way in which the 1957 team did not. This was the more remarkable because of the presence of so many players. I have heard respected Test players, no doubt sure of their niche, say that sixteen is almost too many for a touring party. Further, Murray was unknown to many of the players, and White could have been catapulted into an awkward situation in other circumstances. What made the difference in this tour, as far as morale and pulling together went, was the presence not only of Frank Worrell but also of Berkeley Gaskin.

Everyone now knows of Frank's mature qualities as a leader. He was much more of a disciplinarian when he finally became captain than some people expected from his early days and apparent 'laid back' style. (He had been in trouble more than once at his school in Barbados!) One knows how surprised many people were when, at a reception for him at Sabina Park, he told us about his run-in with a member of the team in Australia. Frank felt that this player was not treating practice in a sensible and serious fashion. Moreover he was sapping the confidence of one of the bowlers by simply hitting him all over the place. Frank had a quiet word with the gentleman in question, suggesting that a run around the track would be better exercise if it were merely exercise that he required. The indiscriminate hitting continued: the player was removed from the nets.

But Frank knew that discipline demanded give and take. He often quoted to me the maxim from Horace's *Ars Poetica* – 'Damus petimusque vicissim': 'We must be willing to give to others what we require of them.' Or what we ask the critics to grant us, we too must be willing to grant them. I remember – for he was good enough to invite me into the West Indies dressing-room – how during lunch at Birmingham Frank prepared Hall for the fact that he was not going to get the new ball when it became due soon after. The captain had decided that Sobers should have it but he did not wait until all were on the field simply to throw the ball to Sobers, leaving Hall disappointed. He very subtly warned Hall.

Of Frank's performance as captain, Graveney, a great friend of West Indies cricket, has this to say: 'Tactically he may not have been a brilliant captain. He was sound without being superb, but he is the one [West Indies] captain I have seen who could get the other ten players pulling and working in the same direction with one common aim – victory.'

But one must say something also about the sterling qualities of Frank's partner in getting the best out of the 1963 players, Berkeley Gaskin. The importance of managers has not always been appreciated and West Indies have sometimes suffered by not having the right one for the occasion. That was not the case in

1963. Berkeley had a knowledge of cricket and of affairs. An important law officer in Guyana, he was a great dresser and, in the very best sense of the word, a gentleman. He had been a fast-medium bowler who tended to deliver off the wrong foot, and to swing the ball into the batsman. In 1947–48 he represented West Indies against England at the Kensington Oval and at Queen's Park. In the first innings of the first game he bowled without success, 11 overs for 30 runs. In the second innings he claimed the wicket of Cranston in a spell of 10–4–15–1. In the Queen's Park game he bowled a total of 58 overs. In the first innings in which England scored 362 (S. C. Griffith 140), his figures were 37–14–72–1 – steady, to say the least. He was well known and respected in inter-territorial cricket and in his native country, then known as British Guiana.

It was a mark of his considerate and intelligent approach to the game, and to life in general, that he was well known and popular in Jamaica which in the cricketing West Indies of those days was about as far from Guyana – a mere 1,600 miles across the sea – as it was possible to be. He was much later to be a most helpful consort to his wife Winnie when she became High Commissioner of Guyana in Jamaica. He liked, as he and his great Jamaican friend Sydney Abrahams, himself no mean cricketer, used to say, to 'show culture', that is, to take the other person's viewpoint and habits into courteous and serious consideration.

He had an interesting way of keeping in touch with all aspects of a game as it proceeded: he did not hide himself in the dressing-room or in the committee's special box. In fact Jamaican cricketers used to tease him for holding 'committee meetings' all over Sabina Park: as an international contest developed its own rhythm, he would be seen, black, debonair, sporting a suitable tie, walking as far around the ground as he could get. He had a word here with a 'brother', a quip there with a beautifully outfitted lady or two, not forgetting to place a respectful kiss on the cheek of some matron – the wife perhaps of a colleague of his in the law business. He would spot an older retired cricketer and ask his opinion of the game. Then back at a quick athletic pace to the dressing-room, to say to some nail-biting neophyte, 'Feeling a bit seedy, young man?' He was to be seen likewise traversing the whole of his beloved Bourda, scene of many of his triumphs.

Anybody who has sat too long in a claustrophobic press box, taking in his colleagues' opinions and prejudices, and dealing with these rather than the ongoing game, will immediately realise the central importance of a regular good walkabout.

In 1963, as I approached the gates at Edgbaston with my wife, who should be standing there but Berkeley, no doubt looking for some West Indian official whose dignity required the presence of the manager to usher him through the gates. He showed my wife quickly to the best seat at his disposal, and took me to the dressing-room to say hello to Frank. This was the man whom Frank was fortunate to have with him in England, even as Jerry Alexander had been to have him on the difficult India–Pakistan tour of 1958–59.

Sobers, in his *Twenty Years at the Top*, tells a wonderful story about Gaskin as manager in India: 'I liked Berkeley. He has a sense of humour and did his best to be strict with the young players . . .' Sobers then goes on to tell how he and Eric Atkinson, tired of the lack of alcohol in India, managed just before Christmas to find a family who had a secret supply. He and Eric then had a night out during a Test in which Sobers was 136 not out overnight. They got back to the hotel at 2:00 a.m., no doubt congratulating themselves on returning so early. There was not a soul about and they were pleased with themselves.

Let Gary continue the story: 'Next day I went out and reached 198 in just over five hours before Joe Solomon ran me out. In the dressing-room Berkeley was there to greet me. "Good thing you got those runs", he said. "I saw you come in late!"'

Gary generously continues to say that Berkeley was still a good enough bowler to help out in the nets. In fact he clean bowled Gary one day, picked up his coat and walked off saying, 'That's it. My job is done'. It was his combination of cricket knowledge and know-how, and his humanity, which made him such an excellent partner with Worrell.

On that 1963 tour there were arguments about bumpers and chucking. Frank dealt with these diplomatically, but also firmly. He seems to have 'cooled' Griffith considerably when umpire Buller complained about bowling which he considered to have been intimidatory. In a subsequent tour a word or two from the captain would have helped greatly. There were times, later on, when the West Indian fast bowlers overdid the short-pitched ball; overdid them not necessarily because they were being intimidatory, but because they were clearly wasting their energy bowling fast risers so far outside the off stump that it would take a very inept batsman to get his bat near enough to the ball to put slip and gully to the test. Some batsmen, like Close, were to insist on sticking out their chests at the 'bouncers'. No wonder they got hit.

Often I felt that the protests of the English press were not unlike the 'dives' for penalties which the British football broadcasters love to discover even when a player – foreign, of course – has been tripped. But even if the press was being less than fair and helpful, I never did understand why subsequent captains found it impossible to have a word with their bowlers when they were clearly wasting the ball and their energy. It is also important to recall – since the English press likes to give the opposite view – that it is not by any chance only the West Indies who have been accused of overusing the short-pitched ball.

For instance, of the West Indies débâcle in Australia in 1951–52 much has been said about the schedule which gave West Indies but one first-class game before the Tests started. There were also the not unusual divisions on the team. (Frank Worrell gives a good insight into these in Ernest Eytle's book about Frank!) But one is likely to forget that not only were the Australian fast bowlers much quicker than England's whom West Indies had defeated in 1950, they were also much more prone to use the short-pitched ball. As *Wisden* 1953 has it: the bumpers from the Australian bowlers were 'too frequent for happy relationships'. And *Wisden* 1958 even more interestingly points out that in the fourth Test of the disastrous West Indies 1957 tour to England 'Kanhai was treated to a very heavy dose of short-pitched balls by Trueman'. Kanhai was, of course, young, inexperienced and promising, and he was injured. So much for line and length!

About chucking I was never sure. Griffith was the West Indian most often accused. I have always found it difficult to judge from the boundary ropes or the press box whether a bowler chucks or not – except in very obvious cases. It seemed to me clear that Cuan McCarthy had an illegal action, as did Tony Lock with his faster ball. The former was soon no-balled out of the game: but it took quite a while before the latter was made to change his action.

One of the difficulties about Griffith was that it was said that his action was all right except for his especially fast bouncer which got up all of a sudden from the exact spot at which the ball had previously reared no higher than the stumps. But is it possible for a bowler to change his action without it being noticed? Well-known players say, 'Of course it is possible, and happens when the quickie tries for that extra yard of pace'. Some said, on the other hand, that because the chuck was used only at certain times it was more difficult for the umpire or any other observer to spot it. It is not the kind of argument that is likely to be settled except through video playbacks and all that.

I well remember an occasion in the West Indies before Griffith became so famous. I was invited to lunch by a very important cricket committee – I do not think that I should say in which territory. During lunch my hosts expressed concern about Griffith's action and a lively discussion ensued. Two gentlemen said that his action was completely legal; two said just the opposite, and one said he could not make up his mind. It was decided that, as trial and other matches were taking place, the five disputants should contrive an occasion to see Griffith in the nets. A special practice was arranged in connection with the trials, and Griffith, although he did not know it, was very closely watched. When next we met opinions were completely unchanged: two felt that he chucked, two said he most certainly did not; and one person could not make up his mind! There was a feeling, however, that he should be selected to play in England: the umpires there would most certainly pronounce on the fairness of his action. What then took place?

It has been asserted that once the team got to England there was a goodwill, 'gentlemen's' agreement not to call anyone until the season had got going, perhaps until the Tests. It is impossible to check out completely this sort of thing.

The English authorities subsequently issued a statement, during a later tour, to the effect that they had never instructed umpires not to no-ball any bowler during Griffith's first tour. Further, *Wisden* 1967 tells us that – 'During the [first Test in 1966] Griffith was no-balled nine times for overstepping the crease. In turn, each umpire scrutinised his action from square-leg, sometimes crossing to point.' Yet at no stage did they call

Griffith. This certainly suggests that at the very least the umpires considered his regular action was legitimate. It would be naive to believe that any bowler under surveillance would let fly with a suspect ball, if he did have it in his armoury.

But the strong reaction to Griffith's action on the part of such people as Benaud and Dexter needs some explanation in the light of his not being no-balled by Buller & Co. After all, Buller did not hesitate to speak to Worrell at the Oval about Griffith's short-pitched bowling. He is reported to have answered Griffith quite sharply when the latter claimed the right to bowl 'two every over'. Of course, captain Worrell, ever the diplomat, had the last word after the Oval Test in 1963, a last word it would be well for all to remember: 'As far as I am concerned the umpires are the sole judges of fair and unfair play.' If Griffith bowled with an unfair action, either intermittently or regularly, why did the umpires not call him? One may also ask why did it take them so long to get Lock to straighten out his action? And to deal with Meckiff? And of course Griffith was called once – in his native Barbados!

The 1963 team, however you rate it alongside other West Indies teams, thrilled the fans, showed great consistency, and was a model of really pulling together. It was also the last team on which Sir Frank Worrell toured. His contributions with bat and ball had, understandably, faded (his top Test score was an undefeated 74 out of 501 in the first Test; his best bowling figures were 13–6–12–2 at Lord's). His great contribution was as captain, as the one who, with Gaskin, moulded the team into a real unit, and brought the best out of people like Solomon and Butcher who tend to be forgotten because they were surrounded by such media-worthy giants. When Worrell's team won the first Test, at Old Trafford, by 10 wickets, West Indies had for the first time won six consecutive Tests. A splendid record which must be shared with those who helped to win the previous five (against India in the West Indies) – under the captaincy of Frank Worrell.

Frank was, as is well known, greatly popular. Yet a few people held back a little in their praise of the great man. His native Barbados did not seem always to appreciate his qualities or contribution. Perhaps because, especially in his early years, he seemed so 'laid back'. Even in his later days his cool attitude could give the quite false impression of standing aside, of not being quite involved. But most of all he had learned to be most diplomatic, and, alas, diplomats are not always universally appreciated. In making sure they do not make enemies, they sometimes lose the opportunity of making close friends.

Unfortunately we have him no longer with us – or we might have had some further insights into the failures of 1957 and the controversies about chucking. It would be wonderful to know what he really thought of Charlie's action, and of the comparative rating of the many teams he played for, then captained, and in the end managed.

What a contrast between that 1963 tour and the one in 1957. One would hardly think that the team came from the same place as the 1950 and 1963 teams. In 1957, under the captaincy of John Goddard, the victor of 1950, two games were drawn, and England won the other three, all by an innings – the last at the Oval by no less than an innings and 237 runs!

And yet the first Test, at Edgbaston, did not appear to start that badly. England scored only 186 in their first innings to which West Indies replied with 474, Collie Smith getting 161 and Walcott 90. But obviously England took that 186, plus the recollection of their utter defeat in 1950, to heart. What was much more devastating to the West Indies, and undoubtedly to the spirit of cricket, was that they decided to try to take Ramadhin out of the game of cricket. In doing so they set on its way a trend now much disliked by English gurus and fans alike: the elimination of the deceptive arts of the spinner and of the truly deceptive slow bowler.

Ramadhin took 7 for 49 in 31 overs in the first innings. Four of these were bowled; the others all caught. More to the point: P. B. H. May fell to the wily Ramadhin for 30, and Colin Cowdrey for 4 (both caught). Action was needed, and the action of inaction was opted for, and, if one may use such a word, vigorously taken in the second innings. The pad stretched forward; the bat was not used. The English umpires would not give the batsman out lbw playing forward. And May and Cowdrey eventually scored 411 together: England got 583 for 4 declared in the second innings off 258 overs.

Goddard, who has been understandably faulted for his handling of the bowling, did one supremely sensible thing when he went into bat in the second innings. He refused to play the ball – except with his pads, and to all intents and purposes dared the umpires to give him out.

But by that time the damage to Ramadhin and to West Indian morale had been done. Ramadhin had to be taught a lesson for humiliating England's batsmen in 1950; and he was. I have had to state elsewhere, regretfully, that despite all the colonial propaganda, English teams and players simply hate to lose. They are the best winners in the world; never crowing over the opposition, and finding good points in them – but losing, no thank you! Understandable, perhaps, if only they did not pretend otherwise, and if they did not accuse others of being bad losers.

There must have been fifty appeals turned down – how fortunate the umpires were not from Pakistan, with Pakistani batsmen at the wicket! It is likely, of course, that every one of the appeals was misdirected, especially as English commentators and umpires seem to feel that one is allowed to appeal only if one feels that the batsman is without doubt out! (You must have heard about the distinguished Australian cricketer who was patronised by an umpire in England: 'You appealed, I noticed. How could you possibly see from the covers if the batsman was leg before?' 'Of course I could not,' replied the fielder, 'and that is exactly why I appealed!')

It might have been simply that the umpires had made up their minds beforehand that when a batsman is playing well forward no one can say with certainty that the ball would hit the wicket, and therefore, as they seemed to do, automatically turned their backs on every appeal! One, perhaps quite wrongly, did not feel that each appeal was being taken on its merits.

What upset many of us who had to teach the young all that wonderful stuff about playing the game, and the importance of conventions as well as rules, was the pair who adopted those padding tactics. They were university graduates whom we admired and respected; and they were obviously acting on a pre-arranged plan. England were 113 for three, 175 runs behind, when Cowdrey came to the wicket. Insole at no. 3 had been bowled for the second time in the game by Ram. Enough was enough. The bats were hidden; the pads brought out. The game was drawn, and one of the cleverest bowlers to confuse English batsmen had been broken. All is fair in love and war; and what's all that lore about certain things not being cricket?

England won the next game, at Lord's, by an innings and 36 runs. Cowdrey added another 152 runs to the 154 he had made at Edgbaston in an England innings which at one time looked to be tottering, with both Graveney and May out without scoring. But Richardson and Evans made amends, and England scored 424 in reply to a West Indies first-innings score of 127. The West Indies second innings of only 261 was due mainly to an excellent 90 from Everton Weekes.

Ramadhin bowled 22 overs in England's only innings for 83 and just the wicket of Wardle at no. 9, although it is true to say that this was not a spinner's wicket; Valentine, who should not really have played, bowled only 3 overs costing 20 runs. For England, the seamers caused the damage: Statham 4, Trueman 4, and Bailey 11 (for 98) in the match.

The next Test, at Trent Bridge, was drawn. It was a batsman's match: Richardson 126, Graveney 258, May 104; Worrell carried his bat for 191 – all of these scores were in the first innings. In the second innings Collie Smith at last got some more runs, 168. Neither Ram nor Val took a wicket, and once again the fast men did the damage for England: Statham 6, Trueman 9 in the match.

Worrell's 191, made without a chance, came after he had bowled 21 overs and then went on to open the innings, and bat through it with his usual elegance. West Indies had had trouble with their batsmen. Weekes was not really fit, and an opening pair was not easily found: in the first Test Pairaudeau and Kanhai put on but 4 in the first innings, and 1 in the second. In the second Test Asgarali put on 7 runs with Kanhai in the first innings and 0 with Collie Smith, who had been promoted in the order, in the second. In the third Worrell and Sobers put on 87 before Sobers went for 47 (bowled Laker). They managed 22 in the second innings. In the fourth Test they were not so successful, putting on 16 and 40.

Leeds was a disaster, being over in mid-afternoon of the third day with an England win by an innings and 5 runs. Beginning in conditions perfect for seam bowling – heavy atmosphere plus a good cross-wind – it developed into a low-scoring affair, the two West Indies innings mounting to 142 (Loader 6 for 36, including that Test rarity, a hat-trick) and 132 against England's solitary 279.

Interestingly, umpire Davies cautioned Trueman for intimidatory bowling – four bouncers to Kanhai in one over. For West Indies the only real bright spot was Worrell's 7 wickets for 70 in 38.2 overs.

At the Oval, as we shall see in chapter 12, the West Indies were again disgraced, and a most disappointing series came to an end, not without recriminations; but the future was not as gloomy as it looked at the Oval on 24 August 1957. For early in 1958, with a new captain, F. C. M. Alexander of Jamaica and Cambridge, in charge, the excellent Conrad Hunte in the opening position, West Indies defeated Pakistan in the West Indies 3–1, with one game drawn. Gary Sobers batted as never before: 52, 52, 80, 365 not out, 125, 109 not out, 14, 27!

Three things stand out from the 1957 tour: one, Ramadhin still held the doubtful record of bowling the most balls in a Test; two, he never recovered his old form; three, Goddard was an unhappy choice as captain seven years after his handling of the bowling and his field placing in 1950 – at one stage he did not use a leg-slip to Ram's bowling, which suggested to the batsmen that he was not going to turn the ball to leg. The cracks already just under the surface of the West Indies team widened considerably, and morale plummeted. One trustworthy witness from the England side, on being asked how he explained the poor performance of the West Indies in 1957, said simply: 'There were so many divisions in the camp!'

9

Sobers: Runs and Shadows

1966 and 1969

As we go deeper into the 1960s, two factors become apparent. First and more obvious is the gathering strength of West Indies cricket. There was a time when very few thought they could defeat those 'who had given the game to the world'. But by now it had been shown that the sacred groves could be entered and conquered, and as a result confidence grew and talent flourished. The second factor was bred from the first. Crowds, being human, love success, take more note of successful teams, go to see them in greater numbers. Which, of course, means that with their growing success West Indies teams were increasingly good money-spinners. Tours thus became more frequent, sometimes with only three years between them (and remember, we are dealing here only with series in England; between times there were visits by England to the Caribbean).

Sobers called the 1963 Worrell team the best he had ever played in. How did he fare when he had taken over the captaincy in 1966 and 1969? In plain figures, the earlier series resulted in three West Indies wins, one to England, and one draw; 1969's three-Test tour went to England 2–0 with one draw; but in the case of 1966 we face the old problem of taking into account the strength of the opposition. England was at its lowest ebb in years, says *Wisden*. So although in many ways the West Indies did well, because of the poor competition which they met, I very much doubt that the 1966 team was one of the great ones.

But let us look at their performance in some detail before coming to that conclusion. Overall the results were rather unenterprising: 15 games drawn, 4 lost, 8 won; and it must be said that the Tests were not that wonderful, except perhaps the one at Lord's. Sobers, however, was at his pinnacle, finishing with a Test average of 103.14. His scores in the series have to be listed to be appreciated:

Old Trafford, 161
Lord's, 46 and 163 not out
Trent Bridge, 3 and 94
Headingley, 174
The Oval, 81 and 0.

His bowling was also impressive: 269.4 overs for 545 runs and 20 wickets for an average of 27.25. In the first Test, after his 161, he bowled his three varieties of ball over 49 overs, taking 3 wickets; he also held five catches. In fact over the series he took more catches than anyone on either side including the wicket-keepers.

Others who performed well included the lively Seymour Nurse (Test average 62.62), Butcher (60.00), and Kanhai (40.50).

The main Test bowlers, besides Sobers, were:

	O	R	W	Av.
Gibbs	273.4	520	21	24.76
Hall	175.3	555	18	30.83
Griffith	144.3	438	14	31.28

The England team for the first Test was not outstanding though an improvement came with the inclusion of Graveney for the second Test. But they searched for an opening pair, and used three captains – always a bad sign. Milburn scored a century, Graveney two, the wicket-keeper, John Murray, in the last Test, one. Six West Indians reached Test centuries, including 209 not out by Butcher, and Sobers alone scored *three*.

In his Test career Sobers scored twenty-six centuries; ten against England, five of them in England. Of these, he says, in his book *Twenty Years at the Top*, 'The two at Lord's were the best, with the 1966 effort the best of all'. David Holford, his cousin, was with him on this occasion, reaching his only Test century – and rarely was one more needed.

Gary had been able to inspire Holford with the confidence which he rightly says is what every batsman needs to achieve his potential, however gifted he might be. He says that when Holford came to the wicket he put it to him that the Lord's wicket is very much like the one at Bridgetown and that as he had made many runs there he should have no trouble at Lord's.

I don't suppose that the argument would bear the most careful logical scrutiny. It reminds one of the old Barbadian planter visiting London with his wife in the old days before the motor-car had taken over. There was a terrific noise of coachmen and drivers controlling their animals, and of street criers promoting their wares. The confusion was intense; the planter surveyed the scene with much satisfaction, and confided to his wife: 'Maude, it's just like Bridgetown on a Friday morning.'

But there can be no contradicting Gary over the importance of confidence, which perhaps he built up in Holford as much by example as by chatter and argument. I have heard many players say how much they seemed to improve when batting with George Headley, and how much he would build up their confidence. One example of this has often been said to be the innings which Ivan Barrow played with him in 1933 at Old Trafford when they put on 200 for the second wicket, Barrow becoming the first West Indian to get a century in England in a Test.

The first Test, won so easily at Old Trafford by the West Indies – by an innings and 40 runs, with two days to spare – was a wonderful opening to Sobers's first captaincy in the 'old country'. Gibbs, still in 1990 the only slow bowler to get over 300 wickets in Test cricket, reaped 10 in the match for 106 runs in 69.1 overs. The wicket did favour spin: Holford got 4 for 83, and Sobers 3 for 103, both in the match. But the presence of Allen and Titmus, who got 7 between them, did not in any way inhibit the old batting firm of Sobers (161) and Hunte (135). But Sobers was lucky to be dropped four times; Hunte had but one chance, early on.

This was Colin Milburn's first Test. He began in the worst possible way – run out for 0 – but came back in the second innings with a characteristically robust 94. It was in this game, too, it should be remembered, that the umpires Buller and Elliott took turns at square-leg so as to scrutinise Charlie Griffith's action; sometimes they crossed to point. He was no-balled nine times . . . for over-stepping the crease!

Milburn was mainly responsible for the draw which England gained in the second Test at Lord's. He batted with real verve and courage in their second innings, hooking Wes Hall and Charlie Griffith almost at will for 126 not out.

Despite many interruptions for rain, it was a splendidly contested match. In the first innings Nurse made 64 and Sobers 46 in the comparatively low total of 269, Higgs taking 6 for 91 in 33 overs. England's 355 gave them a lead of 86; Graveney, recalled after three years of being mysteriously ignored by the selectors and entering the field to a heartwarming welcome, scored 96. Parks supported him well with 91. When WI were 95 for 5 in their second knock it looked bleak for them, but then Sobers (163 not out) nursed Holford to 105 not out and was able to declare at 369 for 5.

This left England to get 284 to win in four hours. Rain reduced that by a full hour, but at 67 for 4 the pressure was very much upon them. Milburn, however, was in full and rumbustious flow and, joined by Graveney, now batting virtually one-handed with a badly bruised thumb, saw them to 197 for 4 and safety at final stumps.

In the third Test, played at Trent Bridge, West Indies put themselves in the good position of 2–0, with one draw, for they won the game by 139 runs. The good thing about this victory was the fact that they extricated themselves from a fairly dodgy position, having scored only 235 in the first innings to which England replied with 325. Lashley, playing his first Test in England, missed his 50 by 1 run and Nurse scored a lively 93. Snow and Higgs did the damage with 4 wickets each.

Although England led by 90 their batting left much to be desired: apart from, Graveney (109), Cowdrey (96), and D'Oliveira (76), only Underwood (12 not out, playing his first Test and Parks (11) reached double figures.)

In the second innings, West Indies, lost 2 wickets for 65, but so recovered that they could declare at 482 for 5, leaving England half an hour on Monday and all day Tuesday to make 393. When they were all out for 253, eighty-five minutes of play still remained. Sobers had another fabulous match: 5 catches, 5 wickets, and 94 runs in the second innings. Basil Butcher, who had always served the West Indies so well, got 209 not out in the second innings, taking part in three century-plus partnerships, with Kanhai, Nurse and Sobers.

The fourth Test started at windswept and rainy Leeds on 4 August; on Monday the 8th it was over – a disaster for England. As the 1967 *Wisden* put it: '. . . this was a sorry performance and one felt at the end of the match that the selectors would have to take drastic action.' (And they did! They dropped Cowdrey, Milburn, Parks, Titmus, Underwood and Snow.)

The first day's play was restricted by rain and bad light to three and a quarter hours. And West Indies were still having trouble to get a really good opening stand; even though the first wicket fell at 37, Lashley had made only 9. Further, Kanhai and Hunte went with the total no more than 122. Early next morning Butcher was caught by Parks off Higgs who had worried the West Indian batsmen in the previous Test: 4 wickets down for 154! But Nurse and Sobers then took the score to 419. As previously noted, Sobers was in rare form in this season, and here at Leeds he excelled. His score of 174 was without blemish; he hit twenty-four 4s and scored 103 between lunch and tea. He scored 174 out of 265 for the fifth-wicket stand, and by wonderful cutting, driving, and hooking reached his 1,000 for the season.

Like all great athletes Sobers made it all look so easy that perhaps we did not appreciate fully his lithe artistry. His build and ability belied the feeling that great batsmen of the highest order tend to be small, compact men like Bradman and Headley. And, oh yes, he took 8 wickets for 80 runs in the game. Perhaps the English selectors were a little hard on the players they dropped for the team which lost by an innings and 55 runs. Gibbs took 6 for 39 in the second innings. And, please note, all who believe in fast bowling, and those who think that the West Indies can win only when using them, that neither Hall nor Griffith, who bowled 20 overs between them, got a wicket in the second innings!

Umpire Elliott, after consultation with his colleague Buller (the same pair who had watched so carefully at Old Trafford), did caution Charlie Griffith for throwing. The delivery had been to Graveney. Apparently Griffith cut his pace considerably after this. I carefully note this, because the impression is often given, quite accurately, that Griffith was never called, except by Cortez Jordan in Barbados; but he was *cautioned* in this game. He took 2 wickets in the first innings, and none in the second. For England, D'Oliveira's hard hit 88 (out of a 240 total), and Barber's 55 out of the second innings of 205, were the only scores over 50.

And so West Indies went to the Oval having won three and drawn one. But the Oval game, as we shall see later, was for them a bit of a disaster.

In 1969 the Old Trafford first Test foreshadowed what was to come. England won by 10 wickets at Old Trafford. Geoff Boycott and John Edrich got them off to a splendid start off some fairly indifferent bowling by a West Indies now without Hall and Griffith: the opening stand was worth 112. Graveney continued the good work with 75, batting at no. 4; and Basil D'Oliveira, now a sort of hardy perennial, scored 57. England made 413 in their first innings.

The West Indies opening partnership of Fredericks and Carew was broken very early as the former fell, hooking, to Snow for a duck; Carew did not tarry long, for he made but 1 run. Wickets fell at 0, 5, 58, 72. The 100 was not achieved until the 6th wicket had fallen, and West Indies followed on having totalled only 147. The fast bowlers, Snow and Brown, had done the damage, taking 4 wickets each. The opening of the second innings looked as if once again West Indies might come from the back to make a race of it: Fredericks (64) and Carew (44) added 92 for the first wicket, but although Butcher and Sobers both scored 48, no one played a really long innings, and Boycott and Edrich brushed off the 10 runs required with ease.

Clive Lloyd, playing his first game for West Indies in England, scored 32 and 13. Foster, the Jamaican hopeful, had a most undistinguished game: 4 and 3, and did not again make the Test team on this tour.

The second Test, played at Lord's, was rather different. West Indies batted first, and the left-hander Fredericks, back on form, contributed 63 to an opening stand with Camacho (67) of 106. Then came Davis's 103 and the innings finally totalled a not unreasonable 380. England battled unevenly. They were 37 for 4 when Hampshire came in – and what a time to begin one's Test career. But he joined the select band of those who have scored a century on their debut, making 107 before being lbw to Shepherd. His captain Ray Illingworth made a gritty 113 and Knott 53, but the innings folded still 36 behind. The wickets had been shared between five bowlers.

Second time out, West Indies declared at 295 for 9. Lloyd's 70 and Fredericks's 60 were the main contributions; Davis fell mightily this time for 0. Needing 332 to win, England were still 37 short (for 7 wickets) at the close, Boycott having made his second century of the series and his fellow Yorkshireman Phil Sharpe 86. In the time/runs equation, the declaration was well judged. It was a tempting target, and if England had made a slightly brisker start they might well have made it. (As a reflection upon Gary's whole attitude, remember that he was one down in a three-match series, yet was still willing to gamble!)

Conditions for most of the final Test at Leeds were overcast, which together with a green wicket made batting none too easy. The West Indies seamers performed well (Holder 4–48, Shepherd 3–43) and restricted England to 223, of which only John Edrich with 79 passed 50. But England's Knight was a match for them and in taking 4–63 was instrumental in gaining the home side a lead, useful in the conditions, of 62. Batting a second time, England lost Boycott without a run on the board, but a consistent performance from the rest brought them to 240, leaving WI 303 to win. Sobers had remarkable figures: 40–18–42–5.

With the low scoring, the time factor was of no great relevance. In fact the wicket was now at its easiest of the whole match, and when West Indies did not lose their fourth wicket until 219 runs were on the board they looked favourites to square the series. Illingworth, however, showed a cool captain's head, and despite 71 from Camacho and 91 from Butcher he led his side to a 30-run victory. After Sobers went for 0, driving wildly before he had had a look at things, the danger man was Clive Lloyd, but Illingworth put himself on (off-spinner against left-hander) and had him caught behind. The match as good as won, Underwood was once again unleashed, to finish with 4–55 off 22 overs of which 12 (just over half!) were maidens.

So what of the two sides? Surely that of 1966 was the stronger. Any team with Sobers at his best and backed up by Hunte, Butcher, Nurse and Kanhai, with Hall, Griffith and Gibbs to lead the attack, must be a very nasty proposition for anyone. It would have been good to see them against a stronger England. By 1969 the two pacemen were gone, Sobers was weary and the batting, missing all but Butcher of the back-up, was no real match.

So despite some good solo performances, because of the weakness of the opposition, and the indifferent all-over results, I would not rate the 1966 team as one of the great ones.

The 1969 tour was a three-Test series – oddly enough. West Indies, to put it mildly, did not do well. Two Tests were lost, one by 10 wickets, another, which could have at least been drawn, by 30 runs, and the other drawn. West Indies had four centuries scored against them, and made only one (C. A. Davis, 103 at Lord's). Butcher battled bravely at Leeds for 91, but got little support from anyone else, including the umpires, and his captain who tarried too long in the dressing-room and then made 0 when even 10 from him might have made the difference! Not a distinguished tour.

Sobers, the captain, had perhaps gone stale. On the whole tour he scored 432 runs in 15 innings. In the three Tests he scored 150, with an average of 30. Gibbs, now an old campaigner, did not distinguish himself either. No, not a distinguished tour, nor a very lively time for West Indies cricket. *Wisden* put it well: 'They finished last summer not having won any of their previous nine engagements against England and having lost four.' But remember, in 1963 and 1966 they won six of the ten Tests they played against England.

Perhaps the most devastating comparison to be made between 1966 and 1969 is in the results of the first-class games:

	P	W	L	D
1966	27	8	4	15
1969	19	2	3	14

For interest:

1963	30	15	2	13
1950	31	17	3	11

The 1963 team, led by Worrell, was the one that Sobers so admired. The captain in 1950 was Goddard.

10

Recovery

1973 and 1976

The 1973 touring team, captained by Kanhai and managed by Esmond Kentish, suggested the possibility of rejuvenation, and recovery of old form. And one is grateful for that – especially grateful to Kanhai and Kentish; but it was not a great team. The first Test, played at the Oval, contrary to usual custom, was the first West Indies win since 1969 (twenty Tests) and the first over England since 1966!

So the team did well and started West Indies back on the trail. The old stalwarts Gibbs and Sobers were on the way out, and Clive Lloyd was on the way in. Sobers played only in the Tests, and distinguished himself with the bat: he scored 306, only 12 runs less than Lloyd whose total was the highest on the team. Sobers averaged 76.50, Lloyd 63.60, Fredericks 50.20. Newcomer Boyce was the star bowler with 19 Test wickets; Gibbs took 9, Sobers 6.

The party for this half-season tour had an extremely good spirit. Kanhai was 37; Gibbs was 38; his promising cousin, Clive Lloyd, was ten years younger. Julien was but 23 and Kallicharran 24. The team lost only one first-class game, drew 10, and won 7.

The Oval first Test having been won by 158 runs (see chapter 12 for the story) much to the delight of the fans, West Indies drew the next Test at Edgbaston – to the chagrin of many English commentators who seem to feel that England are the only team entitled to play for a draw, especially when a series is to be protected! Fredericks outshone his colleagues in the first innings, reaching 150 out of 327. Only Julien with 54 approached him. The total, although not large, proved just too much for England who fell 22 runs short of it. West Indies then scored 302, Lloyd making 94, Sobers 74, and Kanhai 54. England scored 182 for 2. As in the Oval Test there were five Guyanese on the team and the only

Jamaican was the left-handed Ron Headley, the son of George and a member of the Worcestershire county team.

The final Test, at Lord's, not only saw West Indies well on the way to recovery in the international arena, but also became known as the 'Bomb-Scare Test'. But not even the IRA and their threats could hold the West Indies back – they won decisively by an innings and 226 runs, with a day and a half to spare.

On 25 August, the Saturday afternoon, all was going along peacefully, with slightly more electricity in the air than is usual of a summer's afternoon at Lord's, when an authoritative, calm, and oddly reassuring voice asked us to leave the ground quietly. A telephone message had warned that a bomb had been planted. The warning was being taken seriously, and the packed ground had to be inspected and checked. As ever in England, except at some overheated soccer encounters, there was not the slightest hint of panic – this was the more impressive as the IRA had mounted a menacing bomb campaign in London. Eighty-nine minutes were lost, the call proved to be a hoax, and the game went on relentlessly in the favour of the West Indies.

West Indies batted first, and in this, their only innings, gave their fans hope for the future and their opponents a warning of what was to come. Perhaps they had not been taken quite seriously enough – they had been having a lean time of it on the international scene. The innings was a splendid mixture of old and new, and heaped coals of fire on the heads of those critics who had complained of a putative 'go-slow policy' at Edgbaston. The first 3 wickets fell in this fashion: 1 for 8, 2 for 87, 3 for 225. Kanhai was mostly responsible for that partnership of 138; but Lloyd, who was to become captain, was with him, eventually getting his fifth 50 against England. The 'old captain' was in rare form and eventually made 157.

Again there was a slight blip: to 4 for 256 and then 5 for 339, 6 for 373, 7 for 604, and at the declaration 8 for 652. In the meantime the old and new had come together again in the form of Sobers and Bernard Julien. The former must have felt deep down that this was his last trip to the wicket at Headquarters for the team he had captained. Despite disagreements with them, he had done them proud. He now started his innings, coming in at his favourite no. 6 position, quietly, but was soon showing all the old grace, and despite having to retire for a while because of stomach cramps, carried his bat for 150 – the last of his twenty-six Test centuries. Julien was lucky early on to be dropped. But he batted fluently to get his maiden Test 100. He and his senior partner put on 155 in under two hours for a seventh-wicket record, West Indies v. England. But Julien was yet to bowl! In England's second innings of 193, he took 3–69 in 18 overs.

Boyce, just bordering on 30 years of age, also did well for West Indies with the ball, taking 8–99 in the match. In the second innings he dismissed Amiss, Knott and Boycott, in his second burst of genuine speed, for 6 runs in 23 balls.

Only Fletcher offered real resistance for England; 68 in the first innings and 86 not out of 193 in the second. Illingworth in his last game as captain did not have a good match, getting but 1 wicket, and seeing the West Indies put on their largest score yet in England. Underwood lasted, in the second innings, for a stand of 47 runs in the hope that Fletcher, handling the fast bowling well, could get his century. But the game ended with him being bowled by Gibbs for 14, and Fletcher still 14 runs short.

Unfortunately Foster, for the West Indies, once again failed in a Test, even though on the tour he scored 828 runs in first-class games at an average of 63.69. Sobers took six catches – two of them off Gibbs, keeping the memory bright of the times he stood at leg-slip, in what John Arlott used to call the pick-pocket position, ready to scoop up any deflection coming from the bat of a groping player deceived by the flight of the tall, dancing Gibbs.

There were one or two oddities about this tour. First of all it was a three-Test affair. West Indies had not been doing well: Australia had won 2–0 in the West Indies in 1972–73; two seasons earlier India had defeated them 1–0, again in the Caribbean; in 1968–69 Australia won 'down under' 3–1, with one drawn. Yet West Indies chose this short series not only to defeat England utterly, but also, with the emergence of Lloyd, Kallicharran and Julien, to signal what was to come.

Again, the maturity of West Indies cricket upset people like veteran critic Norman Preston. He said in *Wisden*, in reviewing the tour: 'They certainly failed. . . to live up to the carefree and sporting tradition of their predecessors.' He is referring to the Edgbaston game when West Indies, following one of the longest-standing of English cricket traditions, played to draw the second Test, having won the first, and having been given only a three- Test series!. Be *carefree*, my boy, and we might just call you a 'calypso collapso' cricketer. We might even applaud your sporting failure!

It was ever thus! Sixteen years later those English critics who had been moaning so boringly about the use of four fast bowlers by West Indies were applauding the way in which, virtually unrelieved by spin, Fraser, Lewis, Small and Malcolm were bowling down some people. Isn't it time to legislate that all Test teams must use at least one leg-break bowler, one off-spinner, and one left-hand orthodox bowler? It would add so much to the variety of the game! As would the law-enforced addition of at least one left-handed bat.

O wad some power the giftie gie us
To see ourselves as others see us!

But then, Scottish poets don't play cricket, do they?

In the bowling averages for the 1973 tour one notes that Gibbs, not so successful in the Tests, took 24 wickets, Holder 28 and Inshan Ali, unfortunate to be selected only for the first Test, as many as 38.

The least important oddity was that there were six left-handers in the West Indies batting line-up in the first Test, including a left-handed opening pair.

I have spent a long time on this tour because it was an end, and a beginning; and it was altogether an enjoyable interlude with the great and generous Rohan Kanhai as captain, and the thorough and urbane Esmond Kentish as manager, helping to recreate West Indian confidence in themselves and in their cricket.

Clive Lloyd's 1976 team were to take up where Kanhai & Co. had left off, and to sweep the board really – losing but 2 games on tour, winning 18 and drawing 6. The comparative figures for Goddard's 1957 team were: 3 lost; 14 won; 13 drawn. Of the Tests, the 1976 team drew the first two, won the next three.

What with the bowling of Holding and Roberts, and the batting of Fredericks, Greenidge, and Richards in the Tests, it is really difficult to know where to start, or how to give an idea of the sterling performance of this party during the hottest summer for many a year. I shall not forget how brown the ground about seemed as I drove into Old Trafford – where West Indies were to win by 425 runs! Could this be the wet Manchester of my memories, or had I taken a wrong turn somewhere?

Unfortunately one has to say that the English opposition was not as good as in many other years. In Tests their top-scoring batsman was David Steele with a total of 308 runs at an average of 30.80. Knott was next highest with 270, average 30.00; then came Woolmer 245 (27.22) and A. W. Greig 243 (30.37). (Edrich did have an average of 48.33; but his aggregate was only 145 – from four innings.) Underwood, Snow and Willis were their most successful bowlers. Underwood took 17 wickets at an average of 37.11, Snow 15 at 28.20, Willis 9 at 26.00.

Without being unkind, for those three were fine bowlers and cricketers, one wonders if their presence and performance explain the following West Indies batting figures:

	Runs	Av.
Richards	829	118.42
Greenidge	592	65.77
Fredericks	517	57.44
Lloyd	296	32.88

Notice that even Lloyd, who was seventh in the list, has a better average that Steele, and is only 12 runs short of his aggregate! Steele, incidentally, had begun his Test career the year before, at the age of 33.

When we get to the West Indies first-class batting figures we begin to get an idea of what the English bowlers were up against. Six West Indians scored more than 1,200 runs; Greenidge got 1,952; Richards 1,724.

This was the year mostly remembered in England as the 'year of the bumper'. The image that stays in English minds is of the veteran Close swaying back, eyes shut, as the lethal ball hurtles past his chest in the gathering gloom. Close: the old hand recalled to try to handle the West Indies fast battery, 'old' being the true word, for he was aged 45 and had last played Test cricket nine years previously! Which says something about English cricket at that time, and about the selectors. Not that their captain, Tony Greig (an early South African entrant into the

England side, by the way), helped too much when he announced his intention to 'make them grovel'. Those few words put the final inch of steel into the West Indies side and virtually settled the series before it had begun.

Even so, England managed, briefly, to hold off a landslide. At the Trent Bridge first Test WI immediately took the initiative with a first innings of 494 built largely around a massive third-wicket stand of 303. This was Richards's first big innings of the series, 232. Kallicharran made 97, but oddly no one else reached 50. England replied with 332, of which Steele grafted courageously to an obdurate 106 and Woolmer made 82. Next highest score was extras: 38, including 29 no-balls! Daniel was the leading bowler, taking 4 for 53.

Richards was top scorer again with 63 in 176 for 5 declared, which left England with little choice but to try to bat it out for a draw. That they did so was due almost entirely to Edrich and Close, both not out for 76 and 36 respectively.

Lord's, another draw but a tighter game, was Roberts's triumph – 10 for 123 in the rain-interrupted match. England's opening innings was propped up by Close with 60 in a total of 250. Richards was out of the side, injured, and despite Greenidge's 84 and Lloyd's 50, West Indies could manage only 182, Underwood taking 5 for 39. Going in again, England made 254 (Steele 64, Close 46), but not quite fast enough. West Indies needed 323 – highest innings of the match – to win, and by the end had lost 6 wickets for 241, Fredericks 138. Rain had clearly proved West Indies undoing.

The third Test, at Old Trafford, saw the WI steam roller really getting under way. Greenidge scored two 100s, Richards one, Holding had first-innings figures of 14.5–7–17–5 and Roberts second-innings figures of 20.5–8–37–6. Such performances need no embellishment.

West Indies took first innings and made 211, Greenidge 134. In England's truly awful 71 in face of Holding's rampage, only Steele with 20 got to double figures. Second time out, Greenidge got 101, Richards 135, in 411 for 5 declared. By this time we were near the end of the third day, and in poor light Close ('promoted' to open in this game; one suspects an element of expendability) and Edrich showed considerable courage in face of some very hostile bowling indeed. This is where the swaying-back image came from to linger in the English mind; certainly it seemed to many – not all of them English – that a word of warning from the umpires would not have been out of place. Be that as it may, those two went on next day to a very creditable 54 but England finished the fourth day on 125–9; and it was all over after ten minutes on the next day, the innings – with a target of 552 – closing at 126 for a WI win by 425 runs.

So to Leeds. Close and Edrich were dropped (shell-shocked?) and Woolmer and Steele were in due time sent out to face the Wagnerian music. First, though, Fredericks and Greenidge put on 192 for the first West Indies wicket; the former 109, the latter 115 for his third 100 in three Test innings. Richards took only a canter here for 66, and the total was 450.

England looked in the direst trouble at 80 for 4 but they improved to 321 for 6, largely due to a defiant 116 each from captain Greig and Alan Knott, so that they finished at 387. The West Indies second innings of 196 featured 5 wickets for Willis at a cost of 42 runs, but in England's second innings only Greig made any great impression with 76 not out so that they went down by 55 runs; the wickets being shared out among the four WI pacemen.

The Oval Test, starring Richards (again) and, for England, Amiss, making an astonishing comeback against true pace after his battering from the Australians, is described in chapter 12.

Now, fifteen years after his first assault on England in England, we have tended to get accustomed to Richards's supreme batting ability, and to some of his idiosyncracies. The *Wisden* of 1977 says of him: 'Self-confidence, without arrogance, is one of Richards's hallmarks.' Some sections of the press now regularly characterise him as arrogant. I can't say that I have ever found him so in conversation, or at press conferences. But his confidence on the field can look like strutting; especially in understating England, where as Chesterton put it, 'If a man has something sensible to say he often feels he should stammer it out'! Also some sections of the press are quite ambiguous over class and quality. A little of each is good; but consistency in them is to be, as we would say in the Caribbean, 'carried down'.

But certainly 1976 was the year in which Richards, who became 24 that year, could have developed a 'swell head'. In nine months to the end of the series in England, he had scored 1,811 runs in Tests:

In Australia: 101, 44, 2, 30, 101, 50, 98

In West Indies v. India: 142, 130, 20, 177, 23, 64

In England, he made a total of 829, in four Tests and seven innings. During the same series he made eight Test centuries, including two double-centuries, and was just two runs short of another.

At that time only Bradman in 1930 had exceeded that total of runs in a series in England by scoring 905 for Australia in seven innings. Like Richards he had but seven innings, whereas Hammond, who scored 903 for England in Australia in 1928–29, had nine. But it was not only the number of runs Richards scored which marked his greatness. It was, even at that early date, his grace, his footwork, his obvious enjoyment of putting bat to ball, his scoring all round the wicket, and his ability to use the rapier as well as the broadsword.

But although his innings at Trent Bridge and at the Oval were a revelation and iridescent, other batsmen also performed excellently, as we have seen. And the bowlers did just as much to discomfort the not too strong England team as did the batsmen. Holding and Roberts joined the many outstanding opening bowlers who hunt in pairs: Larwood and Voce, Francis and Constantine, Lindwall and Miller.

Holding's Test performance was 159.3 overs, 356 runs, 28 wickets, average 12.71. Roberts's was 221.4–537–28–19.17. These two took a total of wickets which exactly doubled that of Daniel and Holder combined. The four of them took 84 Test wickets between them; the other bowlers, 8.

From our point of view, thinking of the relative merits of West Indies teams touring England, the difficult question to settle is the one concerning the quality of opposition they have met during various tours. Without belittling in any way the achievement of the 1976 party, it seems clear to me that they did not meet many players of the 1950 calibre: Hutton, Washbrook, Compton, Sheppard, Simpson, Evans seem – how shall we put it? – to compare favourably with John Edrich, Close, Steele, Greig and Knott.

A new era had really started in cricket. West Indies were building up, England were not looking like their old selves, and there were about to be two big arguments: one about Kerry Packer's World Series, and the other about the West Indies fast bowling. The latter started during this 1976 tour.

The Kerry Packer interlude or disruption is too large for me to tackle on this occasion, but I did write about the other controversy, which was not only about the West Indies fast bowling but also about an interesting and dangerous conflict of cultures – still with us – which showed itself in arguments about how crowds should behave at Tests, about what level of noise is acceptable, and so on. I am sure that this conflict, as well as the raised prices at cricket, accounts for the falling off in attendance at Tests of Caribbean heritage people.

The controversy still goes on with, for instance, some very harsh regulations being introduced at the Oval. Because it continues, and because few people on all sides seem to understand that one is often impinging on deep habits – in fact, on ways of life – I would like to introduce now what I said then in Tony Cozier's 1977 *West Indies Cricket Annual*:

'The West Indies tour of England in 1976, like so many other things in life, looks and feels in retrospect not quite as it did when it was going on. Then the absorbing matters seemed to be the batting of Richards, the thunderous bowling of Roberts and Holding, the various postures of Tony Greig, and the variety of responses, rather sharper than one expected, to the noise, pan-beating, and generally raucous demeanour of the 'cheering section' which followed the West Indies wherever they went.

Now, in retrospect, one remembers all these things, but not in quite the same way, and one is tempted to focus on the rather different things: the overwhelming reliance of the West Indies attack on pace, and, of course, the unbelievable dearth of Test-class spinners and the way in which the England batsmen never looked like coping with pace.

One also recalls moves by either captain and both selection committees which were as near to bizarre as cricket activities are likely to be.

Consider, for instance, the England selectors bringing back the undoubtedly plucky Brian Close to face the pace and bouncers mainly by standing flat-footed and sticking out his manly chest. Or think of our own West Indian selectors persisting until the third Test with the, once more, plucky but incapacitated Kallicharran.

Further, inexperience alone cannot take the blame for the waste of energy and opportunity that afternoon at Old Trafford when Roberts, Holding and Daniel bowled bumper after bumper at batsmen who could have been dismissed by the well directed ball on, or just outside, the off-stump. Forget the hysterical reaction of some sections of the English press, who seem to have forgotten rather quickly Larwood, Voce, Trueman *et al*; the fact is that, whether within the spirit and laws of the game or not, that particular bowling exhibition was a waste of energy. It hardly gave the batsman a chance to get out!

It was 'exciting', it was an exhibition, but it was counter-productive, and brings into question whether the leadership of a captain need only be encouraging – whether, in fact, the firmness of restraint is not sometimes as much needed as the encouragement of the arm around the shoulder or the quick and obvious applause at the well bowled ball or brave bit of fielding . . .

And now, what about the noisy West Indian crowds, and the near hysterical reaction of some of the English folk – including some of the press?

One of the things we are dealing with here is a clash of cultures, and expressions of frustration and deep tensions and prejudices. Long ago on the first night that I walked the war-darkened streets of London with a Jamaican friend, he complained bitterly, at the top of his voice, that 'if we was in Jamaica now you bound to hear a few radio blaring and thing. This place too damn quiet!'

He was 'only' looking for what he was accustomed to. And so were some quite reasonable English people who were accustomed at cricket (say, in contrast to soccer) to long periods of quiet now and again broken by discreet volleys of applause or muffled exclamations of 'Good shot'. With that kind of English fan who had his customary quiet ways of relaxing utterly shattered, not by raucous shouting or clapping or jumping now and again, but by regular staccato beer-can bashing and drum beating, regardless of what was going on in the game, I felt much sympathy.

But, alas, the matter was much more complicated than that. Such an English person, on the whole, would have felt uncomfortable at most league soccer games where English youths regularly create nuisances by violence as well as noise. One of the sub-cultures of England enjoys English cricket and its old ways;

another is all for the kind of soccer 'hooliganism' which has brought international bans on English clubs.

Contrariwise, I know of one Jamaican fan who was, once upon a time, wont to travel from England to the Caribbean for the Test series, but who now will not go to Lord's to see his beloved West Indies play. 'The crowds have spoiled it all,' he says. 'I don't go to the games to see people rush on the field, simply displaying themselves and making one hell of a lot of noise.'

Some people, in the best tradition of ball games, view, even if only unconsciously, the playing area as sacred, the wicket as a special gate opening to another world, where through old rituals and duly observed forms a struggle is enacted, the forces of nature as well as man battled with, graceful art displayed, persons tested and new techniques developed.

The real trouble with the noise the West Indians made – and they were joined by some natives – was that it started out at a high pitch of intensity and continued there. One felt that it was not really related to the game and its progress, to the ritual and its rites. It was no doubt directed towards a self-assertiveness which arises out of the bewildering circumstances in which West Indians and black English people now find themselves in what is, to so many of us of whatever colour, a changed Britain. And in many ways, not only in cricket, a sadly changed one . . .

One felt that the 'noisy spectators' were trying to say something. They wish 'to be looked upon'; amidst their uncertainty and the threats of 'repatriation', they want to be associated with style, with verve, with success, with something literally 'to shout about'. Perhaps they forgot that others too wish to have their ways of doing things, their culture preserved.

A difficult question. But those who know the innate humour of West Indians, when not threatened, and the traditional tolerance of Britons, when not being invaded, must feel that the contact between the two can and will foster the best elements of both.

The sad thing about the 'confrontation' during the hot, lovely summer was that not a few Englishers simply continued to froth at the mouth, while many West Indians simply went on banging away. Too many people in both groups seemed not to realise that the other might have a point. Perhaps both groups really took themselves and their customs and their teams too seriously. The young English lad who ran on to the field to present John Edrich with an oversize bat struck just the right note. Pity some West Indian had not presented Roberts and Holding with a well marked off-stump at Old Trafford.

For myself, I was saddened to see so many English people behaving as if they really thought that the too noisy West Indian 'cheering section' was going to burst their bounds, take a few captives, and boil them there and then for lunch! And equally was I saddened to find so many West Indians falling for the trap of playing the role of being noisy, carefree, troublesome – a role some 'Europeans' are anxious to put upon them, and thereby, perhaps, disqualify them from real membership of a highly organised, industrial society, where tension is not released by noise at cricket, but rather by rackets in the massage and sauna parlours of cities large and small! . . .

If the great world cannot exist 'half slave and half free', neither can the world of games flourish in conditions in which the intricacy and grace of cricket are reduced simply to proving social, racial or national points to one's honoured opponents on the field.

In any case cricket is the game in which one ball, and one ball only, is quite enough to remove a Bradman, a Headley, a Richards, a Hutton. This we must always remember, even in connection with West Indies success in 1976, and as we continue to build teams for the future.

We are not being true to our real selves, but to an 'image' created for us, when we continue to be careless of sound techniques and intelligent and creative discipline. After all F. R. Martin, Wes Hall, Allan Rae, Frank Worrell, George Headley and Jeff Stollmeyer – to name a few – were also West Indians. Creative discipline and sound technique serve in rain or shine, on 'green tops' or glass-smooth surfaces, and when combined with grace and speed and cunning can gladden the heart and call forth bursts of spontaneous, wonderful recognition.

One of the big differences in recent West Indies cricket has been the uniformity of the teams and tactics: four fast bowlers without change; catching and ground fielding without blemish. In 1963 Hall and Griffith were not exactly slow; Worrell and Sobers could both be quick, but also use medium pace effectively, and with style. Not to mention left-hand spin of great variety. It is hard to remember that that team also boasted the inimitable Lance Gibbs, with his dance of a run-up, his high delivery, and the lovely loop in his flight. He was not only delightful to watch; he managed to be among the world leaders, bagging 309 Test wickets at an average of 29.09, despite the fact that when he was playing there was no shortage of fast bowlers on West Indies teams – but they were not the only bowlers one could count on. Variety is perhaps what the most recent West Indies teams have lacked. But they have not lacked tension and excitement in any of their games'.

11

Clive Lloyd's Continuing Reign

1980 and 1984

The 1980 tour, with Lloyd as captain, was rather disappointing: West Indies won one Test; the other four were drawn. Perhaps England were stronger than expected, perhaps the sense of disappointment came from too much cricket – as much for the spectators as for the players. Certainly, in the winter preceding the tour, West Indies had been in Australia for three Tests, winning two of them; from there they went to New Zealand for three more, finishing only in March before opening their England tour just two months later. (They had been defeated in Dunedin in a close game: New Zealand, wanting 104, sank to 73 for 8 but still won by 1 wicket – one wonders, would a fresh West Indies side have allowed a result like that?) Whatever the reason, this team did not seem to measure up to 1950 or 1976, even when considering the relative strengths of the England teams.

The first Test was perhaps the most interesting of this rain-washed series. On the Trent Bridge wicket England batted first and could muster only 263, although when Botham went at the fall of the fifth wicket, the total was 204. The new England captain had hit the ball hard for the top score of 57, but had been slightly chancy and was eventually caught by Richards off Garner. Garner, on that first morning had taken 2 for 11 in 7 overs, but did not bowl again until 3:40. He eventually took 3 for 44, Roberts getting 5 for 72.

It looked as if West Indies were about to live up to their pre-tour reputation, and even perhaps win by a wide margin. The first wicket fell at 19, but when Richards and Greenidge took the score to 107 one was hoping for a big score. These two who eventually scored 64 and 53 respectively, had little support from the others except for Deryck Murray who also scored 64 – a valuable if painstaking innings which saved West Indies from looking rather pedestrian. They in fact let England off the hook by scoring no more than 308. Willis, who took 4 for 82, at one time on the second day bowled five overs for 4 runs.

But England just did not take advantage of the situation, and managed to score in their second innings 11 runs less than in the first! Boycott top scored with 75, extras were next with 52, of which 19 were byes!

So West Indies were set a 'mere' 208 – just 100 less than they had scored in the first innings. Their performance was nearly as up and down as the weather. For having got to 109 for 2 by close of play, and needing 'only' 99 on the last day, with but few fans in the stands to enjoy the excitement, they could not win until 2:30 – thanks to Andy Roberts's fighting 22 not out made in forty-two minutes off thirty-five balls. By that time they had lost 8 wickets, and escaped with the help of a missed catch or two. Both teams were later to complain about the difficulty of picking up the flight of the ball in the outfield in weather which was already starting to be unpleasant.

The outcome was much more exciting than expected. It only rewarded the relative few who attended, but underlined why so many, who can afford the time, still prefer the long, sometimes slow Test-type cricket to the well supported one-day game.

Andy Roberts took 8 wickets in the game, and Joel Garner 7 (for 74). Willis took 9, and Botham 4.

The second Test, played at Lord's, was marred by rain. Between the Saturday afternoon – when England began their second innings 249 runs behind West Indies having replied with 518 to their 269 – and the close on Tuesday night we had a bit over three and a half hours of cricket which saw England to 133 for 2. But disappointing though this was, particularly to West Indian fans, we did have a few highlights.

Gooch scored 123 out of 269; and what a treat his batting was: he batted for eighty-three minutes less than Tavaré, who made 42, and faced forty balls fewer. Yet Tavaré is one of those hopefuls about whom Englishmen so often enthuse. Both were facing an in-form Holding who took 6 for 67 in 28 overs in the first innings; Garner collected 6 in the match for 57 in 39.3 overs.

Haynes and Richards put on 223 for the second West Indies

wicket. Haynes scored a steady and sensible 184, but I trust he will not mind our concentrating on this occasion on how Richards lighted up the gloom at Lord's.

Wisden, with 'Richards, of course, operated on a higher plane than anyone else', paid handsome tribute. Coming in at the fall of Greenidge for 25 (out of 37), he quickly put an end to English joy. He 'exploded into action'. Botham tried to block the on-side scoring openings, but as with all the truly great batsmen theory became irrelevant as the off-side was promptly blasted for five 4s. After reaching 50, he struck four boundaries to all points off an Underwood over, whereupon bad light brought an interruption. Only an interruption, however, not a halt, for the fusillade continued as Richards went to his century in just five minutes over two hours. In all he gave us 196 minutes of classic strokeplay before the end came almost ludicrously when he spooned an innocent ball from Willey to square-leg. His 145 contained 100 runs in 4s; there was also one 6. It was an innings that makes a nonsense of the adjectival storehouse; 'majestic' perhaps comes as close as any.

The drawn third Test, at Manchester, was a dreary affair – good for ducks, and writers who can only work while imbibing dry wine to guard against the wet outside. Over a third of the scheduled playing time was lost in rain. Lloyd, 'at home' away from home, made 101 in the West Indies innings of 260. It was the only century in the game. When he had scored 66 he reached 5,000 Test runs; at that time the only other West Indians to have achieved that distinction were the old stagers Sobers and Kanhai. A true captain's innings, especially as he had decided to ask England to bat first! England made 150 (Rose 70) and 391 for 7 (Boycott 86).

Unfortunately conditions were such, and promised so to continue, that any comparison between the teams, and between this touring party and others, was becoming more and more difficult.

At the fourth Test, at the Oval (traditionally the scene of the final Test) rain again intervened; chapter 12 gives the details.

And so to Headingley in the hope that we could find a sunmaker to banish the rain for six whole days during the fifth Test. But alas fourteen hours of the game were lost – half of the time already given over during the series to sitting in the damp, seeking inward consolation and wondering how the great game of cricket ever took on in the English climate.

Play was not possible until 2:45 on the second day when Richards, captain in the absence of the injured Lloyd, asked England to face the music in unpleasant circumstances. Roberts was unable to play, but this did not give off-spinner Parry a chance to make the Test team; West Indies continued their policy of using only fast and seam bowlers: Holding, Croft, Garner, Marshall and King. But one can see why they persisted. England lost 7 wickets for 89 runs, before Bairstow – another English wicket-keeper who likes to hold things up with the bat – and Emburey stopped the rot. The innings closed at 143 in under three and a half hours.

West Indies, in a very odd first innings, managed to score just 102 runs more than England – despite the fact that the opening pair put on 83! They declined to 207 for 9; it was Holding's 35 and Croft's stubbornness that pushed the score to 245, not as low a score as it sounds, considering the encircling gloom.

Gooch (55) and Boycott (47) offered staunch resistance, and England declared at 227 for 6 to put an end to this stop–start match – and season. But I think that there were too many interruptions, and too much time lost (including all Monday), for us to waste time on ifs and buts.

Injuries were too much in evidence. Lloyd suffered, as did Garner and Croft; Rowe, disappointingly, had to return home to Jamaica. He never did seem to realise his fantastic ability much appreciated in Barbados, where the style with which he did everything in his 302 v. England in 1973–74, including 'leaving alone', was much applauded.

Despite its record (played 16, won 8, drew 8), this 1980 party was not really one of the top ones to represent the West Indies in England – but this might be a harsh judgement in view of the weather that summer!

Clive Lloyd's 1984 side, managed by Jackie Hendricks, was, as they say, a different cup of tea. They had a notable record: 5 Tests, 5 Tests won; 14 first-class games played, 8 won, 6 drawn.

The Test averages are equally impressive:

Greenidge	81.71	from 572 runs
Gomes	80.00	from 400 "
Lloyd	51.00	from 255 "
Richards	41.66	from 250 "

Marshall	18.20	for 24 wickets
Garner	18.62	for 29 "
Harper	21.23	for 13 "
Holding	22.87	for 15 "

One of the main problems in comparing touring teams is to take into account the varying quality of the opposition – of the England teams which are engaged from year to year. England's team for the first Test in 1950 was: Hutton, Simpson, Edrich, Doggart, Dollery, Yardley, Bailey, Evans, Laker, Hollies, Berry. The English team for the first Test, 1988, was: Gooch, Broad, Gatting, Gower, Lamb, Pringle, Downton, Emburey, DeFreitas, Jarvis, Dilley.

It is my strong feeling that, despite the effects of the war and food rationing and all that, the 1950 England team was superior to the 1988. It is also worth noting that two of the 1988 team did not 'learn their cricket' in England. Lamb and Robin Smith, of course, grew up in South Africa. The category 'learn their cricket in England' is Trevor Bailey's invention. It is the interesting test which he would apply to those wanting to play for England: Greenidge would qualify, but not Lamb or Smith.

But let us stay with the West Indies. There can be no doubt that the greatest development in 1984 – and also in 1988 – was in the opening pair of Haynes and Greenidge, backed up by the fielding and out-cricket, and the availability of many first- class fast bowlers.

Fielding improved almost beyond recognition; West Indies used to have a few outstanding fielders, but the general standard was not good enough, catches were dropped, batsmen were not always forced to work for their runs. In Australia, in 1951–52, for instance, in the first Test five catches were dropped off Valentine and Australia won by just 3 wickets. In the second Test when the score was 27 for 2 Walcott dropped Hassett behind the wicket; Hassett went on to contribute 132 to a total of 517, and again Australia won the match.

But the excellent opening pair has been central. Haynes and Greenidge were not only prolific scorers and stroke-players, they were also good against all kinds of bowling. Stollmeyer and Rae get closest to comparing with the modern pair, but good as they were they did not face really fast bowling in England, and did not do so well against Lindwall and Miller on the faster Australian wickets. (Stollmeyer's long career, starting in 1939 in England, yielded him an average of 42.33 from thirty-two Tests.)

Hunte was the other outstanding West Indian opener. He showed his quality between 1957 and 1968 in most cricket venues, and ended up with an average of 45.06 from forty-four Tests. It is often forgotten that he scored 260, run out, in that innings v. Pakistan when Sobers got the world record Test score of 365 not out. But Hunte could not regularly find an opening partner who really stayed with him. In the game just mentioned Kanhai, at no. 2, made 25 before Hunte and Sobers got together to add 446. In that series Hunte had Sobers, Kanhai and McMorris opening with him.

There can be little doubt that the opening pair of Haynes and Greenidge is the best we have had so far. How, then, do we rate the other members of the 1984 team? First, we should recall that they won all five Tests, two by an innings. When they seemed to be in dire straits at Lord's, having been set 341 to get in their second innings, Greenidge came across with a magnificent 214 and H. A. Gomes 92, both not out. Once again the team was almost unchanged during the Tests, M. A. Small coming in for Holding at Lord's and W.W. Davis for Marshall at Old Trafford. Greenidge, Haynes, Gomes, Richards, Dujon, Lloyd, Harper, Baptiste, Holding, and Garner were the regulars.

We have already commented on the strength of the opening pair, and especially on a stroke-making team this is particularly important. What then of nos. 3, 4, and 5? Even allowing for the genius of Richards, do they measure up to the power, grace and productivity of the three Ws? Gomes, Richards, Dujon – are they really the equivalent of the 1950s trio? I don't think so, notwithstanding the magnificence of Richards. Recall the merciless cutting of Everton Weekes, the sledgehammer hooking of Walcott, and the dreamy ease of Worrell's off-drive. Even if we move Lloyd up the order to take Dujon's place, I don't think that it would affect the comparison as far as batting goes. But we have to remember that Lloyd is one of the greatest fielders the West Indies ever had – those catches snatched from the air, that swoop, pick-up and throwing down of the wicket, all in one move . . . even at times when his somewhat top-heavy stature has left him prone on the turf!

What of the other six members of the 1950 and 1984 teams? How do they compare?

On the former, after the Ws we had Christiani, Gomez, Goddard, as against Lloyd (or Dujon), Marshall, Harper. Christiani did not do well in the Tests; perhaps because he batted at no. 6 in three of the four. But he was a capable bat; his touring performance overall shows this. He was fourth in the first-class averages (45.58), following the three Ws. He scored four centuries during the tour, two being at Lord's v. Middlesex. But no doubt either Lloyd or Dujon could be considered at least his equal with the bat. He was lively in the field and a good team man.

Gomez, in 1950, was an outstanding all-rounder. Malcolm Marshall, at the beginning of his career, was, I thought, going to be more than his equal – as an all-rounder. But Marshall's batting has simply not developed as it should have. There is no doubt that he has more than made his contribution as a bowler, over 300 Test wickets in his career to date, at a strike-rate better than Fred Trueman's. But I think that as an all-rounder Gomez was at least his equal. Remember Gomez's performance in 1950: only Ram (135) and Val (123) took more wickets than he with his 55 in 680.3 overs at an average cost of 25.58 per wicket. He scored three centuries and averaged 42.92 in first-class games, coming just after the three Ws and Christiani. In the Tests he averaged 41.40.

Harper, in 1984, was another who promised much but did not quite come off. First he faltered with the bat, and then later, unfortunately, with the ball. But of course he was always a magnificent fielder. I should think that comparing Goddard and Harper we would have to give the edge to Goddard (as player, not as captain), or consider them equal.

The final three in 1984 were Baptiste, Holding, Garner; in 1950, Ramadhin, Valentine and either H. H. Johnson or Prior Jones. And here, of course, the comparison becomes almost impossible as one seems to be comparing mangoes with ortaniques. There can be no doubt of the world-class quality of the fast bowling of Holding and Garner; but about the bowling of Ram and Val in 1950, remembering especially when it took place, one is really at a loss for words. The effect they left on the English cricketing psyche was quite remarkable: first of all, they were slow bowlers, when the English, secure in their stereotypes, were expecting new versions of Constantine, Martindale and Francis. Second, the England batsmen just could not play them in 1950 – and they were not bowling bouncers, but practising what the English love to tell us is one of the fine arts of cricket, spin bowling.

It was their strike-rate in the Tests that summer in England which is difficult to appreciate fully: Val took 33 wickets in 422.3 overs, a wicket every 12.80 overs. Ram took 26 in 377.5 overs, one every 14.5 overs. As between them they took hardly four minutes to complete two overs, wickets seemed to be falling much more quickly than showers on a bad English summer's day.

Between Baptiste, however, and either Jones or Johnson in 1950, one would have to give the decision to Baptiste.

The England team that was so clearly beaten in 1984 was not a constant: Fowler, Lloyd, Randall, Gower, Lamb, Botham, Miller, Pringle, Downton, Cook, and Willis played in the first Test. Broad, Gatting and Foster came in for the second. For the third Terry and Allott joined the side and Cook was reinstated. For the fourth Cowans took the place of Willis and Pocock the place of Pringle. Tavaré, Ellison, and Agnew rang the changes for the fifth. West Indies did not really face outstanding opposition in that tour – even though Lamb got three centuries, and Botham bagged 8 for 103 in one innings of the Lord's Test. Lamb topped England's batting with an average of 42.88 (for WI, Greenidge 81.71, Gomes 80.00, Lloyd 51.00). That England team must have been one of the weakest to represent what used to be the sole home of the great game, in which, it was supposed, flannelled fools were sweetly applauded by ladies in long white dresses and cartwheel hats.

So how do we in the end compare the two teams? A really difficult task, but perhaps although as individual performers the 1950 team was slightly better, 1984 must get the nod as the more balanced. They had three excellent fast bowlers, two of them outstanding. They also had Harper as spin bowler, and Gomes capable of blocking up an end. Although the 1950 team was good in the field with Goddard outstanding, the later side was even better with Lloyd, Harper and Haynes. But they did meet weaker opposition.

Christopher Martin-Jenkins complained in *Wisden* about the use of fast bowlers by the West Indies, with reference to the unfortunate injury which Andy Lloyd received at Birmingham. Yet neither he nor many of the reporters in the press box at the time mentioned that Lloyd had played the ball onto the earpiece of his helmet.

The West Indies fielding was outstanding – witness Harper's fourteen catches and his ground fielding, swooping and throwing in one action. And Baptiste's direct hit from long-leg at Lord's to run out Geoff Miller. But these were mere examples of a general excellence.

The first Test at Edgbaston rather signalled what was to happen for the rest of the tour. Gower, having won the toss, decided to bat. And 6 wickets fell for 103! Botham (64) and Downton (33) held things up nicely, but the innings yielded only 191 runs. When 2 West Indies wickets went down for 35 one wondered whether a low-scoring game was in store for us. But 206 runs were to taunt the bowlers before another wicket fell. Richards hit 117 (despite a stomach bug), his seventh Test century against England; Gomes scored his first, and when he went, caught Miller at second slip off Pringle, for 143, he received a resounding ovation. His previous highest Test score was 126 against Australia at Sydney in January 1982.

After Clive Lloyd went with a bad shot that had him caught at first slip for a quick 71, including eight 4s, the graph dipped. Wickets fell at 418, 418, 421 and 455. Baptiste and Holding then decided to liven up proceedings, and to play powerful but judicious cricket with the bat. They selected the balls to beat; Baptiste would, for instance, play 'doggo' to Cook, and then as he shortened his length, square-cut him for 4. There was nothing agricultural about the batting of these two fast bowlers. Baptiste was eventually not out 87, with eleven 4s; Holding out for 69, with four 6s and eight 4s; West Indies, 606. Pringle's bowling was tidiest: 31–5–108–5. Next most effective was Willis with 25–3–108–2.

England's second innings improved to 235 (Andy Lloyd absent,

1. John Goddard (left), captain of the 1950 tourists, and the outstanding all-rounder Gerry Gomez. With Jeff Stollmeyer, Gomez provided the link between pre- and post-war West Indies teams, and enjoyed a most successful tour in 1950 with bat and ball.

2. 'Those two little pals of mine Ramadhin and Valentine.' Unknown before the 1950 tour, they took 258 first-class wickets between them that year, including 59 in the Test matches, and each bowled more than 1000 overs.

3. Allan Rae, seen here being stumped by Godfrey Evans off Norman Yardley for 68 in the third Test in 1950, which West Indies won by 10 wickets. Rae scored 377 runs in the series at an average of nearly 63, forming a solid opening partnership with Jeff Stollmeyer.

4. Clyde Walcott cuts a ball past the diving figure of Ken Barrington during West Indies match against Surrey in 1957. Walcott never quite scored the runs in England that his performances against Australia in 1954–55 predicted, although he kept wicket with distinction in 1950.

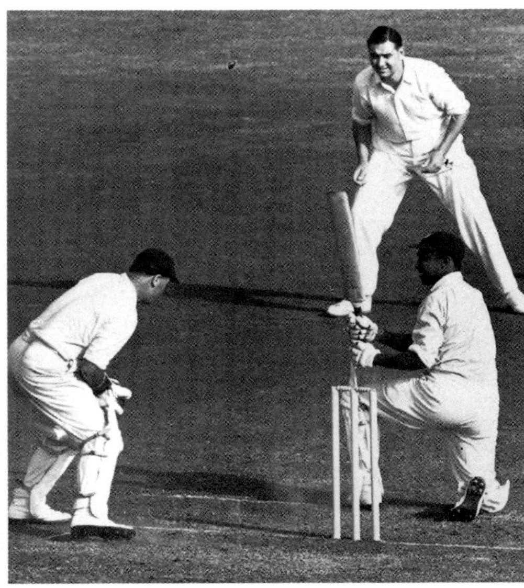

5. Frank Worrell sweeps past Godfrey Evans and Colin Cowdrey during his magnificent 191 not out in the third Test at Trent Bridge in 1957. Worrell had already bowled 21 overs in England's first innings, and was opening the batting only as a stop-gap due to the poor form of Kanhai, Pairaudeau and Asgarali.

6. Sonny Ramadhin bowling to Peter May during the first Test at Edgbaston in 1957. May and the non-striker, Colin Cowdrey, effectively negated the threat of Ramadhin by their controversial defensive play, in a second innings stand of 411, after the spinner had taken 7 first-innings wickets. He took only 7 more wickets in the series.

7. Wes Hall, West Indies flamboyant fast bowler, who toured England in 1957, 1963 and 1966, when he was a central figure in the epic drama of the drawn Lord's Test of that year. The non-striker is Surrey's Micky Stewart, manager of England during the 1988 series.

8. Jerry Alexander, the Cambridge Blue who was later to captain West Indies, appeals for lbw against Cowdrey off the bowling of Worrell during the 1957 tour. Cowdrey was given not out.

9. Gary Sobers made his fifth and last tour of England in 1973, sixteen years after his first in 1957. Fittingly he marked his final Test appearance in England with an innings of 150 not out at Lord's, and topped the Test batting averages with 306 runs at 76.50.

10. West Indies captain Rohan Kanhai sweeps a ball from Derek Underwood during his innings of 157 in the third Test at Lord's in 1973. Sobers and Bernard Julien also made centuries as West Indies amassed a total of 652 for 8 declared, to win by an innings and 226 runs.

11. Lance Gibbs takes his second wicket in consecutive balls as the England captain, Ray Illingworth, is caught at short-leg by Gary Sobers for 0 in the final Test of 1973 at Lord's. Sobers took six catches in the match, mainly in the 'pick-pocket position' of leg-slip.

12. The West Indies team before the start of a match during their 1957 tour. *Front row, left to right*: A.L. Valentine, C.L. Walcott, J.D.C. Goddard, F.M. Worrell, D. St E. Atkinson. *Back row, left to right*: B.H. Pairaudeau, G. St A. Sobers, W.W. Hall, D.T. Dewdney, F.C.M Alexander, N.S. Asgarali, O.G. Smith.

13. England's opening batsman, Bob Woolmer, is the first of Michael Holding's 14 victims in the fifth Test at the Oval in 1976, lbw for 8. Woolmer was one of seven openers tried by England in the series, of whom only Dennis Amiss, with an innings of 203 in that same Test, suggested any permanence against the West Indies pacemen.

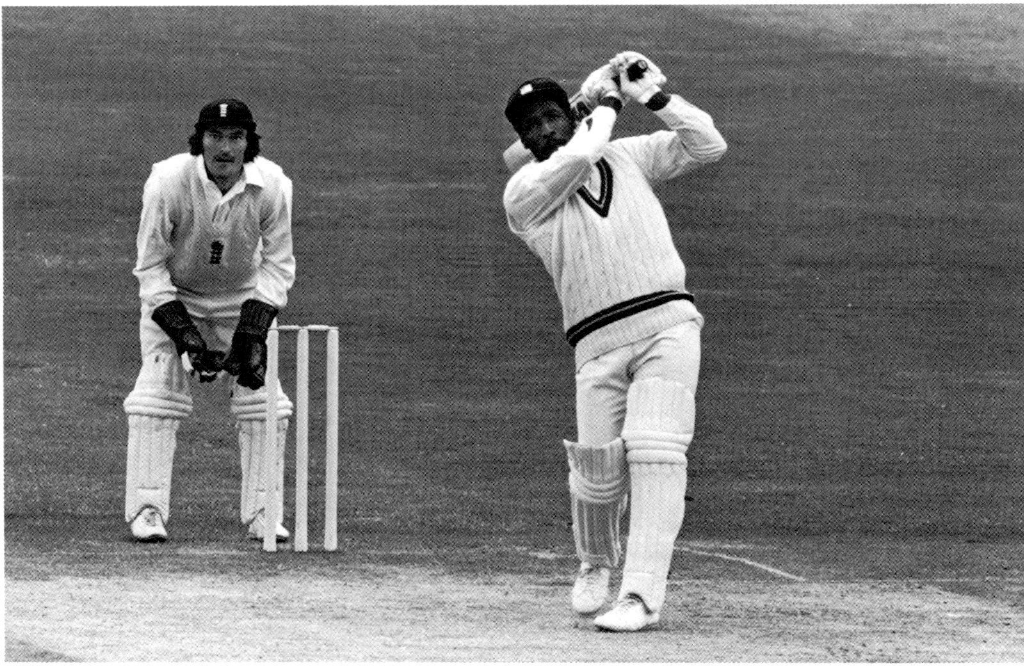

14. Viv Richards began the 1976 Test series with an innings of 232 at Trent Bridge, and ended it with a colossal total of 829 runs at an average of 118.42. Here he demonstrates his mastery of England's bowling by lifting Derek Underwood for 6, as Alan Knott looks on in admiration.

15. Andy Roberts took 28 Test wickets in 1976, including 10–123 in the second Test at Lord's. Here he celebrates the dismissal of the England captain Tony Greig for 0 in the first Test at Trent Bridge.

16. Gordon Greenidge hooks Chris Old for 6 at Lord's in 1976, showing his liking for the ground where he scored a remarkable 214 not out to win the second Test in 1984.

17. Clive Lloyd, the West Indies captain in 1976, causes David Steele and Brian Close to take evasive action as he sweeps a ball from Derek Underwood during the second Test at Lord's in that year. Lloyd's team took up where Kanhai's had left off, losing only two games on tour and winning the Test series 3–0.

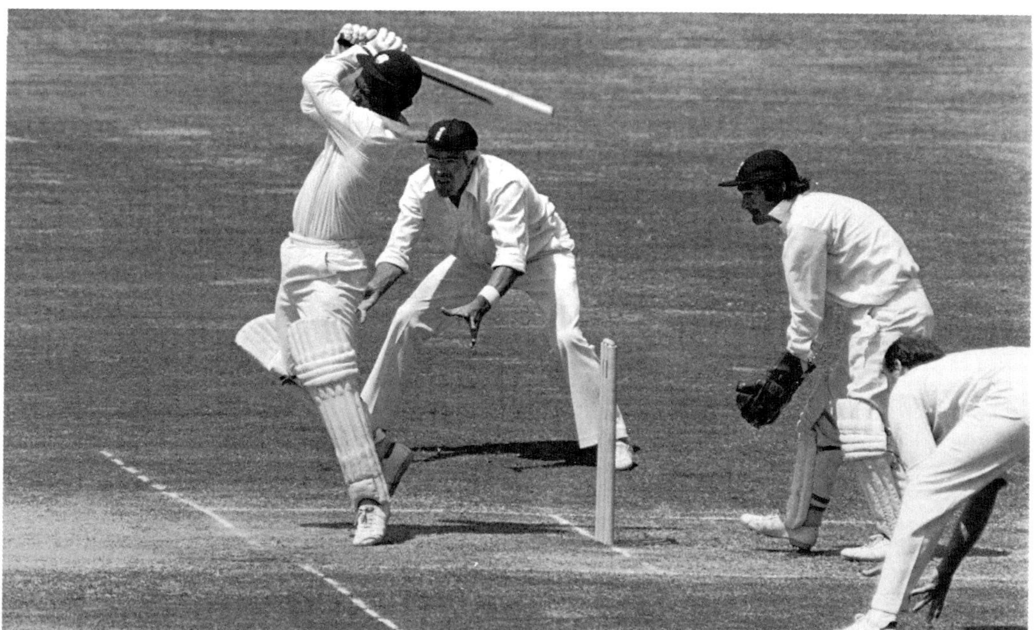

18. Roy Fredericks rocks onto the the back foot to smash the ball through the off-side during his magnificent innings of 138 in the second Test at Lord's in 1976. The left-handed Fredericks was a prolific partner for Gordon Greenidge in Test matches, never more so than in 1976 when he scored more than 500 runs in the series at an average of 57.44.

19. England's Pat Pocock is bowled by Joel Garner for 0 in the fourth Test at Old Trafford in 1984, a match which West Indies won by an innings and 64 runs. Garner's pace allied to awkward bounce brought him 55 Test wickets on his two tours of England in 1980 and 1984.

20. *left* Jeff Dujon scored a marvellous century in the fourth Test at Old Trafford in 1984 to underline his claim to be West Indies finest wicket-keeper-batsman. *Right* Malcolm Marshall defied a broken thumb to take 7–53 in England's second innings at Headingley in 1984 and set up a West Indies win by 8 wickets. Although absent from the fourth Test, Marshall took 24 wickets in the series.

hurt), but West Indies won by an innings and 180 runs, in four days.

The second Test, played at Lord's, was memorable indeed. And England looked much more like a Test team, even if they could not in the second innings, when they needed to, contain Greenidge.

England led by 41 runs in the two first innings which were rather low-scoring – 286 to 245. And having, in their second innings, scored 300 for 9 their skipper, David Gower, must have felt quite safe in giving West Indies 330 minutes to try to make 342 runs. They took on the challenge, and lost only 1 wicket, by the run-out route – not saving the game by a backs-to-the-wall Dunkirk effort, but winning it. One says the West Indies did this but it was very much a Greenidge effort – 214 not out. Gomes played the quiet role, but scored a more than adequate 92, also not out. Botham who had got 8 wickets in the first innings could do nothing in his 20.1 overs in the second. He had bowled 27.4 in the first and then scored 81 runs. He was appointed joint man-of-the-match with Gordon Greenidge.

It was a great game; and both Fowler and Lamb scored centuries for their side. But it must have knocked England back on their heels – over eleven overs of the mandatory last twenty were not required by the batsmen in achieving their victory! Marshall and Garner bowled particularly well at the beginning of England's second innings; but they and M. A. Small had kept up the pressure throughout. Marshall took 8 wickets in the match; Garner 4.

It was as outstanding a triumph as that by the Ramadhin and Valentine team; but it was not quite such a team effort, and I am not at all certain that England at Lord's in 1984 had the likes of Hutton, Washbrook, Edrich, Yardley, Evans and Bedser playing for them. One of the unfortunate things about this game was that despite the tension and the drama out there on the lovely green, and despite the effort and grace of so many in the middle, some notable sports commentators could find nothing better to do than constantly bleat about the over rate and the use of fast bowlers. I do wonder why the crowds, mostly English and West Indian, still flock to see these 'boring' games.

The third Test, at Headingley, did not see England pulling themselves back into the picture. Although Gower won the toss and

Lamb got his second successive century, in the course of which he helped to take the score from 87 for 4 to 172 for 5, England did not get the kind of score they hoped for, even though Marshall bowled but six overs and had to leave the field with a broken thumb. In fact England collapsed to 270.

As in the Lord's Test, England were in contention for most of the game, however, and their supporters must have felt there was a chance to pull the series back to 2–1. But the apparent evenness of the situation disappeared after England's third wicket fell for 104 in their second innings. It was amazing in a way.

West Indies (Gomes 104 not out) had scored 302 in reply to England's 270 (Lamb 100). At 104 for 3 in their second innings, then, England were 72 runs ahead. Since West Indies' fastest bowler had been told by the doctors to stay out of cricket for ten days because of the double fracture to his left thumb, we were all surprised to see him casting off some of the protection on it and coming down the stairs to take his place at the wicket to help, in his one-handed way, Gomes get to his 100. West Indies had lost wickets thus: 5 for 201, 6 for 206, 7 for 206 – still 64 runs behind England, and no one expected Marshall to be able to bowl in the second innings. Holding then decided to have a go: he struck five 6s in his 59, removing England's lead. But Gomes was left sitting on 96, when Marshall arrived and in allowing Gomes to get his 104 also struck a one-handed 4!

But worse was to come for England in that second innings: from 104 for 3 they did as follows: 106 for 4, 107 for 5, 135 for 6, 138 for 7, 140 for 8, 146 for 9 and 159 for all out! Their lead had been reduced to 127. Who had done this to them? Mainly the one-handed Marshall: 26–9–53–7.

Allott, bowling better than ever, had managed 6 for 61 in the West Indies first innings. But Marshall's performance dominated the scene. Some time was needed for us to realise that not since Armstrong's Australians in 1921 had England lost the first three Tests of a home series.

The fourth Test, played at Old Trafford, followed the same sort of pattern: England looking as if about to take over and then all of a sudden West Indies putting the foot down and moving decisively away so that they did not even have to bat a second time.

Lunch was taken on the first day with West Indies at 77 for 4 in

26 overs. Gomes, Richards, and Lloyd were out, to bad shots off Allott. England could hardly have hoped for more. But they had not dismissed Greenidge, and the fifth wicket did not fall until 267 had been posted on the board. In fact at 3:20 they had given up using a slip fielder. Greenidge had put his head down, Dujon was showing the fluidity and variety one had always expected of him. When he was eventually out for 101, Winston Davis, covering for Marshall, unable to play because of that broken thumb, came in as night-watchman. He held on and next day, despite interruptions for light, scored his career best of 77 out of a 170 sixth-wicket partnership with the evergreen Greenidge. That was virtually the end for England, for the score mounted to exactly 500, Harper adding a useful 39 not out.

England then scored 280 and 156. Garner collected 6 wickets in the match, Davis 2, and Harper, at last living up to his potential, 6 – all in the second innings! Four wins in a row, and the Oval to come.

12

A Home from Home

Kennington Oval

All over the world, not least of all in the West Indies, stately Lord's is known as Headquarters. And many a cricketer would prefer to make a century there than anywhere else. But in a sense the Oval, the *Kennington Oval*, has a special place in the hearts of West Indians.

It is not commonly known that the settlement of West Indians in Brixton, close to the Oval, is not a new phenomenon. True, the number and concentration have increased greatly, but West Indians were living there at the end of the First World War. Many are members of Surrey CCC, and any West Indies game at the Oval comes closest to reproducing the crowds and crowd reaction native to the Caribbean. I remember on one occasion, while trying to get back to the press box, being caught in the midst of drums and trumpets, and being invited to 'take a blow on the horn'. But it is not only on the terraces that the West Indies flavour is strong. In the pavilion your quieter, more 'respectable' West Indian is also to be found – a lawyer, a doctor, a schoolmaster and coach, one-time West Indian players such as John Cameron, or the mayor of Lambeth. They might be quieter, but not exactly quiet; and the fear of women which cloaks Lord's has no place at the Oval.

Lord's is green: the Oval tends to be grey, the outfield slightly bumpy and at times burnished brown. The surrounds of Lord's are tree-dominated, although in recent years a large hotel on one side contrasts with the grand houses on the north which are reputed to sell at fantastic prices. The old greyish 'gasometer', more correctly called a gas holder, as John Arlott constantly reminded us, is what used to dominate and characterise the Oval. But, in the distance, on a clear day from a high vantage point one can see Vauxhall and Big Ben and the surrounds of the great river.

What of the cricket itself, and of West Indies Tests there?

In August 1939, as terrible war was about to engulf Europe and the world, West Indies came to the Oval with their best tour result (in England) so far, having lost the first Test at Lord's and drawn the second at Old Trafford. They had the chance therefore of squaring the rubber. The match – over three days, like all the Tests – turned out to be a high-scoring affair: England first innings, 352 (Joe Hardstaff 94); West Indies 498, then the highest WI Test score in England. Headley was run out by his partner Victor Stollmeyer for 65 when set for a century or two. This so concentrated Stollmeyer's mind that, although he had been ill for most of the tour, he made 96 good runs before being stumped.

But the pair that lighted up the encircling gloom were Ken Weekes of Jamaica (but born in New York), and Learie Constantine, 137 and 79 respectively. Weekes was in such form in his left-handed unorthodoxy that when the team later played in Toronto on its hasty retreat from the threat of war in Europe, he converted quite a few baseball addicts to the slower moving game of cricket by constantly scoring 'home runs', hitting the ball clear out of the Fry Cadbury Park!

At the Oval, England's 1939 second innings was a massive 366 for 3 declared, the young Hutton (165) and the old master Hammond (138), both not out, dominating the attack. Constantine took 6 wickets in the match. The game ended in a draw.

Of the West Indies players in that game, only J. B. Stollmeyer and Gerry Gomez were to be in the triumphant 1950 side, whose match here was nearly as important to West Indies cricket as was the Lord's victory earlier in the season. It is detailed in chapter 7.

The 1957 Oval Test, like most of that tour, was a disaster: England won by an innings and 237 runs in three days. For England, Richardson made 107 and Graveney 164 in a total of 412. In neither innings could West Indies muster a total of 100. Sobers shone in the darkness, scoring 39 and 42. Both Everton Weekes and Jerry Alexander fell for a pair to the Laker-Lock combination. Dewdney avoided a similar fate only by scoring a single in the second innings. Laker got 5 wickets, Lock 11; not unlike the havoc they were to visit upon the Australians on this very wicket.

By 1963, the West Indian fans at the Oval had grown greatly in number. And they were very much aware, when the game started on 22 August, that England had the chance of squaring the rubber, West Indies having won two, England one, with the Lord's game drawn. In fact at the end of the first innings, England having batted first and scored 275, things did not look good for West Indies who could reply only with a meagre 246, Hunte 80, and Butcher 53. But Hall, Griffith and Sobers kept the English second innings to 223, and then Hunte, that great exemplar of the elegant and quiet West Indian, was in fine form for 108 not out. His partner as opener was Rodriguez, a clever selection by Worrell. Rodriguez failed in the first innings but in the second 78 runs were put on before he fell to one of Tony Lock's many catches. Hunte and Kanhai then added 113, and Butcher chipped in with 31 not out. Thus England's doom was sealed – with a day to spare. On that Monday 23,350 spectators packed the ground: the gates had to be closed. The noise and crowds outside the Oval Underground, with touts offering non-existent tickets, was 'like Bridgetown on a Friday morning'. The red double decker buses were held up in long queues.

About two thirds of the fans were clearly of West Indian heritage and were staunch and lively supporters. It can be imagined what happened when Butcher's successful off-drive brought the game to an early end! Spectators trooped across the grounds towards the pavilion and the dressing-rooms, there to call for their heroes, each one of whom, as he appeared, they cheered to the not overcast skies.

West Indies thus won the series 3–1 with one match drawn, a splendid recovery from the débâcle of 1957. This was the last glimpse that the Oval crowd was to get of the elegant Frank Worrell, somewhat faded with bat and ball (9 runs and 5 overs for no wickets), but ever so successful as leader of men.

It was not only in the going of Worrell that, perhaps, the fans were witnessing the end of an era. In 1957 West Indies had been quite feeble once Cowdrey and May had played 'pad ball' with them, but all of a sudden in 1963 they once again showed that they were really a cricketing power to notice. Not that that could ever make them or any other team invincible! Further, Hall and Griffith were in power, and there were complaints, including some from umpire Buller, about short-pitched bowling. The other irritation to the English cricketing Establishment, and to the England teams, was often just beneath the skin, and needed a careful eye to detect: most of the West Indies team were already playing in England, either in the leagues or the county competition.

I certainly know of at least one English selector who did not relish this situation. As he used to say in tones more of sorrow than of anger, 'We always have to pick a Second Eleven, because the best playing in England are qualified to play for others. But what annoyed some players much more than selection problems was the fact that the 'overseas cricketers' were habituating themselves to English conditions. What an unfair practice! Almost as bad as asking English cricketers, footballers and athletes to perform in hot countries!

The 1966 game was an inexplicable let-down for West Indies. They came having won three of the previous Tests, two by an innings, and having drawn one. They then disappointed their vocal Oval fans by losing by an innings and 34 runs. Lance Gibbs, sometimes visibly critical of Sobers's captaincy, did not manage to take a wicket. From the West Indies point of view the trouble was with England's first innings, and their own second. England's no. 4, Graveney, made 165 whilst their nos. 9, 10, and 11, J. T. Murray, Higgs and Snow, scored respectively 112, 63, and 59 not out, so that after they had been 166 for 7, they made a total of 527. As *Wisden* puts it: 'Never before in Test cricket had the last three wickets produced 361 runs . . . Murray, moreover, became the third no. 9 to make a Test hundred.' The other two were G. O. Allen (122) and Ray Lindwall (100).

Before all that, West Indies had opened the match with 268 – Kanhai 104, Sobers 81. In their second innings, though, Sobers, who had been superb with the bat for the whole season, was caught Close, bowled Snow for 0. He might have asked too much of himself in bowling 54 overs, but he did take 3 wickets. Gibbs's figures were: 44–16–115–0! Only Butcher (60) and Nurse (70) got more than 50, and the next highest scorer was Griffith at no. 9 with 29 not out. Jackie Hendriks collected a pair, bowled on each occasion. Total: 225. Result: defeat with a day and a half to spare.

Perhaps tiredness and staleness had set in. Whatever the

reason for this odd performance after winning three Tests by a good margin, the usual Oval crowd did not have the usual reasons for their wonted celebrations.

The 1969 tour was a three-Test trip and there was no game at the Oval. But in 1973, another three-Test tour, the usual arrangements were reversed, and the *first* was at the Oval. From West Indies' point of view it was a rather careless game, even though it was won by 158 runs. WI batted first and put up the respectable score of 415 despite some good bowling by Arnold. Lloyd, with Kallicharran, took the score from 64 for 3 to 272 for 4. Lloyd scored 132, Kalli 80, and Boyce coming at no. 9 made a more than useful 72. He then troubled the English batsmen, taking 5 for 70 in 22 overs, and England fell for 257.

But the West Indies second innings was poor indeed. Only three batsmen scored more than 25: Ron Headley 42, Kalli another 80, and Sobers 51. Total 255. So England needed 413 to equal the score. They managed 255 by the time they were out soon after lunch on the last day, Hayes in his first Test 106 not out. Boyce starred again, taking 6 for 77; Gibbs, 3 for 61. West Indies won by 158 runs to the delight of the West Indian supporters who waited around long after the last wicket fell, celebrating the spendid start to the tour. There were six left-handers on the team, and all but Inshan Ali played county cricket.

The 1976 Test was a delightful celebration. Drums beat, horns blew. I am not sure whether a few conch shells also announced and greeted the dire straits of England. Without a doubt a few jackasses also brayed. West Indies came to the shadow of the gas holder having drawn the first two Tests and then won the third by 425 runs, and the fourth by 55. The massed West Indian heritage crowds came to the Oval to enjoy a victory, especially as they had heard of the exploits of the 'new boy' Viv Richards. He had scored 232 and 63 in the first Test, missed the second, 4 and 135 in the third, and 'failed' in the fourth getting 'only' 66 and 38. He did not fail the Oval fans. In a total of 687 for 8 declared, he scored 291. No other West Indian got a century.

West Indies won by 231 runs, despite 203 (out of 435) from Amiss in the first innings, and two half centuries from our old friend Knott. Amiss's innings was one of rare courage. Eighteen months earlier he had had a terrible time against Australia's

Lillee and Thomson. His confidence against real pace never really recovered (indeed it was he who, as a result, pioneered the wearing of helmets), and it received a further setback when at the start of the season he was hit on the back of the head by Holding in the MCC v. West Indies game at Lord's and had to be helped from the field. Now on the slow Oval wicket of the time he showed, in his only Test of the summer, a new technique against the pacemen, playing back on the stumps, open-chested to most deliveries.

Roberts got but 1 wicket in the game, Holding 14 for 149, and Holder, whom one tends to forget, 3 for 104. The crowds had much to celebrate: West Indies had finished the series without losing a Test: three won, two drawn.

In 1980 (fourth Test) the rain interfered, there being no play at all on Saturday 26 July. England seemed to have the better of the drawn game: they scored 370 in the first innings, the first wicket yielding 155 (Gooch 83), and 209 for 9 declared in the second. West Indies' first innings was merely 265, of which 41 were extras (no-balls 28). Garner covered himself with glory in scoring 46. Marshall got 45; Bacchus 61. They did not have a second innings.

West Indies suffered from injuries in an unprecedented way: on the Monday, when they needed to press their advantage home, England being 92 for 9, Lloyd was off the field and Croft and Garner, who nonetheless each got 5 wickets in the match, were injured. Willey made England's second century of the series (100 not out), batting at no. 8 in the second innings, and it was good to see Bacchus topping the West Indies only innings. Altogether it was a lack-lustre performance which matched the weather but not the sterling and loudly cheering battle we had become accustomed to at the Oval.

In 1984 the West Indies came to the Oval in great form. They had won the four previous Tests, two of them by an innings-plus. It is true that the second, the Lord's Test, had looked in great danger until Greenidge, in the second innings, took over and scored the first of his two double centuries in the series. At the Oval it was his opening partner Haynes who shone with 125 in the second innings, and so with Dujon and captain Lloyd made sure of a fifth victory, on this occasion by 172 runs. The weather was hot, the noise almost deafening, the alcohol, despite rules and threats, flowed freely.

Honours were even in the first innings. The West Indies having batted first could get only 190, Lloyd top scoring with 60 not out. England then replied with 162. It said much for the maturity of West Indies cricket that they made sure to keep England below their score, mainly through Marshall's devastating form. He took 5 for 35 in 17.5 overs. And the fielding was sharp.

Again at the end of play on the first day one wondered if we were really in for a low scoring game at last. But Haynes played his masterful innings, and although there was no other score over 50, enough of his colleagues contributed something to the cause to make the total 346, a lead of 374 runs with ten hours of the game remaining. England did not go down without a fight from Broad and Tavaré and Botham. But something got into Holding, and, skating along the Oval turf on his resumed long run-up, in seventeen balls he dismissed Broad, Gower and Lamb at a personal cost of 5 runs in an innings of 202.

England came out of the series not only having lost 5-0, but also giving the impression that they had lost touch with the game and with their great traditions in the game. What disappointed West Indies was that Richards scored a total of only 23 in the match. In fact the batting did not impress except for Lloyd in both innings, and Haynes and Dujon in the second.

By 1984 it had become noticeable that the old-time West Indies support had fallen off, even at the Oval. In 1988 this tendency was even more marked. No doubt many factors were at work. But one would be quite willing to suggest at least two dampeners: one, the rise in the price of tickets; the other, the very culture-bound, Anglocentric regulations about drums, about 'noise', about going on to the pitch, about banners, about drink, about, in short, the necessity to take one's interest in the matches and the results very quietly and with as little show of emotion as possible. Perhaps Tests should now be started with the hymn 'O God, our help in ages past', or 'Rock of Ages', or much better, 'Abide with me'!

One of the most ironic and hypocritical recent tendencies is the attempt to cut down and control the drinking of your ordinary fan, while at the same time making sure that the liquid demon flows in the hospitality boxes, which are paid for as much to supply guests with drink as to give them a better view of the game. But then, of course, those of us who are invited into such boxes, like those who inhabit the press boxes, know how to hold our drink, do we not?

By 1988, whose match is discussed in chapter 7, the crowds at the Oval were not quite what they used to be. Was it an economic matter, or a loss of enthusiasm for Test cricket? Or was the tea party trying to take over from the festival; the sharp handclap from heckling or cheering comment? Which team do you cheer for, Mr Tebbit – sorry, which team do you *clap* for?

13

West Indies and Test Cricket: a Special Contribution?

One is tempted to answer immediately with a strong affirmative. But in doing so one must be careful to avoid the usual generalisations. The West Indies teams have shown a certain élan which at times strongly contrasts with England teams which insist on 'putting up the shutters' and playing it safe. But the matter is much more complicated than that.

Unfortunately it is hard to make the simplest statement without generalising. Yet generalisations can be so misleading, and they so easily lead to stereotypes: English batsmen are dull and over-careful: WI batsmen are enterprising and carefree. Denis Compton over-careful? Ted Dexter dull? And what of Botham? Allan Rae carefree? Haynes and Greenidge, at the Oval in 1988, carefree? Yet there is often a hint of truth in the stereotype – that is what makes it so dangerous.

On the whole, especially since the influence of Len Hutton as captain, England batting does tend to err on the side of 'no cutting, no hooking'. Trevor 'Barnacle' Bailey is easily contrasted in the minds of some with the one and only L. N. Constantine. And as Learie was the West Indian best known to English fans for a long time, his penchant for hitting hard and for entertaining the crowds was what came to be associated with West Indies batting. But even in Learie's day there were players like F. R. Martin, first-class players who had a cautious approach to the game. Frank Martin opened the West Indies innings in the fifth Test, at Sydney, in 1931, saw his partner C. A. Roach go at 70, and took his bat out for 123 when his captain declared at 350 for 6. (Constantine made 0 in that innings, and Headley was lbw for 105.)

I and many others were brought up to be aware of over-generalisations and stereotypes. But many radio and TV broadcasters now don't seem to mind dealing in all kinds of stereotypes: 'Italians don't have the temperament to win the World Cup'; 'West Indians will drop their heads at the first sight of pressure'. I can remember our Latin master in the fourth form pointing out how dangerous was the invitation given the reader, in the *Aeneid*, to judge all Greeks by the deviousness of one – 'ab uno disce omnes'. But my first practical experience, in sport, of the dangers and misleading character of accepted stereotypes was while covering the Olympic games in Rome in 1960.

Accepted wisdom then was that the black athletes (from the USA especially) must win all sprint races, whereas Anglo-Saxons and Scandinavians were the long-distance people. But it was a German who won the 100 metres and an Italian the 200, in the most conclusive manner, while an unknown Ethiopian, in the darkening Roman evening, lighted up the TV screens as he took over the marathon! Had 'white' peoples genes changed, or was the Ethiopian not really 'black'? Of course, genes have little to do with it: but just try to convince your ordinary fan of this – or your ordinary sports writer.

The thing is that when a group appears to play in a certain way, or to excel at a certain game, it is likely to have something to do with their genetic inheritance, but much more to do with their cultural experience, and most to do with the circumstances under which they most commonly play. The love of seam bowlers in English cricket has to do with green wickets being more common in England than anywhere else except perhaps New Zealand. But it also has to do with the old county cricket schedules in which it would have been silly for more than one player to bowl really fast week in and week out, and in which it was useful simply to hold an end quiet with seam bowling. Similarly there are now things about English batting which have much more to do with the plethora of one-day games in their regular schedule than anything else. It also tends to mean that there are not a few English bowlers who can give you a very sound ten or twelve overs, but who are not very penetrating and tend to fall off beyond the twelve-over spell – or to pull muscles and otherwise become injured.

Much of this is well illustrated by the black youngster in the Indiana library in the 1950s. He took out book after book on basketball, although he had been thought to be more or less illiterate. The intrigued librarian enquired of the young man the reason for this intense interest and study. 'It's my way out,' the young man answered, 'it's my way out.' Do you remember the old story about calling down a Yorkshire coal pit for a new fast bowler? Physical build and brawn are of course often involved, but so are the cultural and social conditions in which the athlete lives and has grown up. But in any case, why is it so easily forgotten that even within given 'racial' groups physical characteristics vary widely? George Headley, neat and black and dancing, was very much more in build and movement like Don Bradman than Joel Garner. And Ted Dexter's movements were not exactly those of Sir Len Hutton; more like Sir Gary Sobers, shall we say?

Then there is the whole question of certain personal qualities, the origins of which we know little. Ian Botham, for example, like Constantine before him, had the gift of imposing himself on a game in such a way as to get the best – or nearly the best – of batsmen to hit long hops to square-leg's waiting hands. At Sabina Park when he came on to bowl in 1986 it took only one ball for a US colleague who was enjoying the hospitality of our commentary box to say: 'I know nothing about cricket but this man is obviously going to impress his personality on the game.' And he did.

But has West Indies made a special mark on the game? It certainly has the reputation, and has had it for some while, of flamboyance in batting, dangerous speed in bowling, briskness in the field, and a certain lack of consistency overall – what one of the most offensive writers on the game used to characterise as 'calypso collapso'. Perhaps he wrote before the England collapses of 1988. But he was certainly writing during the Ram–Val melting away of the England batting. The only thing that was right about the implication of his comment is that West Indies tend to go down, when they do, with all guns firing, whereas England's collapses give the impression of coming from over-cautiousness and the refusal to strike pale half-volleys to the boundary. After all, in 1950 Hutton was clean bowled by Val, *middle stump*, at Lord's, leaving the ball alone: in fact, shouldering arms!

These contrasting attitudes might be thought to reflect a difference in the two societies. But they might be concerned with quite other matters. In England, for instance, it is always worth holding on, except in the rarest of summers, because a brisk shower might be just around the corner. And one would look a fool to get out just before rain stopped play for half an hour or a few hours, or for the day! As a rule – but there are no iron laws about this kind of thing – when it rains in the West Indies the grounds become drenched, so if there is rain in the offing one had better make the runs now.

But a difference in attitude there is: Englishmen have been heard, and English women also, to rejoice because England had broken a losing spell by *managing to draw a game*. There is quite a common West Indies attitude which would consider this rather pettifogging. Their way of ending a dry spell would be to go for the win – and of course risk a loss in the effort. Clearly to some mentalities *not to lose* is more important than to win! And to a few wonderful people, decreasing in number every day, the style with which one plays is just as important as winning or losing. But this latter attitude is harder to maintain the greater the external prizes for winning, or excelling as man-of-the-match, become.

It is not only an inner moral habit which determines many of the general attitudes to playing games today; money is very much involved, as well as the possibilities of a greater fame which leads to being 'marketable'. This fame, fanned by the media and encouraged by advertisers and promoters, probably has more of an influence than even higher payment 'by results'.

But payment and the means of making a living have always played their part. George Headley did not go on one tour because the West Indies could not, or would not, pay him enough or pay his league club to release him. Learie went out to the West Indies to play against England on one occasion only because Sir Pelham Warner, who was born in Trinidad, wrote to the Board from England complaining that Learie was not selected to play. (They said they could not afford to pay him.) Sir 'Plum', graduate of Queen's Royal College, Trinidad, had been supporting the idea that MCC should visit the West Indies. Why should he continue to do so when he knew that West Indies were not selecting their strongest team by leaving Constantine out?

In West Indies cricket one of the things that might have contributed from time to time to a less planned approach to the game, and to a more cavalier attitude at times, was that it was almost completely amateur, in the sense of being unwaged. One's living therefore did not depend entirely on one's performance. One had some other job – if one had a job at all!

It is not perhaps widely known that on some of the first West Indies tours players had to find their own passages. Learie's father, Lebrun, once was unable to join a tour he had been selected for because he had not enough to leave to keep the family going. He saw his 'team-mates' onto the boat at Port of Spain, and, having bid them farewell, was about to head home. He was eventually whisked by fast launch to the disappearing ship when the necessary money was collected on the wharfside. It is said that one or two other players were selected precisely because they could not only play but could also pay! With this kind of history, plus island jealousies and mutual ignorance about each other, it could hardly be wondered at that at times a certain instability and lack of cohesion was more than apparent.

The attitudes of teams so constructed, and accustomed to playing perhaps only on the weekends, could not compare with teams of regular professionals plus a few comparatively well-to-do amateurs – in the matters of strict discipline, concentration and sticking to a task that lasted three days, six days a week, for the better part of a summer. But what such teams could bring to the task was freshness, an appetite for the game, a willingness to concoct new solutions – to improvise.

And improvising, rather than recklessness, was the mark of Learie Constantine. It might look as if he were being cavalier when in fact he was intelligently trying to find a new solution. C. L. R. James gave an excellent example of this: when Learie was playing for Nelson he once found that the bowler was so controlling his line and length that it was impossible to score by piercing the off-side field. He considered and played forward and back, but to no avail. What he then did was to go outside his off stump and glide the ball just past his leg stump to the fine-leg boundary. He did this with a pendulum swing of the bat. When you think of it this was a most sensible thing to do; it was splendid improvisation. But it was not the acceptable thing to those calling themselves orthodox. I have been told by people who bowled long at Hammond that if you pitched up to him *on any line* he would attempt, often successfully, to drive you through the covers. And he was the very image of orthodoxy! But you could probably get him stumped with a googly just outside the leg stump! In fact C. B. Clarke dismissed him in just this fashion during the 1939 tour.

It is not that Learie's judgement was always faultless; and he had a generous, if exhibitionist, inclination to entertain the fans. This got him into trouble on occasion. Once in a big charity match in London I was at the other end when he was given out lbw very early in his innings. He was making one of his favourite shots: he would put his left toe down the wicket, just outside leg stump, and swing a perpendicular bat, starting in the direction of point and picking up the ball for a 6 over square-leg. The wicket this day was none too good, the ball did not come through as evenly as he expected, the umpire gave him out. He was livid – although I did not realise this until returning to the dressing-room at the luncheon break. But he had made the shot much too early in his knock, and he should have known that we were not playing with Test umpires.

This business of improvisation, of zest, of style, of stroking the ball rather than pushing or poking or prodding – these I would say tended to be the things that many West Indies batsmen brought to the game. But you must then resist the 'explanation temptation', especially the physio-genetic explanation. Kanhai was sometimes as extravagant as Learie, and often more brilliant: the one of Indian heritage from Guyana, the other from Trinidad with African forebears. Stollmeyer was one of our most elegant and fluent of stroke-makers: he was from Trinidad and came from an originally Dutch planter family – his nephew now plays football for the USA! Ivan Barrow, a splendid square-cutter, in 1933 got WI's first Test century in England just before George Headley, and put on 200 with him for the second wicket in the process. He was from Jamaica, and a Jew. George himself, as is well known, was born in Panama, of African ancestry: his mother was from Jamaica, his father from Barbados, and he spent his early years in Panama and Cuba. His second name was Alphonso – not a common name in the Anglophone Caribbean.

Even the three Ws, from tiny Barbados (168 square miles), did not come exactly from the same stable socially. Everton Weekes probably would have led too hard a life to come to fame in cricket (and international bridge!) were it not for the fact that during the war he joined the Barbados forces. Frank Worrell went to school at Combermere, where for many years the famous West Indian writer and editor, Frank Collymore, taught and played cricket. But Combermere was not quite Harrison College, to which Clyde Walcott moved after a year there. Further, Walcott did not meet Everton Weekes until both of them went to Trinidad for trial matches in 1945, four years after Walcott had first played in Trinidad. All this, notice, in a place as small as Barbados – about which clearly generalisations could be dangerous!

As far as West Indies bowlers go: the first thing is to remind ourselves that fast bowlers first dominated the scene and have done so especially in the recent past. But one surely does not have constantly to remind the English press and fans of Ramadhin and Valentine – two people of different genetic inheritance! It is even more amazing that one has to point out that one of the few slow bowlers to be among the top wicket-takers in all Tests is Lance Gibbs of Guyana and the West Indies: 309 wickets at 29. 09 in 79 Tests. May one note that Trueman played but 67 Tests.

But Ram and Val and Lance Gibbs were not the first or only ones. A list would have to contain C. R. ('Snuffie') Browne and O. C. (Tommy) Scott from the old days. At Old Trafford in 1928 Browne and Scott took 2 wickets each, as many as the total taken by the fast bowlers: Francis none, Constantine 1, and Griffith 3.

F. R. Martin was also an outstanding slow bowler, as were the Trinidadian Achong and the Jamaican left-hander Mudie. The latter took 3 for 40 at Sabina when West Indies defeated England by an innings and 161 runs in March 1935. And in 1939 in England West Indies had two outstanding slow bowlers: J. H. Cameron, who had played for Cambridge, and C. B. (Bertie) Clarke, who was later to play county cricket and who might well have gone on the tour to India in 1948–49. In 1950, besides Ram and Val, there was also the 'legger' with a good googly, 'Boogles' Williams of Barbados. His figures in first-class matches on that tour were 301.2 overs, 856 runs, 31 wickets, at an average of 27.61. Compare these with Worrell's: 480.1–970–39–24.87. (He was a good batsman too: in Barbados he and Walcott shared a large partnership in which he got 185 and Walcott 120.) And, of course, even in the heyday of 1984 when West Indies swept the board, and when Marshall, Holding and Garner were dispensing their thunderbolts, there was a useful off-spinner on the team, Harper. He took 13 wickets in the five Tests, 6 of them for 57 runs in 28.4 overs at Old Trafford in the second innings.

But what of the fast bowlers, and the fact that for a while West Indies used four of them in harness? This gambit was much opposed by English critics who support the traditional – including the traditional 'rights' of the chosen few under apartheid! I don't myself think that the success of the West Indies bowlers was mainly based on their speed, but on the fact that each one of them was so good. Never before did a batsman not feel relief at seeing off an opener and looking forward to 'first change'. The speed no doubt added to the tension, but a similar effect was had when Val and Ram were really in form: they kept coming at you, demanding full concentration all the while. The nearest thing I have seen to it was Lindwall, Miller, Johnston, Toshack – but the last named was not in any sense dangerous. He was mainly a negative bowler who had to be watched, but whose chief task was to keep an end sealed until the new ball, then available after 55 overs, was due.

I always said that, despite all the complaining – over the apparent destruction of the beauty of spin bowling, especially leg-spin – as soon as they found four good enough fast or medium-fast bowlers England would use them just as the West Indies had. And in the tour of the West Indies in 1989 that is exactly what England did: Angus Fraser, Devon Malcolm, Gladstone Small, Phil DeFreitas and the replacement Chris Lewis.

From the point of view of cricket, the main weakness in depending on one kind of bowling lies only in the fact that conditions can change suddenly, and one might not have the necessary adaptability. Thus the decision to play Valentine instead of Dewdney at Lord's in 1957 was disastrous. Of the 20 wickets England took, only 1 fell to a slow bowler, Wardle. Bailey had 11 wickets in the game, Trueman 4, and Statham 4. England knew the Lord's wicket, and did not let aesthetics or tradition stop them from beating West Indies by an innings and 36 runs.

But Marshall, Garner and Holding were not only fast; they were exceptionally good bowlers. They along with Trueman have the best strike-rate among bowlers who have taken over 200 wickets in Tests. Marshall has taken 1 wicket for roughly every forty-six balls bowled; Garner and Holding, one for every fifty balls! Andy Roberts had a strike-rate slightly inferior to these. If we add to these, say, Baptiste, or more recently Walsh and Ambrose and Benjamin, then what we have always is a foursome of excellent bowlers who are also fast. But I doubt that the situation would be much different if one could find on the same team four accurate and difficult-to-play slow bowlers. After all in 1950 some batsmen complained of the relentlessness of the bowling of Ram and Val. And some broadcasters complained that there was no time for comment, so quickly were overs being bowled – so relentless was the pressure!

It's the *pressure* that matters. But admittedly if to the difficulty of 'reading' the bowling is added an element of physical pressure, then the batsman's difficulties increase. Modern slow bowlers tighten the screw by placing well-protected fielders very close to the bat. Is not the 'bat/pad' catch now as common as the slip catch? Whether a certain field placing, or short-pitched balls, are fair is a matter that must be left to the umpires who are the sole judges of fair and unfair play. What has always amazed me is that England's pained whingeing and superior moral sentiments about short-pitched bowling have mainly taken place in England where, so far, English umpires – 'the best in the world' – are indeed sole judges of fair and unfair play. Why have they not ruled in the fashion which would please the erstwhile cricket correspondent of *The Times*?

What the West Indies have contributed to cricket, particularly to English cricket, is not, as many letters to *The Times* suggest, nor as one of that paper's main correspondents is always saying, unfair fast bowling – I would abhor that.

What they have contributed is the refusal to follow the tradition, loved by batsmen from all over the world, of allowing a breather after the first two bowlers have done their best, a sort of brief tea-break before getting on with the main business of getting runs and taking wickets – always, of course, within the spirit and letter of the law and always with a sense of style and aesthetic satisfaction. Farnes, Bowes and Voce were the only old-time English fast bowlers I had the pleasure of seeing in action. I heard all about Larwood and 'have seen the film'. I wonder if a foursome of Larwood, Voce – what a bowler! – Farnes and Bowes would be any less effective, frightening and wonderful to watch than Holding, Roberts, Garner and Marshall!

But in an odd way, perhaps the greatest contribution which West Indies have made to the great game, again especially to English cricket, is the one started in 1950: that of showing to people ever so sure of themselves, and of their right to win, that the mighty can fall – even in their own territory. Good *can* come out of Nazareth! This is such an important point for both David and Goliath!

Whenever, alas, there is a world sporting event being broadcast by British commentators, one need listen for no more than five minutes to realise how many of the British, especially the English, like to suppose that any group they don't know, or which they think of as 'Third World', or not out of the 'top drawer', need not be taken too seriously, and would be happy to be patronised by them.

West Indies, by winning at Lord's in 1950, and subsequently keeping up the good work – though, of course, not always winning –made the very simple point so admirably put by the Caribbean poet Cesaire:

> No race [*and I would add nor group, nor country*]
> holds the monopoly of beauty, of intelligence,
> of strength
> and there is a place for all at the rendezvous of
> victory.

It is a hard ideal to live up to, and one hopes that the West Indies and all their opponents on the field will always do so. This – and aesthetic and somatic satisfaction – is what the very essence of games should be, rather than their being promoted as the generators and sustainers of a virulent form of tribalism which is only seen for what it really is when the 'hooligans' take to a logical conclusion all that they have been hearing on the radio and television about their own superiority and right to win, which generally is only frustrated by *naive* or *cheating* foreigners. You might wonder at the use of the word naive. I am only quoting what the television commentators called the Camerouns World Cup football team before they matched every move England could make.

And the word no doubt would have been used about West Indies cricket – or would it have been, 'instinctive'? – before that day at Lord's made memorable by, among others,

> Those two little pals of mine
> Ramadhin and Valentine.

14

A West Indies Team

1950–1988

One amusing way of reminding oneself of the strength of West Indies cricket since 1950 is to try to select a representative team, taking into account only players from the tours to England between then and 1988.

I wonder what would be the reaction to the following team?

> Greenidge, Rae, Richards, Worrell, Sobers, Weekes, Marshall, Holding, Hendriks, Garner, Gibbs.

Certainly there is going to be an objection to Rae. But I would always want, within reason, one of my openers to be left-handed, and I think Rae a better proposition than Fredericks – especially on a side of such stroke-makers, since Rae always was a solid anchor man. Clearly the other two openers who would have to be considered are Haynes and Hunte.

Of the batsmen, Richards, Worrell and Sobers must be certainties. Of the bowlers, Marshall, Holding and Gibbs must also be certainties.

I don't think that there can be any argument about the wicket-keeper, Hendriks. Or can there be? Here is a good example of the difficulty which selectors face! As far as Alexander and Deryck Murray go it is a matter of whether one wants a wicket-keeper who also bats. If one does then Alexander would get the nod over both Hendriks and Murray, but perhaps not over Dujon. Alexander's Test average is 30.03, Murray's 22.90, Hendriks's 18.62, that of Dujon, still playing, over 30. (Collie Smith's was 31.69, and he was considered a good bat.) Dujon's batting has seemed to fall off; Alexander's seemed to improve, and remember that he topped the averages in Australia on a team which contained Worrell and Sobers among other stars. But then again Sobers says that Hendriks was the best West Indies wicket-keeper he ever saw.

On such a strong batting side, the batting of the wicket-keeper might not be a consideration, in which case Hendriks would probably get the nomination. Incidentally it is one of those inexplicable matters of history that Alexander, Dujon and Hendriks all went to Wolmer's Boys' School in Jamaica, which was also the school of Ivan Barrow, another West Indies wicket-keeper. Both Dujon and his father before him played for Kingston Cricket Club, Sabina Park, Jamaica, as did Alexander and Hendriks. Barrow was a Melbourne man, the club of Holding and Passailaigue.

Weekes and Garner are odd people to be somewhat doubtful about. But should Lloyd be considered for Weekes's place? He was such a fantastic fielder, and a left-hander. And can Garner be chosen over Roberts or Ramadhin? Garner has one of the best strike-rates in cricket: he was also very economical, and an outstanding field.

Whom have we not even mentioned? Valentine, Hall, Griffith, Gomez, Harper, Baptiste, Ambrose, Walsh, Butcher, Kanhai, Kallicharran, Rowe, Nurse?

My team underlines the variety as well as the strength of West Indies cricket in as much as both Worrell and Sobers were perfectly good spin bowlers, left-handed at that – and not bad quick bowlers either. Both of them started cricket as bowlers! So that although the team conforms to the old formula of five batsmen, one all-rounder, a specialist wicket-keeper and four bowlers, because of Worrell, and to some extent, Richards, it has many more than four bowlers, and a great variety of bowling.

Although Learie Constantine in a famous *Wisden* article inveighed against the publication and use of averages, they can give us some idea of a player's performance over a stretch of time. So here are the relevant averages of the team I have selected.

The batsmen: Greenidge, 46.86 (at the end of 1988); Rae, 46.18; Richards, 52.66 (at the end of 1988); Worrell, 49.48; Sobers, 57.78; Weekes, 58.61. (Headley's was 60.83 in twenty-two Tests.)

The bowlers: Marshall, 290 wickets at 20.41 (at the end of 1988); Holding, 249 wickets at 23.68; Roberts, 202 wickets at 25.61; Gibbs, 309 wickets at 29.09.

The averages of other batsmen who would have to be considered: Walcott, 56.68; Fredericks, 42.49; Hunte, 45.06; Haynes,

39.67 (at the end of 1988); Butcher, 43.11; Nurse, 47.60; Lloyd, 46.67; Kanhai, 47.53; Kallicharran, 44.43.

Notice the high average of Walcott, though he tended to do better outside England. For instance, his scores against Australia in the West Indies (1954-55) were phenomenal: 108, 39, 126, 110; 8, 73; 15, 83, 155, 110. Total 827 runs for an average of 82.70. As *Wisden* put it: '. . .He performed feats achieved by no other player in history when both at Port of Spain and Kingston he hit a century in each innings of a match and altogether five in the series'. But in the 1950 series in England which is often thought of as the 'Three Ws Series' his Test average was 45.80. Compare that with the following: Worrell, 89.83; Rae, 62.83; Weekes, 56.33; Stollmeyer, 50.83.

But in a touring party of seventeen players, he would have to be included. Who would the others be? I'll put up at least one 'Aunt Sally'. I hope that the reader will have great pleasure in throwing rotten oranges at him and in selecting one which all his cricket friends will agree with.

> Greenidge, Rae, Richards, Worrell (Capt), Weekes, Sobers, Marshall, Holding, Hendriks, Garner, Gibbs, Walcott, Hunte, Kanhai, Dujon, Roberts, Ramadhin.

Manager would be Berkeley Gaskin, (of the 1963 team) and his assistant would be Jerry Alexander whose excellent work as manager in India Clive Lloyd has described and praised. The captain and these two were great friends, and they would pull together and help the team to produce its best efforts.

These are some notable omissions from my seventeen, as no doubt the reader has noticed. What, for instance, of J. B. Stollmeyer, Clive Lloyd, Gerry Gomez, Haynes, Valentine? What say you, dear reader? Remember that a touring party of sixteen would be even better, and then decide whom you are going to throw out of the balloon.

Perhaps by this you might have developed some sympathy for selectors! And don't forget that I have not in any way considered West Indian territorial 'representation'. I wonder how many selection committees in the Caribbean have had that kind of freedom! In fact the territories work out: Barbados, eight; Guyana, two; Trinidad, one; Jamaica, four; Antigua, two.

15

Before and After

Reflections and Recollections

The 1988 tour was my last and writing about it has brought to mind many bits of cricket that I would like to share with you. The more so as the banning of the Gooch-captained England team to India and the fiasco of the rebel tour to South Africa in 1989–90 have shaken the world of Test tours – even though at the same time there has been much papering-over of the cracks in the walls.

The first English batsman really to thrill me was Maurice Leyland. It must certainly be over fifty years since I saw him at Sabina Park, during one of Yorkshire's visits to Jamaica. He comes back to me as having an openness of style quite uncharacteristic of many left-handers, an ability to hit clean through the ball. He seemed to me to *drive* the ball to fine-leg, not by turning around or paddling it as Colin Cowdrey often did. But with a pendulum swing which seemed to be directed straight past the bowler or at mid-on. Gary Sobers played a similar shot, but on the off-side, rocketing the ball all along the grass, bisecting third-man and point while apparently straight driving. He used this stroke at Kensington Oval, Barbados, to great effect against the 1970–71 Indians in scoring an unbeaten 178.

Some of my schoolfellows were very much impressed with Hedley Verity, who seemed to us to keep a rather long thumb nail – for lifting the seam, we thought! I was not impressed. He seemed too steady and unenterprising – a revealing view which explains why, even if I had been blessed with talent in cricket, despite my love of the game and hard practising I would still not have got very far. I much preferred the bowling of the West Indian Tommy Scott, not mainly for chauvinistic reasons but because he was always, it seemed to me, trying to do something with his leg-breaks and top-spinners. To watch him bowling with George

Headley at silly mid-on was a treat. I can still see Lionel, Lord Tennyson stamping his left foot in disgust at Melbourne Park, as Headley took the ball off his bat despite all his efforts to guide the top-spinner down to his toes.

Voce's action seemed to me a dream, as he almost brought both arms together behind his back just before his left hand hurled the thunderbolt. It has always seemed odd to me that English journalists write as if England have never had real fast bowlers. The ones I saw, Farnes, Bowes, Voce, Trueman, Statham, were not exactly slow. I never saw Tyson – nor Larwood and, later, John Snow. But I remember clearly how one of our teachers at St George's, Jamaica, an American Jesuit who was very fond of cricket, dismissed 'body-line bowling' as a great indecency. 'We'll soon be playing in a suit of knight's armour', he used to say with a dismissive raising of an arched eyebrow (*John Woodcock, please note*). He also thought, taking his argument from the catcher in baseball, that wicket-keepers stood entirely too far back! And he would have seen Francis and Martindale rearing away at Sabina.

But even though I thought Manny Martindale a thrilling bowler as he leapt into his delivery stride, and Learie Constantine electrifying as he caught the ball at about ear level, facing away from it on his return to his bowling mark, I can't imagine any fast bowlers more beautiful and effective than Lindwall and Holding. Lindwall's great feat was his rhythm which allowed him so wonderfully to produce the really fast ball without apparent change in action. With one such ball from the pavilion end at Lord's in 1948, he clean bowled Bill Edrich, playing forward defensively. A fruity voice had just shouted from the Father Time area after a bouncer or two, 'Why don't you bowl at the wicket, sir?' Lindwall – I have not the slightest idea whether he had heard the remark – immediately obliged. Holding's effortless tall twinkle across the grass as he ran up to deliver, his high action and neat delivery, managed somehow to suggest the smoothness of ice skating. Yet he was considered by some English critics a 'boring bowler' – because he did not bowl as many overs in an hour as they have decided 'are good for the game.' They would prefer to see Emburey – a fine and sporting man – wheeling in at seventeen overs an hour, whether he got a wicket or not! Well, every man to his own taste, as long as he does not endow it with the aura of high and incontrovertible principle!

Of the slower bowlers one remembers that at Sabina Park in 1935 Hollies bowled 46 overs for 114 runs. Sabina was even smaller then than it is now, and George Headley scored 270 not out, Sealy 91, and R. S. Grant 77. So Hollies must have been right on the spot with his leg-breaks to have conceded only 2.47 runs per over. I don't remember his bowling very clearly. But I do know that for years after, Louis Teape, our Senior League competition captain and a great admirer of Headley's, always held up Hollies's bowling to Headley in that game for our emulation. We always compared it to Tony Lock's containment of Everton Weekes in the first Sabina Park Test in 1954, which was something to behold. True it is that the crowd dubbed Tony Lock 'Shylock' because of his then doubtful action especially when propelling his fast change. But nonetheless the battle between him and Weekes was worth almost a month of one-day games.

Weekes made 55 in the first innings, and 90 not out in the second. He was in powerful form. But you could see him go forward to drive only to find the ball not quite there. Then he would think of a square-cut, only to find the ball too close to him. Then he would go back to late-cut, and decide against it. It was a wonderful duel, and I remember Lock bowling a series of maiden overs to a Weekes who was in full flow! Lock bowled 41 overs for 76 runs and 3 wickets in the first innings and 14 overs for 36 runs and 2 wickets in the second. That is a total of 55 overs at just slightly more than 2 runs per over. And he was bowling to Stollmeyer, Weekes, Walcott, Headley and Gomez.

In the second innings we saw one of cricket's odd-men-out who are known to be excellent, and who perform outstandingly once, and are not heard of again – sometimes because they are not given a chance, sometimes because they seem to have shot their bolt, or simply have had more important things to do: Esmond Kentish of Jamaica. He played only two Tests, but on the day in question, at Sabina, he took the wickets of May, Graveney, Evans, Lock and Trueman for 49 runs in 29 overs.

It was on the same ground in the first innings of the last Test of that series that Frank King put up one of the greatest displays of attacking fast bowling I have ever seen. He had Hutton, who eventually made 205, in all kinds of worries late in the afternoon of the first day.

I actually witnessed Gary Sobers's 365 not out at Sabina Park in February 1958. It was exhilarating. But it was the sort of occasion of which details are hard to recall. The excitement was so great towards the end of the innings, the crowd so vociferous, that it was hard to keep track of the actualities. Then as Sobers reached the magic score the crowds rushed onto the field. Once they were cleared the Pakistan captain, A. H. Kardar, started his delaying tactics, claiming that the wicket had been injured by the invasion. Sabina Park was rock-hard in those days, and Hunte – it is often forgotten – had scored 260 elegant runs before being run out. He and Sobers put on 446 runs for the second wicket! Play did not resume until the next day so that Kardar could be satisfied that the wicket had been repaired and was really playable. His antics did not help him much: Pakistan lost by an innings and 174 runs. West Indies put up their highest score ever, 790 for 3. Eric Atkinson took 8 wickets in the match for 78 runs, and Jerry Alexander, then captain, took six catches behind the wicket, four off Atkinson.

In the next game at green Bourda, Georgetown, it should be remembered, Sobers scored 125 and 109 not out. Hunte got 114 in the second innings. Eric Atkinson did not play – one supposes that he was injured; he did suffer from a nagging groin problem. Gibbs, playing in his third Test, took 7 wickets for 136. Sobers was really phenomenal in that series: 52, 52, 80, 365 not out, 125, 109 not out, 14 and 27. The last two scores were made at Queen's Park Oval where Pakistan won by an innings and 1 run, Fazal Mahmood taking 8 wickets in the match.

Among the England batsmen who have frustrated West Indies hopes on famous occasions one cannot but remember Hutton's 205 (Sabina Park, 1954), Gooch's 123 (Lord's, 1980), and Gower's 154 not out (Sabina Park, 1981). Hutton's was a patient, masterly knock. Having survived the early thunderbolts of Frank King he set about reducing the West Indies first innings of 139 to a nonsense. Hutton's innings was outstanding, but gave the impression of overcautiousness – perhaps because he was the first professional to captain England, and England needed a victory in that game to save the series: they had lost the first two games comprehensively. Sobers, just three years before his world-beating innings, was still played mainly as a bowler. He batted at no. 9 in both innings, getting 14 not out in the first, and 26 in the second. He took 4 wickets for 75 in 28.5 overs in the first innings. One is reminded of the fact that Frank Worrell batted at no. 9 or 10 for Combermere School in Barbados.

But important though Hutton's innings was, it did not have the style of the Gooch and Gower innings referred to above. Gower went in at no. 4, when England had been led by 157 in the first innings. The more fluently and aggressively he dealt with Holding, Garner, Croft, Marshall & Co., the clearer it became that England would force a draw despite their poor first-innings showing of 285 – of which Gooch had scored 153!

Just one year earlier, at Lord's, Gooch had similarly been the only England batsman to hold off the West Indies challenge, and he did it on a greenish wicket and with style, the ball seeming always to be attracted to the very middle of his bat. In fact fans at that game were lucky indeed. They saw not only Gooch's 123 out of a total of 269, but also for West Indies a second-wicket stand of 223 between Haynes (184) and Richards (145).

But I grew up at a cricketing time when one great name, and his feats, dominated the world game, just as Headley dominated the West Indian one – Donald George Bradman.

I used to walk a good distance to the cable office on the waterfront in Kingston to read carefully the flimsy blue copy paper with the Australian scores pinned up on the board for all to see. We had no radio, and television did not exist. What mystery and romance those names held for me: Ponsford, McCabe, Woodfull, Kippax, Grimmett and Ironmonger – it was years before I noted the humble origins of that last name! But always, of course, it was Bradman. Bradman who scored 223 in the third Test against West Indies in January 1931 (Headley then scored 102 not out in a total of 193). In the fourth Test Bradman got 152, but was bowled for 0 by Griffith in the second innings of the fifth. Headley had scored 105 and that unsung West Indian player, F. R. Martin, who opened with Roach, 123 not out.

So when in 1946 I found myself in England, having come over for post-graduate studies, on the first civilian ship to arrive from Jamaica after the war, I realised all of a sudden that in 1948 I would have the chance to see Bradman. I joined Allan Rae and Harold Fraser, with whom I played for the West Indies Wanderers, early in the morning in the Lord's queue to see the legend himself play against MCC. I was not disappointed. As Bradman came down the white steps, and his green Australian cap and tiny figure became visible, even before he had touched the incredible green of Lord's, there was a deafening outburst of applause, and the pavilion and ground rose to him.

Bradman was then a few months short of 40, and had not played in England for ten years. As he took his guard, turning towards his wicket, with his back to the bowler, to mark it with his boots in his characteristic fashion, a silence fell, and Bill Edrich ran in sharply from the Nursery end. Learie Constantine had always said that Bradman did not like the rising ball. In fact Learie had claimed to put to an end Bradman's threat to break his own highest Test score by getting him with such a 'bouncer' first ball in the morning after he had already scored 223 – the only wicket Constantine took in that game in 1931 in Brisbane. Edrich too apparently had a theory about Bradman and the fast rising ball, and his first delivery was a bouncer, rising to about Bradman's left ear. The bat came around in a beautiful arc as he swivelled with a minimum of effort. The ball crashed to the turf about two yards from him, and then on to the midwicket boundary for 4.

What must he have been like at 25 or 28? I had always heard from English detractors of Bradman that he was too much of a 'machine', and had too much of a killer instinct. This appeared to me, on actually seeing the man, to be sheer nonsense. One of the things that surprised Harold Fraser and me on that occasion was that Bradman actually 'passed the time of day' with the bowlers and fielders between overs, but once he faced up, it was clear that his whole attention was given over to the ball. George Headley was the only other batsman I have seen who so completely gave the impression that the bat was part and parcel of his body. But Bradman seemed to have more power. Comparisons are odious, though. It is just that one was forced to be in awe of Bradman in the flesh, as one had wondered 'is it true what they say about him?'

Those people with an interest in cricket statistics know that 487 (unbroken) is the record for the sixth-wicket stand. They might have heard vaguely that it was achieved in Jamaica in 1931–32. Seeing it achieved is one of my earliest memories of cricket: Melbourne Park, intense heat, an enormous crowd, Passailaigue (261 not out) sweeping 6s, and George Headley (344 not out) placing the ball wherever he wished. And both, with perfect understanding, stealing single after single.

Seven years later I was a raw undergraduate, walking across the snowbound campus of Holy Cross College, Worcester, Massachusetts. Suddenly a Yankee voice, high-pitched, came out of the dark: 'Is Mr Headley still batting?' I was taken back until I recognised a young Jesuit lecturer in his black robes. As a teacher at my High School in Jamaica, he had reluctantly accepted my father's invitation to join us for the game at Melbourne Park, on Ash Wednesday 1932.

Now on his after-dinner walk in the freezing weather he was accompanied by two colleagues who understandably wanted to know who this Mr Headley was! 'Ah', replied the young Jesuit, using baseball terms to enlighten his American colleagues, 'He is Ty Cobb, Babe Ruth and Joe DiMaggio all wrapped up in one.' Babe Ruth, some will remember, was a pitcher who became one of the greatest hitters in baseball. It took many years and a more lively ball to catch up with his records. Ty Cobb was a great all-rounder and stealer of bases, never being satisfied with a single when there was the slightest chance of stretching it into a double, and DiMaggio was a great New York out-fielder and hitter. Baseball would not have been an alien metaphor to Headley. Legend has it that he played the game as a young lad in Panama. He must at least have watched it in Cuba before he was sent to Jamaica, at the age of 12, by his mother, so that he would have an English education!

Suddenly the snows of that New England winter were warmed by the heat and chatter, and rum drinking, of that great day as the Reverend gentleman explained to his colleagues how Passailaigue 'hit the ball out of the park', while 'Mr Headley stroked the ball all around the field'. Clarence Passailaigue, bow-legged, of ruddy complexion, and rather rough looking; George Headley, very black, very neat, lithe and agile. The one no doubt with long-ago Haitian connections when white families fled that country to Jamaica and Cuba and Trinidad; the other born in Panama of a Jamaican mother and a Barbadian father both helping to build the great Canal.

What a mad world we live in; for surely Headley and Passailaigue, according to South African ideology defended by British lovers of freedom should never have been allowed to play on the same team or even against each other. And on that snowbound campus in 1939 the argument was still raging about whether 'Negroes' should be allowed to play baseball in the big leagues! (One of my classmates, who wanted to uphold the status quo, on being taxed with thinking 'Negroes' inferior, replied vigorously 'Not so! They are so damned good we'll never get a game.')

And all these English cricketers, who admittedly aren't paid all that much – is it true they just can't exist without playing in apartheid South Africa? And all the Lords and 'leading' sports writers who see nothing wrong in it at all! All this in the name of the great game of cricket, and of civilisation, and God help us, Christianity! A word to the wise is always sufficient. But what does one say to the idiots?

And what about those whose idea of good does not go beyond 'looking after their families' and 'helping kith and kin'. That latter idea sounds so simple and sound. But it is in the end totally divisive, and means finally that 'black' people must band together against 'white' people and vice versa.

However, I have to say that I am acutely aware of how easy it is, in fighting fascism, to become a fascist, even if one claims to be very left wing! And in fighting racism one must not become racist! I was much upset by the kind of legalistic hounding of Zola Budd that took place; it simply underlined for me how easy it is to become fascist and indecently nationalist! Those English people who were baying at her mainly because she runs so much better than most English women are quite beyond contempt. Racism is only one form of 'groupism', of an inhuman and artificially induced 'herd instinct': another form is xenophobia, which some English groups cultivate with a vengeance. And which some people, who should know better, have been trying to foster in the West Indies and among Caribbean heritage people in the UK.

'Damus petimusque vicissim', Frank Worrell used to say,

quoting one of the old mottoes of a West Indian cricketing county. Horace first wrote that about the art of writing poetry 'we poets do not ask from the critics anything we are not willing to grant them'. While distinguished cricket writers call West Indian players in England 'mercenaries', and while Micky Stewart is on record as saying that he would like all overseas players banned from county cricket, is it not odd that English cricket players, and their strong lobby, should assert an unalienable right to play anywhere 'since they have to earn a living'?

In 1950 we all thought that fascism and the virulent racism of the Nazis had been defeated. The West Indies seemed a microcosm of what might be a brave new world: an Indian, and a grandson of indentured labourers among the descendents of slave and slave owner and late-comers, among the Weekeses and the Goddards, the Valentines and the Stollmeyers, the Gomezes and the Christianis, the Trestrails and the Worrells! And back at home there were Achong and Tang Choon and Asgarali, and Barrow and Abrahams. But even in the West Indies racialism and racism were later to be issues raised in the name of justice, and at the same time used to create and exploit divisions.

In 1950, the jubilee year of West Indies tours to England, some of the performances were as outstanding as any of those in the Olympics of 1948. Against Leicestershire West Indies scored 682 in the first innings, 39 runs short of the Australian 1948 record against Essex. Roy Marshall scored 188; Worrell (241 not out) and Weekes (200 not out) shared a partnership of 309; Weekes's first hundred took him 65 minutes, the fastest in that season. Ten of the West Indies first-class victories were by an innings. The three Ws scored twenty centuries between them. But it was not all knock-about and 'brutality'. As *Wisden* put it: 'For beauty of stroke no one in the history of the game can have excelled Worrell' and went on to remark that his masterpiece was the 261 he made at Trent Bridge, when he and Weekes added 283 for the fourth wicket.

But the thing for both West Indian and English fans to keep clearly in mind is this. The English press in 1950 expected Johnson, Jones and Pierre, the fast bowlers, to 'do the damage'. Yet they took only 91 wickets in thirty-one first-class games, while Ramadhin and Valentine took 258; in the Tests, Valentine took 33 wickets, Ramadhin 26, Goddard 6, Worrell 6, Johnson 3.

Even more memorable is the phrase from *Wisden* commenting on the 1950 tour: 'West Indies. . . can rightly claim on results alone to be second to Australia' – Australia who in 1948 won four Tests, one being drawn, and who did not lose a single first-class game, winning twenty-three of the thirty-one played, the Australia of Bradman, Morris, Barnes, Hassett, Miller and Harvey!

We have all enjoyed, in 1950 and in 1988, and on many other occasions, 'cricket, lovely cricket', played as cricket by all kinds of nationalities and races. It has been a great experience, and sometimes a consolation against the injustices of the present and the past. But as the distinguished West Indian poet Derek Walcott says about another great embodiment of the human spirit: 'The classics can console, but not enough.'

Surely there is more to life than even the great game of cricket!

As G. C. ('Jack') Grant, the first West Indies captain to take a team to Australia, has put it: 'Believe it or not I often made runs, [when I was over 50 and playing in Rhodesia] but when the Rhodesian Government made its Unilateral Declaration of Independence in November 1965, I ceased to play altogether. Not because I was too old, but because politically I was not on the same wavelength as my fellow players, all of whom were white and most of whom supported Ian Smith.'

Now in later years Grant has been maligned by groupist West Indian writers for being selected to captain the West Indies, just as Jerry Alexander was later to be. The bone of contention is that in Grant's case not only was he white, but he was selected at a time when the powers in WI society would not have a non-white captain. Grant was also, like Alexander, a Cambridge Blue in cricket and soccer. Grant led the first West Indies team to win abroad – in the fifth Test in Australia, in February–March 1931, when West Indies won by 30 runs. F. R. Martin made 123 not out in the first innings, Headley 105, and Grant 62.

At last, as we know, the apartheid system is partly crumbling, and partly being dismantled. One has to be grateful to all sportsmen and sportswomen who have stood firm against the injustices of the system. Those who know South Africa well know that the international ban on sports really spoke to South Africans of all classes and colours. Now we will all have to rebuild – with 'malice to none' and goodwill to all. In this connection, cricket, along with all other sports, must play its part, but it will only do so if we keep it in its proper human place.

Whatever they thought of his selection, Grant was admired by many of his team for his sterling Christian values, and Learie Constantine, a staunch fighter against racial prejudice if ever there was one, on more than one occasion invited Grant to be Director of Education in the new state of Trinidad and Tobago.

But Grant had insisted on fighting against apartheid in South Africa where he helped to run missionary education. He eventually had to leave for what was then Southern Rhodesia where he carried on the struggle. He was also in trouble there for fighting against the Smith regime which was but another case of wanting to organise society not on the basis of justice but rather on the grounds, first of all, of favouring one's 'kith and kin', and only within that framework looking after 'justice'.

So he knew what he was talking about when he said:

> 'Sad it is that politics should disrupt relationships. But sadder still if we set more store on cricket than on politics, which is basically concerned with human relations and justice.'

And how much sadder when we place personal comfort and gain, and of course trade, above working for human relations and justice for all!

But what now of 1991? Bold men make forecasts about cricket – and the weather in England; yet cowards will not resist requests to pronounce on such matters. Put me down to be both a bold man and a coward!

How are the West Indies going to do in England in 1991? No doubt the weather will play an important part in the series. For instance, recently Richardson looked in really good form in the Caribbean: will he be as sound and fertile on wettish green wickets?

The greatest unknown factor at this time is the selection of the team. West Indies have a real problem: they have been at the top or close to it for some time, yet as their team has matured and in fact aged, they have not been bringing along many bright new youngsters who could quietly slip into the shoes of the veterans who have served West Indies well for some time. 'Don't change horses in the middle of a stream. Don't change a winning team.' These are good pieces of folk wisdom, but if too slavishly followed they leave one with a team no longer able to dominate the scene, and quite unclear about who is to carry on the traditions of our cricket.

The present West Indies team, as selected to play the first two Tests against Australia in the West Indies in 1991, is an ageing team without its previous fire-power in either bowling or batting. They seem to me to need to find replacements at least for Marshall and Greenidge, and possibly for Dujon also. And they need at least one more bowler of true Test quality, although much will depend on the availability of Bishop. In fact both teams have to improve their bowling considerably. The better batsmen on both sides can collect quite big scores; the team that can find bowlers who combine containment with wicket-taking should win easily. But it is not easy to find such bowlers: so many of them, especially in the England team, get hit for at least one 4 an over – even after beating the bat twice in a row.

Another problem faces the West Indies: it has to do particularly with not changing tactics when circumstances change. The use of four fast bowlers was invariably effective – not only because the bowlers were fast, but because they were first-class as well. They were very nearly the best bowlers West Indies have produced – but remember Tommy Scott, Ram, Val, Lance Gibbs, and Worrell and Sobers in their spinning modes. Now that we do not have four excellent fast bowlers our tactics must change. It is just as ridiculous to use four fast bowlers simply because they are fast as it was to continue to use Ram when it became clear that the umpires' interpretation of the lbw laws, together with May and Cowdrey's use of that interpretation, had rendered one of the greatest spin bowlers ineffective. What we might do now is seal off one end completely by using a bowler, and the appropriate field setting, to do just that, while concentrating on getting wickets at the other end by using two really good fast bowlers in relays, and in combination with an off-spinner such as the vastly improved Hooper.

Perhaps Hooper should be helped to concentrate on becoming a first-class off-spinner since Richardson is batting so well. Lara – a left hander – promises to be one of the best, and Logie has come into his own. Bowlers win matches, and although our batting is not what it used to be, neither is our bowling, and the latter is what we must concentrate on if we are to win the series against England. And variety of bowling, but of good bowling, will test the England batsmen more than a dose of the medicine as before when that medicine has lost much of its original efficacy! It would add to the variety if West Indies could find a good left- hander, whether of spin or speed. A sportswriter in Jamaica suggested, just before the 1950 tour, that the selectors 'shake the mango tree a bit more slowly' – he referred to the story that when Yorkshire needed a new fast bowler they sent a message to the nearest coal mine 'to send up a strong lad'. Another slow shake would be useful now, even though it would be hard to produce two more twins to match 'those two little pals of mine'!

In these days, when so much international cricket is being played, one is not quite sure whether the popularity of the game – in its Test match mode at least – is not waning; sponsored boxes are no measure of cricket's true popularity. The 1991 Engalnd – West Indies series is of the greatest importance not only to these two keen cricket rivals but to the game itself, to its honesty, to its subtle grace, and to its supporters. One wonders whether 1991 will be as surprising and stimulating as was 1950.

Facts and Figures
1950 – 1988

Appendix 1 **1950**

Tests: Played 4, Won 3, Lost 1

First-class Matches: Played 31, Won 17, Drawn 11, Lost 3

All Matches: Played 38, Won 19, Drawn 16, Lost 3

Won: England (3), Lancashire (2), Yorkshire (2), Glamorgan, Somerset, Nottinghamshire, Sussex, Leicestershire, Surrey, Gloucestershire, Essex, Kent, Minor Counties, Northumberland, Cumberland, Westmorland.

Drawn: Worcestershire, Surrey, Cambridge University, Oxford University, Hampshire, Northamptonshire, Derbyshire, Glamorgan, Middlesex, South of England, H. D. G. Leveson Gower's XI, Durham, L. N. Constantine's XI, Col. L. C. Stevens's XI, Indian Gymkhana, Club Cricket Conference.

Lost: England, MCC, Warwickshire.

First-class Averages

Batting

	M	I	NO	R	HS	Av	100	Ct	St
E. D. Weekes	23	33	4	2310	304*	79.65	7	31	—
F. M. Worrell	22	31	5	1775	261	68.26	6	11	—
C. L. Walcott	24	36	6	1674	168*	55.80	7	30	18
R. J. Christiani	24	34	10	1094	131*	45.58	4	30	6
G. E. Gomez	27	30	4	1116	149	42.92	3	32	—
R. E. Marshall	20	28	0	1117	188	39.89	3	15	—
A. F. Rae	26	38	4	1330	179	39.11	4	15	—
J. B. Stollmeyer	25	37	1	1334	198	37.05	1	23	—
K. B. Trestrail	19	28	5	629	94	27.34	—	8	—
J. D. C. Goddard	22	21	5	309	58*	19.31	—	21	—
H. H. Johnson	17	16	4	184	39*	15.33	—	5	—
C. B. Williams	20	18	4	152	33*	10.85	—	16	—
P. E. Jones	17	16	4	83	20	6.91	—	14	—
S. Ramadhin	21	15	8	36	7*	5.14	—	3	—
A. L. Valentine	21	19	3	49	9*	3.06	—	7	—
L. R. Pierre	12	7	1	2	1	0.33	—	5	—

Bowling

	O	M	R	W	Av
S. Ramadhin	1043.4	398	2009	135	14.88
A. L. Valentine	1185.2	475	2207	123	17.94
J. D. C. Goddard	295.2	96	618	33	18.72
L. R. Pierre	204	39	557	24	23.20
F. M. Worrell	480.1	170	970	39	24.87
G. E. Gomez	680.3	221	1407	55	25.58
C. B. Williams	301.2	57	856	31	27.61
H. H. Johnson	435.5	102	954	34	28.05
P. E. Jones	388.3	82	980	33	29.69
R. E. Marshall	120.5	36	336	7	48.00
J. B. Stollmeyer	27	3	117	2	58.50

Also bowled: K. B. Trestrail 3–0–17–0; C. L. Walcott 12–6–22–0; E. D. Weekes 9–0–41–2.

Test Averages

England Batting

	M	I	NO	R	HS	Av
L. Hutton	3	6	1	333	202*	66.60
C. Washbrook	2	4	0	255	114	63.75
T. E. Bailey	2	4	1	145	82*	48.33
T. G. Evans	3	6	0	224	104	37.33
W. G. A. Parkhouse	2	4	0	130	69	32.50
R. T. Simpson	3	6	0	171	94	28.50
W. J. Edrich	2	4	0	94	71	23.50
J. G. Dewes	2	4	0	87	67	21.75
G. H. G. Doggart	2	4	0	76	29	19.00
N. W. D. Yardley	3	6	0	108	41	18.00
R. O. Jenkins	2	4	1	53	39	17.66
A. V. Bedser	3	6	0	20	13	3.33
R. Berry	2	4	2	6	4*	3.00
W. E. Hollies	2	4	1	5	3*	1.66

Also batted: F. R. Brown 0, 15; D. C. S. Compton 44, 11; H. E. Dollery 8, 0; M. J. Hilton 3, 0; D. J. Insole 21, 0; J. C. Laker 4, 40; A. J. McIntyre 4, 0; D. Shackleton 42, 1; D. S. Sheppard 11, 29; J. H. Wardle 33*, 21; D. V. P. Wright 4, 6*.

England Bowling

	O	M	R	W	Av
R. Berry	108.5	47	228	9	25.33
W. E. Hollies	119	38	268	10	26.80
D. V. P. Wright	53	16	141	5	28.20
A. V. Bedser	181	49	377	11	34.27
T. E. Bailey	47.2	12	121	3	40.33
R. O. Jenkins	118.2	20	409	10	40.90

Also bowled: F. R. Brown 21–4–74–1; D. C. S. Compton 7–2–21–0; M. J. Hilton 41–12–91–0; J. C. Laker 31–9–86–1; D. Shackleton 49–9–135–1; R. T. Simpson 1.3–0–9–0; J. H. Wardle 47–16–104–2; W. J. Edrich 34–8–81–0; N. W. D. Yardley 31–4–94–1.

West Indies Batting

	M	I	NO	R	HS	Av
F. M. Worrell	4	6	0	539	261	89.83
A. F. Rae	4	7	1	377	109	62.83
E. D. Weekes	4	6	0	338	129	56.33
J. B. Stollmeyer	4	7	1	305	78	50.83
C. L. Walcott	4	6	1	229	168*	45.80
G. E. Gomez	4	6	1	207	74	41.40
J. D. C. Goddard	4	6	2	106	58*	26.50
R. J. Christiani	4	6	1	82	33	16.40
H. H. Johnson	2	3	0	30	22	10.00
S. Ramadhin	4	5	2	10	4*	3.33
A. L. Valentine	4	5	0	15	9	3.00
P. E. Jones	2	2	0	1	1	0.50

West Indies Bowling

	O	M	R	W	Av
J. D. C. Goddard	74.4	29	122	6	20.33
A. L. Valentine	422.3	197	674	33	20.42
S. Ramadhin	377.5	170	604	26	23.23
F. M. M. Worrell	98.2	36	182	6	30.33
H. H. Johnson	65.4	13	142	3	47.33

Also bowled: C. L. Walcott 4–1–12–0; G. E. Gomez 80–25–163–2; P. E. Jones 38.4–7–105–1.

England v West Indies 1950 (First Test)

VENUE: Old Trafford

DATE: 8, 9, 10, 12 June. England won the toss

RESULT: England won by 202 runs

Batted First: England

1 L. Hutton	b Valentine	39	(8) c and b Worrell	45
2 R. T. Simpson	c Goddard b Valentine	27	(1) c Weekes b Gomez	0
3 W. J. Edrich	c Gomez b Valentine	7	(2) c Weekes b Ramadhin	71
4 G. H. G. Doggart	c Rae b Valentine	29	(3) c Goddard b Valentine	22
5 H. E. Dollery	c Gomez b Valentine	8	(4) c Gomez b Valentine	0
6 N. W. D. Yardley*	c Gomez b Valentine	0	(5) lbw b Gomez	25
7 T. E. Bailey	not out	82	(6) run out	33
8 T. G. Evans†	c and b Valentine	104	(7) c Worrell b Ramadhin	15
9 J. C. Laker	b Valentine	4	c Stollmeyer b Valentine	40
10 W. E. Hollies	c Weekes b Ramadhin	0	c Walcott b Worrell	3
11 R. Berry	b Ramadhin	0	not out	4
Extras (B 8, LB 3, NB 1)		12	(B 17, LB 12, NB 1)	30
Total		312		288

Batted Second: West Indies

1 A. F. Rae	c Doggart b Berry	14	c Doggart b Hollies	10
2 J. B. Stollmeyer	lbw b Hollies	43	c sub b Laker	78
3 F. M. Worrell	st Evans b Berry	15	st Evans b Hollies	28
4 E. D. Weekes	c sub b Bailey	52	lbw b Hollies	1
5 C. L. Walcott†	c Evans b Berry	13	b Berry	9
6 R. J. Christiani	lbw b Berry	17	c Yardley b Hollies	6
7 G. E. Gomez	c Berry b Hollies	35	st Evans b Berry	8
8 J. D. C. Goddard*	run out	7	not out	16
9 H. H. Johnson	c Dollery b Hollies	8	b Berry	22
10 S. Ramadhin	not out	4	b Berry	0
11 A. L. Valentine	c and b Berry	0	c Bailey b Hollies	0
Extras (LB 6, NB 1)		7	(B 4, W 1)	5
Total		215		183

Bowling

	O	M	R	W	O	M	R	W
West Indies								
Johnson	10	3	18	0				
Gomez	10	1	29	0	25	12	47	2
Valentine	50	14	104	8	56	22	100	3
Ramadhin	39.3	12	90	2	42	17	77	2
Goddard	15	1	46	0	9	3	12	0
Worrell	4	1	13	0	5.5	1	10	2
Walcott					4	1	12	0
England								
Bailey	10	2	28	1	3	1	9	0
Edrich	2	1	4	0	3	1	10	0
Hollies	33	13	70	3	35.2	11	63	5
Laker	17	5	43	0	14	4	43	1
Berry	31.5	13	63	5	26	12	53	4

Fall of Wickets

	E 1st	WI 1st	E 2nd	WI 2nd
1st	31	52	0	32
2nd	74	74	31	68
3rd	79	74	43	80
4th	83	94	106	113
5th	88	146	131	126
6th	249	178	151	141
7th	293	201	200	146
8th	301	211	266	178
9th	308	211	284	178
10th	312	215	288	183

Umpires: F. Chester and D. Davies Captain* Wicket-keeper†

England v West Indies 1950 (Second Test)

VENUE: Lord's
DATE: 24, 26, 27, 28, 29 June. West Indies won the toss
RESULT: West Indies won by 326 runs

Batted First: West Indies

1 A. F. Rae	c and b Jenkins	106	b Jenkins	24
2 J. B. Stollmeyer	lbw b Wardle	20	b Jenkins	30
3 F. M. Worrell	b Bedser	52	c Doggart b Jenkins	45
4 E. D. Weekes	b Bedser	63	run out	63
5 C. L. Walcott†	st Evans b Jenkins	14	(6) not out	168
6 G. E. Gomez	st Evans b Jenkins	1	(7) c Edrich b Bedser	70
7 R. J. Christiani	b Bedser	33	(8) not out	5
8 J. D. C. Goddard*	b Wardle	14	(5) c Evans b Jenkins	11
9 P. E. Jones	c Evans b Jenkins	0		
10 S. Ramadhin	not out	1		
11 A. L. Valentine	c Hutton b Jenkins	5		
Extras (B 10, LB 5, W 1, NB 1)		17	(LB 8, NB 1)	9
Total		326	(6 wkts dec.)	425

Batted Second: England

1 L. Hutton	st Walcott b Valentine	35	b Valentine	10
2 C. Washbrook	st Walcott b Ramadhin	36	b Ramadhin	114
3 W. J. Edrich	c Walcott b Ramadhin	8	c Jones b Ramadhin	8
4 G. H. G. Doggart	lbw b Ramadhin	0	b Ramadhin	25
5 W. G. A. Parkhouse	b Valentine	0	c Goddard b Valentine	48
6 N. W. D. Yardley*	b Valentine	16	c Weekes b Valentine	19
7 T. G. Evans†	b Ramadhin	8	c Rae b Ramadhin	2
8 R. O. Jenkins	c Walcott b Valentine	4	b Ramadhin	4
9 J. H. Wardle	not out	33	lbw b Worrell	21
10 A. V. Bedser	b Ramadhin	5	b Ramadhin	0
11 R. Berry	c Goddard b Jones	2	not out	0
Extras (B 2, LB 1, W 1)		4	(B 16, LB 7)	23
Total		151		274

Bowling

	O	M	R	W	O	M	R	W
England								
Bedser	40	14	60	3	44	16	80	1
Edrich	16	4	30	0	13	2	37	0
Jenkins	35.2	6	116	5	59	13	174	4
Wardle	17	6	46	2	30	10	58	0
Berry	19	7	45	0	32	15	67	0
Yardley	4	1	12	0				
West Indies								
Jones	8.4	2	13	1	7	1	22	0
Worrell	10	4	20	0	22.3	9	39	1
Valentine	45	28	48	4	71	47	79	3
Ramadhin	43	27	66	5	72	43	86	6
Gomez					13	1	25	0
Goddard					6	6	0	0

Fall of Wickets

	WI 1st	E 1st	WI 2nd	E 2nd
1st	37	62	48	28
2nd	128	74	75	57
3rd	233	74	108	140
4th	262	75	146	218
5th	273	86	199	228
6th	274	102	410	238
7th	320	110		245
8th	320	113		248
9th	320	122		258
10th	326	151		274

Umpires: D. Davies and F. S. Lee Captain* Wicket-keeper†

England v West Indies 1950 (Third Test)

VENUE: Trent Bridge
DATE: 20, 21, 22, 24, 25 July. England won the toss
RESULT: West Indies won by 10 wickets

Batted First: England

1 R. T. Simpson	c Walcott b Johnson	4	run out	94
2 C. Washbrook	c Stollmeyer b Worrell	3	c Worrell b Valentine	102
3 W. G. A. Parkhouse	c Weekes b Johnson	13	lbw by Goddard	69
4 J. G. Dewes	c Gomez b Worrell	0	lbw b Valentine	67
5 N. W. D. Yardley*	c Goddard b Valentine	41	b Ramadhin	7
6 D. J. Insole	lbw b Ramadhin	21	st Walcott b Ramadhin	0
7 T. G. Evans†	b Ramadhin	32	c Stollm'er b Ramadhin	63
8 D. Shackleton	b Worrell	42	c Weekes b Valentine	1
9 R. O. Jenkins	b Johnson	39	not out	6
10 A. V. Bedser	c Stollmeyer b Valentine	13	b Ramadhin	2
11 W. E. Hollies	not out	2	lbw b Ramadhin	0
Extras (LB 12, NB 1)		13	(B 11, LB 10, W 2, NB 2)	25
Total		223		436

Batted Second: West Indies

1 A. F. Rae	st Evans by Yardley	68	not out	46
2 J. B. Stollmeyer	c and b Jenkins	46	not out	52
3 R. J. Christiani	lbw b Shackleton	10		
4 F. M. Worrell	c Yardley b Bedser	261		
5 E. D. Weekes	c and b Hollies	129		
6 C. L. Walcott†	b Bedser	8		
7 G. E. Gomez	not out	19		
8 J. D. C. Goddard*	c Yardley b Bedser	0		
9 H. H. Johnson	c Insole b Bedser	0		
10 S. Ramadhin	b Bedser	2		
11 A. L. Valentine	b Hollies	1		
Extras (B 2, LB 10, NB 2)		14	(NB 5)	5
Total		558	(no wkt)	103

Bowling

	O	M	R	W	O	M	R	W
West Indies								
Johnson	25.4	5	59	3	30	5	65	0
Worrell	17	4	40	3	19	8	30	0
Gomez	3	1	9	0	11	3	23	0
Goddard	6	3	10	0	12	6	18	1
Ramadhin	29	12	49	2	81.2	25	135	5
Valentine	18	6	43	2	92	49	140	3
England								
Bedser	48	9	127	5	11	1	35	0
Shackleton	43	7	128	1	6	2	7	0
Yardley	27	3	82	1				
Jenkins	13	0	73	1	11	1	46	0
Hollies	43.4	8	134	2	7	6	1	0
Simpson					1.3	0	9	0

Fall of Wickets

	E 1st	WI 1st	E 2nd
1st	6	77	212
2nd	18	95	220
3rd	23	238	326
4th	25	521	346
5th	75	535	350
6th	105	537	408
7th	147	538	410
8th	174	539	434
9th	191	551	436
10th	223	558	436

Umpires: F. Chester and H. Elliot Captain* Wicket-keeper†

England v West Indies 1950 (Fourth Test)

VENUE: Kennington Oval
DATE: 12, 14, 15, 16 August. West Indies won the toss
RESULT: West Indies won by an innings and 56 runs

Batted First: West Indies

1	A. F. Rae	b Bedser	109
2	J. B. Stollmeyer	lbw b Bailey	36
3	F. M. Worrell	lbw b Wright	138
4	E. D. Weekes	c Hutton b Wright	30
5	C. L. Walcott†	b Wright	17
6	G. E. Gomez	c McIntyre b Brown	74
7	R. J. Christiani	c McIntyre b Bedser	11
8	J. D. C. Goddard*	not out	58
9	P. E. Jones	b Wright	1
10	S. Ramadhin	c McIntyre b Wright	3
11	A. L. Valentine	b Bailey	9
	Extras (B 5, LB 11, NB 1)		17
	Total		503

Batted Second: England

1	L. Hutton	not out	202	c Christiani b Goddard	2
2	R. T. Simpson	c Jones b Valentine	30	b Ramadhin	16
3	D. S. Sheppard	b Ramadhin	11	c Weekes b Valentine	29
4	D. C. S. Compton	run out	44	c Weekes b Valentine	11
5	J. G. Dewes	c Worrell b Valentine	17	c Christiani b Valentine	3
6	T. E. Bailey	c Weekes b Goddard	18	lbw b Ramadhin	12
7	F. R. Brown*	c Weekes b Valentine	0	c Stollmeyer b Valentine	15
8	A. J. W. McIntyre†	c and b Valentine	4	c sub b Ramadhin	0
9	A. V. Bedser	lbw b Goddard	0	c Weekes b Valentine	0
10	M. J. Hilton	b Goddard	3	c sub b Valentine	0
11	D. V. P. Wright	lbw b Goddard	4	not out	6
	Extras (B 5, LB 6)		11	(B 6, LB 3)	9
	Total		344		103

Bowling

	O	M	R	W	O	M	R	W
England								
Bailey	34.2	9	84	2				
Bedser	38	9	75	2				
Brown	21	4	74	1				
Wright	53	16	141	5				
Hilton	41	12	91	0				
Compton	7	2	21	0				
West Indies								
Jones	23	4	70	0				
Worrell	20	9	30	0				
Ramadhin	45	23	63	1	26	11	38	3
Valentine	64	21	121	4	26.3	10	39	6
Gomez	10	3	24	0	8	4	6	0
Goddard	17.4	6	25	4	9	4	11	1

Fall of Wickets

	E	WI	E
	1st	1st	2nd
1st	72	73	2
2nd	244	120	39
3rd	295	229	50
4th	318	259	56
5th	337	310	79
6th	446	315	83
7th	480	321	83
8th	482	322	83
9th	490	326	85
10th	503	344	103

Umpires: W. H. Ashdown and F. S. Lee Captain* Wicket-keeper†

Appendix 2 **1957**

Tests: Played 5, Drawn 2, Lost 3

First-class Matches: Played 31, Won 14, Drawn 13, Lost 3, Abandoned 1

All Matches: Played 35, Won 16, Drawn 15, Lost 3, Abandoned 1

Won: Worcestershire, Northamptonshire, Oxford University, Essex, Gloucestershire, Glamorgan (2), Sussex, Derbyshire, Ireland, Surrey, Lancashire, Leicestershire, Kent, L. E. G. Ames's XI, Minor Counties.

Drawn: England (2), E. W. Swanton's XI, Cambridge University, MCC, Yorkshire, Nottinghamshire, Surrey, Ireland, Hampshire, Somerset, Middlesex, Warwickshire, Lancashire, T. N. Pearce's XI.

Lost: England (3).

First-class Averages

Batting

	M	I	NO	R	HS	Av	100	Ct	St
F. M. Worrell	20	34	9	1470	191*	58.80	4	10	—
C. L. Walcott	21	36	5	1414	131	45.61	3	28	—
G. St A. Sobers	25	44	6	1644	219*	43.26	3	26	—
O. G. Smith	26	45	9	1483	168	41.19	3	13	—
R. B. Kanhai	22	39	4	1093	95	31.22	—	20	5
N. S. Asgarali	21	37	3	1011	130	29.73	2	11	—
E. D. Weekes	23	40	1	1096	105	28.10	1	17	—
A. Ganteaume	19	32	3	800	92	27.58	—	11	—
B. H. Pairaudeau	18	33	0	781	163	23.66	2	7	—
F. C. M. Alexander	20	30	10	387	83	19.35	—	41	7
D. St E. Atkinson	16	23	4	324	101*	17.05	1	6	—
J. D. C. Goddard	17	21	4	243	61	14.29	—	13	—
W. W. Hall	15	16	3	178	22	13.69	—	3	—
R. Gilchrist	15	16	5	67	20	6.09	—	3	—
S. Ramadhin	4	22	4	105	28	5.83	—	2	—
D. T. Dewdney	16	18	7	49	22*	4.45	—	2	—
A. L. Valentine	16	11	6	19	7	3.80	—	4	—

Bowling

	O	M	R	W	Av
S. Ramadhin	937.1	361	1664	119	13.98
A. L. Valentine	513	160	1180	60	19.66
J. D. C. Goddard	91	31	173	8	21.62
D. St E. Atkinson	605.1	201	1235	55	22.45
F. M. Worrell	406.5	94	949	39	24.33
D. T. Dewdney	317.4	45	974	36	27.05
O. G. Smith	405.3	136	920	34	27.05
G. St A. Sobers	477.3	145	1172	37	31.67
R. Gilchrist	394.2	54	1176	37	31.78
W. W. Hall	292	47	906	27	33.55
N. S. Asgarali	76	24	201	5	40.20

Also bowled: A. Ganteaume 3–0–20–0; C. L. Walcott 8–2–28–0; E. D. Weekes 6–0–32–1.

Test Averages

England Batting

	M	I	NO	R	HS	Av
T. W. Graveney	4	5	1	472	258	118.00
P. B. H. May	5	6	1	489	285*	97.80
F. S. Trueman	5	4	3	89	36*	89.00
M. C. Cowdrey	5	6	0	435	154	72.50
P. E. Richardson	5	7	0	411	126	58.71
D. S. Sheppard	2	2	0	108	68	54.00
T. G. Evans	5	6	2	201	82	50.25
D. B. Close	2	3	0	89	42	29.66
G. A. R. Lock	3	3	0	37	20	12.33
J. B. Statham	3	2	0	20	13	10.00
J. C. Laker	4	3	1	18	10*	9.00
D. V. Smith	3	4	1	25	16*	8.33
T. E. Bailey	4	4	1	5	3*	1.66
P. J. Loader	2	2	0	1	1	0.50

Also batted: D. J. Insole 20, 0; D. W. Richardson 33; J. H. Wardle 11.

England Bowling

	O	M	R	W	Av
P. J. Loader	44.3	17	100	10	10.00
G. A. R. Lock	114.2	59	163	15	10.86
F. S. Trueman	173.3	34	455	22	20.68
T. E. Bailey	117	37	277	12	23.08
J. C. Laker	246.2	99	448	18	24.88
J. B. Statham	158.2	37	433	13	33.30

Also bowled: D. B. Close 2–1–8–0; T. W. Graveney 5–2–14–0; J. H. Wardle 22–5–53–1; D. V. Smith 45–13–97–1.

West Indies Batting

	M	I	NO	R	HS	Av
O. G. Smith	5	10	0	396	168	39.60
F. M. Worrell	5	10	1	350	191*	38.88
G. St A. Sobers	5	10	0	320	66	32.00
C. L. Walcott	5	10	1	247	90	27.44
R. B. Kanhai	5	10	1	206	47	22.88
E. D. Weekes	5	10	0	195	90	19.50
D. St E. Atkinson	2	4	1	55	46	18.33
J. D. C. Goddard	5	8	1	112	61	16.00
N. S. Asgarali	2	4	0	62	29	15.50
S. Ramadhin	5	9	1	47	19	5.87
B. H. Pairaudeau	2	4	0	20	7	5.00
R. Gilchrist	4	7	2	22	11*	4.40
F. C. M. Alexander	2	4	1	11	11	3.66
A. L. Valentine	2	4	2	4	2*	2.00

Also batted: D. T. Dewdney 0, 1.

West Indies Bowling

	O	M	R	W	Av
F. M. Worrell	128.2	25	343	10	34.30
S. Ramadhin	261.3	78	547	14	39.07
O. G. Smith	89	14	223	5	44.60
R. Gilchrist	152.3	19	466	10	46.60
G. St A. Sobers	135	24	355	5	70.10

Also bowled: C. L. Walcott 1–0–4–0; D. T. Dewdney 15–2–43–1; D. St E. Atkinson 125.4–39–267–2; J. D. C. Goddard 58–18–128–2; A. L. Valentine 26–4–88–0.

England v West Indies 1957 (First Test)

VENUE: Edgbaston
DATE: 30, 31 May, 1, 3, 4 June. England won the toss
RESULT: Match Drawn

Batted First: England

1	P. E. Richardson	c Walcott b Ramadhin	47	c sub b Ramadhin	34
2	D. B. Close	c Kanhai b Gilchrist	15	c Weekes b Gilchrist	42
3	D. J. Insole	b Ramadhin	20	b Ramadhin	0
4	P. B. H. May*	c Weekes b Ramadhin	30	not out	285
5	M. C. Cowdrey	c Gilchrist b Ramadhin	4	c sub b Smith	154
6	T. E. Bailey	b Ramadhin	1		
7	G. A. R. Lock	b Ramadhin	0		
8	T. G. Evans†	b Gilchrist	14	(6) not out	29
9	J. C. Laker	b Ramadhin	7		
10	F. S. Trueman	not out	29		
11	J. B. Statham	b Atkinson	13		
	Extras (B 3, LB 3)		6	(B 23, LB 16)	39
	Total		186	(4 wkts dec.)	583

Batted Second: West Indies

1	B. H. Pairaudeau	b Trueman	1	b Trueman	7
2	R. B. Kanhai†	lbw b Statham	42	c Close b Trueman	1
3	C. L. Walcott	c Evans b Laker	90	(6) c Lock b Laker	1
4	E. D. Weekes	b Trueman	9	c Trueman b Lock	33
5	G. St A. Sobers	c Bailey b Statham	53	(3) c Cowdrey b Lock	14
6	O. G. Smith	lbw b Laker	161	(7) lbw b Laker	5
7	F. M. Worrell	b Statham	81	(5) c May b Lock	0
8	J. D. C. Goddard*	c Lock b Laker	24	not out	0
9	D. St E. Atkinson	c Statham b Laker	1	not out	4
10	S. Ramadhin	not out	5		
11	R. Gilchrist	run out	0		
	Extras (B 1, LB 6)		7	(B 7)	7
	Total		474	(7 wkts)	72

Bowling

	O	M	R	W	O	M	R	W
West Indies								
Worrell	9	1	27	0				
Gilchrist	27	4	74	2	26	2	67	1
Ramadhin	31	16	49	7	98	35	179	2
Atkinson	12.4	3	30	1	72	29	137	0
Sobers					30	4	77	0
Smith					26	4	72	1
Goddard					6	2	12	0
England								
Statham	39	4	114	3	2	0	6	0
Trueman	30	4	99	2	5	3	7	2
Bailey	34	11	80	0				
Laker	54	17	119	4	24	20	13	2
Lock	34.4	15	55	0	27	19	31	3
Close					2	1	8	0

Fall of Wickets

	E	WI	E	WI
	1st	1st	2nd	2nd
1st	32	4	63	1
2nd	61	83	65	9
3rd	104	120	113	25
4th	115	183	524	27
5th	116	197		43
6th	118	387		66
7th	121	466		68
8th	130	469		
9th	150	474		
10th	186	474		

Umpires: D. E. Davies and C. S. Elliott   Captain*   Wicket-keeper†

England v West Indies 1957 (Second Test)

VENUE: Lord's
DATE: 20, 21, 22 June. West Indies won the toss
RESULT: England won by an innings and 36 runs

Batted First: West Indies

1	N. S. Asgarali	lbw b Trueman	0	(4) c Trueman by Wardle	26
2	R. B. Kanhai†	c Cowdrey b Bailey	34	(1) c Bailey b Statham	0
3	C. L. Walcott	lbw b Bailey	14	c Trueman b Bailey	21
4	G. St A. Sobers	c May b Statham	17	(5) c May b Bailey	66
5	E. D. Weekes	c Evans b Bailey	13	(6) c Evans b Bailey	90
6	F. M. Worrell	c Close b Bailey	12	(7) c Evans b Trueman	10
7	O. G. Smith	c Graveney b Bailey	25	(2) lbw b Statham	5
8	J. D. C. Goddard*	c Cowdrey b Bailey	1	c Evans b Trueman	21
9	S. Ramadhin	b Trueman	0	c Statham b Bailey	0
10	R. Gilchrist	c and b Bailey	4	not out	11
11	A. L. Valentine	not out	0	b Statham	1
	Extras (B 2, LB 1, W 4)		7	(B 4, LB 6)	10
	Total		127		261

Batted Second: England

1	P. E. Richardson	b Gilchrist	76
2	D. V. Smith	lbw b Worrell	8
3	T. W. Graveney	lbw b Gilchrist	0
4	P. B. H. May*	c Kanhai b Gilchrist	0
5	M. C. Cowdrey	c Walcott b Sobers	152
6	T. E. Bailey	b Worrell	1
7	D. B. Close	c Kanhai b Goddard	32
8	T. G. Evans†	b Sobers	82
9	J. H. Wardle	c Sobers b Ramadhin	11
10	F. S. Trueman	not out	36
11	J. B. Statham	b Gilchrist	7
	Extras (B 7, LB 11, W 1)		19
	Total		424

Bowling

	O	M	R	W	O	M	R	W
England								
Statham	18	3	46	1	29.1	9	71	3
Trueman	12.3	2	30	2	23	5	73	2
Bailey	21	8	44	7	22	6	54	4
Wardle					22	5	53	1
West Indies								
Worrell	42	7	114	2				
Gilchrist	36.3	7	115	4				
Ramadhin	22	5	83	1				
Valentine	3	0	20	0				
Goddard	13	1	45	1				
Sobers	7	0	28	2				

Fall of Wickets

	WI 1st	E 1st	WI 2nd
1st	7	25	0
2nd	34	34	17
3rd	55	34	32
4th	79	129	180
5th	85	134	180
6th	118	192	203
7th	120	366	233
8th	123	379	241
9th	127	387	256
10th	127	424	261

Umpires: D. E. Davies and C. S. Elliott Captain* Wicket-keeper†

England v West Indies 1957 (Third Test)

VENUE: Trent Bridge
DATE: 4, 5, 6, 8, 9 July. England won the toss
RESULT: Match Drawn

Batted First: England

1 P. E. Richardson	c Walcott b Atkinson 126	c Kanhai b Gilchrist 11
2 D. V. Smith	c Kanhai b Worrell 1	not out 16
3 T. W. Graveney	b Smith 258	not out 28
4 P. B. H. May*	lbw b Smith 104	
5 M. C. Cowdrey	run out 55	
6 D. W. Richardson	b Sobers 33	
7 T. G. Evans†	not out 26	
8 T. E. Bailey	not out 3	
9 J. C. Laker		
10 F. S. Trueman		
11 J. B. Statham		
Extras (B 1, LB 10, W 1, NB 1)	 13	(B 7, LB 2) 9
Total	.... (6 wkts dec.) 619	(1 wkt) 64

Batted Second: West Indies

1 F. M. Worrell	not out 191	b Statham 16
2 G. St. A. Sobers	b Laker 47	lbw b Trueman 9
3 C. L. Walcott	c and b Laker 17	c Evans b Laker 7
4 R. B. Kanhai†	c Evans b Bailey 42	c Evans b Trueman 28
5 E. D. Weekes	b Trueman 33	b Statham 3
6 O. G. Smith	c Evans b Trueman 2	b Trueman 168
7 D. St. E. Atkinson	c Evans b Trueman 4	c Evans b Statham 46
8 J. D. C. Goddard*	c May b Trueman 0	c Evans b Statham 61
9 R. Gilchrist	c D. W. Richardson b Laker 1	(10) b Statham 0
10 A. L. Valentine	b Trueman 1	(11) not out 2
11 S. Ramadhin	b Statham 19	(9) b Trueman 15
Extras (B 5, LB 10)	 15	(B 2, LB 10) 12
Total	 372	367

Bowling

	O	M	R	W	O	M	R	W
West Indies								
Worrell	21	4	79	1	7	1	27	0
Gilchrist	29	3	118	0	7	0	21	1
Atkinson	40	7	99	1	1	0	1	0
Ramadhin	38	5	95	0				
Valentine	23	4	68	0				
Sobers	21	6	60	1				
Goddard	15	5	26	0	1	0	2	0
Smith	25	5	61	2				
Walcott					1	0	4	0
England								
Statham	28.4	9	78	1	41.2	12	118	5
Trueman	30	8	63	5	35	5	80	4
Laker	62	27	101	3	43	14	98	1
Bailey	28	9	77	1	12	3	22	0
Smith	12	1	38	0	12	5	23	0
Graveney					5	2	14	0

Fall of Wickets

	E 1st	WI 1st	WI 2nd	E 2nd
1st	14	87	22	13
2nd	280	120	30	
3rd	487	229	39	
4th	510	295	56	
5th	573	297	89	
6th	609	305	194	
7th		305	348	
8th		314	352	
9th		317	365	
10th		372	367	

Umpires: J. S. Buller and F. S. Lee   Captain*   Wicket-keeper†

England v West Indies 1957 (Fourth Test)

VENUE: Headingley
DATE: 25, 26, 27 July. West Indies won the toss
RESULT: England won by an innings and 5 runs

Batted First: West Indies

1	F. M. Worrell	b Loader	29	c Cowdrey by Trueman	7
2	G. St A. Sobers	c Lock b Loader	4	run out	29
3	R. B. Kanhai	lbw b Laker	47	lbw b Loader	0
4	E. D. Weekes	b Loader	0	c Cowdrey b Trueman	14
5	C. L. Walcott	c Cowdrey b Laker	38	c Sheppard b Loader	35
6	O. G. Smith	b Trueman	15	c Evans b Smith	8
7	B. H. Pairaudeau	b Trueman	6	c Trueman b Loader	6
8	J. D. C. Goddard*	b Loader	1	c Loader b Lock	4
9	F. C. M. Alexander†	not out	0	b Laker	11
10	S. Ramadhin	c Trueman b Loader	0	run out	6
11	R. Gilchrist	b Loader	0	not out	6
	Extras (LB 2)		2	(LB 5, NB 1)	6
	Total		142		132

Batted Second: England

1	P. E. Richardson	c Alexander b Worrell	10
2	D. V. Smith	b Worrell	0
3	T. W. Graveney	b Gilchrist	22
4	P. B. H. May*	c Alexander b Sobers	69
5	M. C. Cowdrey	c Weekes b Worrell	68
6	D. S. Sheppard	b Worrell	68
7	T. G. Evans†	b Worrell	10
8	G. A. R. Lock	b Gilchrist	20
9	J. C. Laker	c Alexander b Worrell	1
10	F. S. Trueman	not out	2
11	P. J. Loader	c Pairaudeau b Worrell	1
	Extras (B 2, LB 5, W 1)		8
	Total		279

Bowling

	O	M	R	W	O	M	R	W
England								
Trueman	17	4	33	2	11	0	42	2
Loader	20.3	9	36	6	14	2	50	3
Smith	17	6	24	0	4	1	12	1
Laker	17	4	24	2	6.2	1	16	1
Lock	14	6	23	0	1	0	6	1
West Indies								
Worrell	38.2	9	70	7				
Gilchrist	27	3	71	2				
Sobers	32	9	79	1				
Ramadhin	19	5	34	0				
Smith	8	1	17	0				

Fall of Wickets

	WI 1st	E 1st	WI 2nd
1st	16	1	40
2nd	42	12	40
3rd	42	42	49
4th	112	136	56
5th	125	227	71
6th	139	239	92
7th	142	264	103
8th	142	272	113
9th	142	278	123
10th	142	279	132

Umpires: J. S. Buller and D. E. Davies Captain* Wicket-keeper†

England v West Indies 1957 (Fifth Test)

VENUE: Kennington Oval, London
DATE: 22, 23, 24 August. England won the toss
RESULT: England won by an innings and 237 runs

Batted First: England

1	P. E. Richardson	b Smith	107
2	D. S. Sheppard	c and b Goddard	40
3	T. W. Graveney	b Ramadhin	164
4	P. B. H. May*	c Worrell b Smith	1
5	M. C. Cowdrey	b Ramadhin	2
6	T. E. Bailey	run out	0
7	T. G. Evans†	c Weekes b Dewdney	40
8	G. A. R. Lock	c Alexander b Sobers	17
9	F. S. Trueman	b Ramadhin	22
10	J. C. Laker	not out	10
11	P. J. Loader	lbw b Ramadhin	0
	Extras (B 1, LB 8)		9
	Total		412

Batted Second: West Indies

1	F. M. Worrell	c Lock b Loader	4	(4) c Cowdrey b Lock	0
2	N. S. Asgarali	c Cowdrey b Lock	29	b Lock	7
3	G. St. A Sobers	b Lock	39	b Lock	42
4	C. L. Walcott	b Laker	5	(5) not out	19
5	E. D. Weekes	c Trueman b Laker	0	(6) b Lock	0
6	O. G. Smith	c May b Laker	7	(7) c Sheppard b Lock	0
7	R. B. Kanhai	not out	4	(1) c Evans b Trueman	8
8	F. C. M. Alexander†	b Lock	0	b Laker	0
9	D. T. Dewdney	b Lock	0	st Evans b Lock	1
10	S. Ramadhin	c Trueman b Lock	0	b Laker	2
11	J. D. C. Goddard*	absent ill		absent ill	
	Extras (NB 1)		1	(B 4, LB 2, NB 1)	7
	Total		89		86

Bowling

	O	M	R	W	O	M	R	W
West Indies								
Worrell	11	3	26	0				
Dewdney	15	2	43	1				
Ramadhin	53.3	12	107	4				
Sobers	44	6	111	1				
Goddard	23	10	43	1				
Smith	30	4	73	2				
England								
Trueman	5	1	9	0	5	2	19	1
Loader	7	4	12	1	3	2	2	0
Laker	23	12	39	3	17	4	38	2
Lock	21.4	12	28	5	16	7	20	6

Fall of Wickets

	E 1st	WI 1st	WI 2nd
1st	92	7	10
2nd	238	68	39
3rd	242	73	43
4th	255	73	69
5th	256	85	69
6th	322	89	69
7th	366	89	70
8th	399	89	75
9th	412	89	86
10th	412		

Umpires: D. E. Davies and F. S. Lee Captain* Wicket-keeper†

Appendix 3 **1963**

Tests: Played 5, Won 3, Drawn 1, Lost 1

First-class Matches: Played 30, Won 15, Drawn 13, Lost 2

All Matches: Played 38, Won 19, Drawn 16, Lost 3

Won: England (3), Col L. C. Stevens's XI, Duke of Norfolk's XI, Gloucestershire, Cambridge University, MCC, Oxford University, Somerset, Glamorgan, Ireland, Sussex, Derbyshire, Middlesex, Warwickshire, Yorkshire, T. N. Pearce's XI, Sir Learie Constantine's XI.

Drawn: England, Worcestershire, Lancashire, Surrey (2), Ireland, Hampshire, Essex, Minor Counties, Leicestershire, Glamorgan, Northamptonshire, Nottinghamshire, Kent, A. E. R. Gilligan's XI, Club Cricket Conference.

Lost: England, Yorkshire, Sussex.

First-class Averages

Batting

	M	I	NO	R	HS	Av	100	Ct	St
G. St A. Sobers	24	34	6	1333	112	47.60	4	29	—
B. F. Butcher	22	34	5	1294	133	44.62	2	9	—
C. C. Hunte	21	37	6	1367	182	44.09	3	12	—
R. B. Kanhai	21	32	4	1149	119	41.03	1	12	—
E. D. McMorris	17	29	5	878	190*	36.58	2	5	—
S. M. Nurse	17	29	2	911	116*	33.74	3	15	—
M. C. Carew	21	39	4	1060	117	30.28	1	7	—
W. V. Rodriguez	12	18	4	413	93	29.50	—	8	—
J. S. Solomon	23	35	6	774	62	26.68	—	9	—
F. M. Worrell	18	23	2	522	74*	24.85	—	6	—
W. A. White	9	14	3	228	68*	20.72	—	9	—
D. L. Murray	15	20	4	269	67	16.81	—	42	7
W. W. Hall	20	21	2	264	102*	13.89	1	10	—
L. A. King	18	22	7	202	27*	13.46	—	10	—
D. W. Allan	18	22	5	226	34	13.29	—	46	9
C. C. Griffith	20	23	7	164	27*	10.25	—	7	—
L. R. Gibbs	19	18	6	89	31	7.41	—	13	—
A. L. Valentine	15	11	5	10	6*	1.66	—	5	—

Bowling

	O	M	R	W	Av
C. C. Griffith	701.2	192	1527	119	12.83
S. M. Nurse	13	1	53	3	17.66
L. R. Gibbs	733	216	1564	78	20.05
W. W. Hall	566.4	113	1506	74	20.35
J. S. Solomon	152.5	25	540	26	20.76
C. C. Hunte	441	8	112	5	22.40
G. St A. Sobers	758.3	182	1844	82	22.48
W. A. White	286	83	647	28	23.10
M. C. Carew	32	7	99	4	24.75
L. A. King	493.5	100	1284	47	27.31
A. L. Valentine	306.3	98	822	24	34.25
F. M. Worrell	204	56	480	13	36.92
W. V. Rodriguez	59	6	240	4	60.00

Also bowled: B. F. Butcher 2.3–0–10–1; E. D. McMorris 3–0–26–0.

Test Averages

England Batting

	M	I	NO	R	HS	Av
P. J. Sharpe	3	6	1	267	85*	53.40
E. R. Dexter	5	10	0	340	73	34.00
D. B. Close	5	10	0	315	70	31.50
K. F. Barrington	5	10	0	275	80	27.50
M. J. Stewart	4	8	0	211	87	26.37
J. B. Bolus	2	4	0	105	43	26.25
J. M. Parks	4	8	0	190	57	23.75
F. J. Titmus	4	8	1	145	52*	20.71
G. A. R. Lock	3	6	0	115	56	19.16
J. H. Edrich	3	6	0	103	38	17.16
M. C. Cowdrey	2	4	1	39	19*	13.00
D. Shackleton	4	7	5	20	8	10.00
F. S. Trueman	5	10	1	82	29*	9.11
J. B. Statham	2	4	0	29	14	7.25
D. A. Allen	2	4	1	12	5	4.00

Also batted: K. V. Andrew 3*, 15; P. E. Richardson 2, 14.

England Bowling

	O	M	R	W	Av
F. S. Trueman	236.4	53	594	34	17.47
E. R. Dexter	95	22	227	7	32.42
D. Shackleton	243.2	73	518	15	34.53
G. A. R. Lock	91.5	24	230	6	38.33
F. J. Titmus	101	23	256	6	42.66
D. A. Allen	88.1	32	208	4	52.00
J. B. Statham	81	10	243	3	81.00

Also bowled: D. B. Close 25–5–88–0.

West Indies Batting

	M	I	NO	R	HS	Av
C. C. Hunte	5	10	2	471	182	58.87
R. B. Kanhai	5	9	0	497	92	55.22
B. F. Butcher	5	9	1	383	133	47.87
G. St A. Sobers	5	8	0	322	102	40.25
J. S. Solomon	5	8	0	204	62	25.50
F. M. Worrell	5	8	1	142	74*	20.28
M. C. Carew	2	4	1	57	40	19.00
D. L. Murray	5	8	2	93	34	15.50
W. W. Hall	5	7	1	79	28	13.16
E. D. McMorris	2	4	0	36	16	9.00
C. C. Griffith	5	7	2	32	13*	6.40
L. R. Gibbs	5	7	3	15	6	3.75

Also batted: W. V. Rodriguez 5, 28.

West Indies Bowling

	O	M	R	W	Av
C. C. Griffith	223.5	53	519	32	16.21
L. R. Gibbs	249.3	74	554	26	21.30
G. St A. Sobers	231	50	571	20	28.55
W. W. Hall	178	26	534	16	33.37
F. M. Worrell	45	16	104	3	34.66

England v West Indies 1963 (First Test)

VENUE: Old Trafford

DATE: 6, 7, 8, 10 June. West Indies won the toss

RESULT: West Indies won by 10 wickets

Batted First: West Indies

1 C. C. Hunte	c Titmus by Allen	182	not out	1
2 M. C. Carew	c Andrew b Trueman	16	not out	0
3 R. B. Kanhai	run out	90		
4 B. F. Butcher	lbw b Trueman	22		
5 G. St A Sobers	c Edrich b Allen	64		
6 J. S. Solomon	lbw b Titmus	35		
7 F. M. Worrell*	not out	74		
8 D. L. Murray†	not out	7		
9 W. W. Hall				
10 C. C. Griffith				
11 L. R. Gibbs				
Extras (B 3, LB 7, NB 1)		11		
Total	(6 wkts dec.)	501	(no wkt)	1

Batted Second: England

1 M. J. Stewart	c Murray b Gibbs	37	c Murray b Gibbs	87
2 J. H. Edrich	c Murray b Hall	20	c Hunte b Worrell	38
3 K. F. Barrington	c Murray b Hall	16	(4) b Gibbs	8
4 M. C. Cowdrey	b Hall	4	(5) c Hunte b Gibbs	12
5 E. R. Dexter*	c Worrell b Sobers	73	(6) c Murray b Gibbs	35
6 D. B. Close	c Hunte b Gibbs	30	(7) c Sobers b Gibbs	32
7 F. J. Titmus	c Sobers b Gibbs	0	(8) b Sobers	17
8 D. A. Allen	c Sobers b Gibbs	5	(9) b Gibbs	1
9 F. S. Trueman	c Worrell b Sobers	5	(10) not out	29
10 K. V. Andrew†	not out	3	(3) c Murray b Sobers	15
11 J. B. Statham	b Gibbs	0	b Griffith	7
Extras (B 2, LB 7, NB 3)		12	(B 10, LB 4, NB 1)	15
Total		205		296

Bowling

	O	M	R	W	O	M	R	W
England								
Trueman	40	7	95	2				
Statham	37	6	121	0				
Titmus	40	13	105	1				
Close	10	2	31	0				
Allen	57	22	122	2	0.1	0	1	0
Dexter	12	4	16	0				
West Indies								
Hall	17	4	51	3	14	0	39	0
Griffith	21	4	37	0	8.5	4	11	1
Gibbs	29.3	9	59	5	46	16	98	6
Sobers	22	11	34	2	37	4	122	2
Worrell	1	0	12	0	4	2	11	1

Fall of Wickets

	WI	E	E
	1st	1st	2nd
1st	37	34	93
2nd	188	61	131
3rd	239	67	160
4th	359	108	165
5th	398	181	186
6th	479	190	231
7th		192	254
8th		202	256
9th		202	268
10th		205	296

Umpires: C. S. Elliott and J. G. Langridge   Captain*   Wicket-keeper†

England v West Indies 1963 (Second Test)

VENUE: Lord's
DATE: 20, 21, 22, 24, 25 June. West Indies won the toss
RESULT: Match Drawn

Batted First: West Indies

1 C. C. Hunte	c Close b Trueman	44	c Cowdrey b Shackleton	7
2 E. D. McMorris	lbw b Trueman	16	c Cowdrey b Trueman	8
3 G. St A. Sobers	c Cowdrey b Allen	42	(5) c Parks b Trueman	8
4 R. B. Kanhai	c Edrich b Trueman	73	(3) c Cowdrey b Shackleton	21
5 B. F. Butcher	c Barrington b Trueman	14	(4) lbw b Shackleton	133
6 J. S. Solomon	lbw b Shackleton	56	c Stewart b Allen	5
7 F. M. Worrell*	b Trueman	0	c Stewart b Trueman	33
8 D. L. Murray†	c Cowdrey b Trueman	20	c Parks b Trueman	2
9 W. W. Hall	not out	25	c Parks b Trueman	2
10 C. C. Griffith	c Cowdrey b Shackleton	0	b Shackleton	1
11 L. R. Gibbs	c Stewart b Shackleton	0	not out	1
Extras (B 10, LB 1)		11	(B 5, LB 2, NB 1)	8
Total		301		229

Batted Second: England

1 M. J. Stewart	c Kanhai b Griffith	2	c Solomon b Hall	17
2 J. H. Edrich	c Murray b Griffith	0	c Murray b Hall	8
3 E. R. Dexter*	lbw b Sobers	70	b Gibbs	2
4 K. F. Barrington	c Sobers b Worrell	80	c Murray b Griffith	60
5 M. C. Cowdrey	b Gibbs	4	not out	19
6 D. B. Close	c Murray b Griffith	9	c Murray b Griffith	70
7 J. M. Parks†	b Worrell	35	lbw b Griffith	17
8 F. J. Titmus	not out	52	c McMorris b Hall	11
9 F. S. Trueman	b Hall	10	c Murray b Hall	0
10 D. A. Allen	lbw b Griffith	2	not out	4
11 D. Shackleton	b Griffith	8	run out	4
Extras (B 8, LB 8, NB 9)		25	(B 5, LB 8, NB 3)	16
Total		297	(9 wkts)	228

Bowling

	O	M	R	W	O	M	R	W
England								
Trueman	44	16	100	6	26	9	52	5
Shackleton	50.2	22	93	3	34	14	72	4
Dexter	20	6	41	0				
Close	9	3	21	0				
Allen	10	3	35	1	21	7	50	1
Titmus					17	3	47	0
West Indies								
Hall	18	2	65	1	40	9	93	4
Griffith	26	6	91	5	30	7	59	3
Sobers	18	4	45	1	4	1	4	0
Gibbs	27	9	59	1	17	7	56	1
Worrell	13	6	12	2				

Fall of Wickets

	WI 1st	E 1st	WI 2nd	E 2nd
1st	51	2	15	15
2nd	64	20	15	27
3rd	127	102	64	31
4th	145	115	84	130
5th	219	151	104	158
6th	219	206	214	203
7th	263	235	224	203
8th	297	271	226	219
9th	297	274	228	228
10th	301	297	229	

Umpires: J. S. Buller and W. E. Phillipson Captain* Wicket-keeper†

England v West Indies 1963 (Third Test)

VENUE: Edgbaston

DATE: 4, 5, 6, 8, 9 July. England won the toss

RESULT: England won by 217 runs

Batted First: England

1	P. E. Richardson	b Hall 2	c Murray b Griffith	14
2	M. J. Stewart	lbw b Sobers 39	c Murray b Griffith	27
3	E. R. Dexter*	b Sobers 29	(5) st Murray b Gibbs	57
4	K. F. Barrington	b Sobers 9	(3) b Sobers	1
5	D. B. Close	lbw b Sobers 55	(4) c Sobers b Griffith	13
6	P. J. Sharpe	c Kanhai b Gibbs 23	not out	85
7	J. M. Parks†	c Murray b Sobers 12	c Sobers b Gibbs	5
8	F. J. Titmus	c Griffith b Hall 27	b Gibbs	0
9	F. S. Trueman	b Griffith 4	c Gibbs b Sobers	1
10	G. A. R. Lock	b Griffith 1	b Gibbs	56
11	D. Shackleton	not out 6		
	Extras (LB 6, NB 3)	9	(B 9, LB 9, NB 1)	19
	Total	216	(9 wkts dec.)	278

Batted Second: West Indies

1	C. C. Hunte	b Trueman 18	c Barrington b Trueman	5
2	M. C. Carew	c and b Trueman 40	lbw b Shackleton	1
3	R. B. Kanhai	c Lock b Shackleton 32	c Lock b Trueman	38
4	B. F. Butcher	lbw b Dexter 15	b Dexter	14
5	J. S. Solomon	lbw b Dexter 0	(6) c Parks b Trueman	14
6	G. St A. Sobers	b Trueman 19	(5) c Sharpe b Shackleton	9
7	F. M. Worrell*	b Dexter 1	c Parks b Trueman	0
8	D. L. Murray†	not out 20	c Parks b Trueman	3
9	W. W. Hall	c Sharpe b Dexter 28	b Trueman	0
10	C. C. Griffith	lbw b Trueman 5	lbw b Trueman	0
11	L. R. Gibbs	b Trueman 0	not out	4
	Extras (LB 7, W 1)	8	(LB 2, W 1)	3
	Total	186		91

Bowling

	O	M	R	W	O	M	R	W
West Indies								
Hall	16.4	2	56	2	16	1	47	0
Griffith	21	5	48	2	28	7	55	3
Sobers	31	10	60	5	27	4	80	2
Worrell	14	5	15	0	8	3	28	0
Gibbs	16	7	28	1	26.2	4	49	4
England								
Trueman	26	5	75	5	14.3	2	44	7
Shackleton	21	9	60	1	17	4	37	2
Lock	2	1	5	0				
Dexter	20	5	38	4	3	1	7	1

Fall of Wickets

	E 1st	WI 1st	E 2nd	WI 2nd
1st	2	42	30	2
2nd	50	79	31	10
3rd	72	108	60	38
4th	89	109	69	64
5th	129	128	170	78
6th	172	130	184	80
7th	187	130	184	86
8th	189	178	189	86
9th	200	186	278	86
10th	216	186		91

Umpires: C. S. Elliott and L. H. Gray   Captain*   Wicket-keeper†

England v West Indies 1963 (Fourth Test)

VENUE: Headingley
DATE: 25, 26, 27, 29 July. West Indies won the toss
RESULT: West Indies won by 221 runs

Batted First: West Indies

1 C. C. Hunte	c Parks b Trueman	22	b Trueman	4
2 E. D. McMorris	c Barrington b Shackleton	11	lbw b Trueman	1
3 R. B. Kanhai	b Lock	92	lbw b Shackleton	44
4 B. F. Butcher	c Parks b Dexter	23	c Dexter b Shackleton	78
5 G. St A. Sobers	c and b Lock	102	c Sharpe b Titmus	52
6 J. S. Solomon	c Stewart b Trueman	62	c Titmus b Shackleton	16
7 D. L. Murray†	lbw b Titmus	34	(8) c Lock b Titmus	2
8 F. M. Worrell*	c Close b Lock	25	(7) c Parks b Titmus	0
9 W. W. Hall	c Shackleton b Trueman	15	c Trueman b Titmus	7
10 C. C. Griffith	c Stewart b Trueman	1	not out	12
11 L. R. Gibbs	not out	0	c Sharpe b Lock	6
Extras (B 4, LB 5, W 1)		10	(LB 7)	7
Total		397		229

Batted Second: England

1 M. J. Stewart	c Gibbs b Griffith	2	b Sobers	0
2 J. B. Bolus	c Hunte b Hall	14	c Gibbs b Sobers	43
3 E. R. Dexter*	b Griffith	8	lbw b Griffith	10
4 K. F. Barrington	c Worrell b Gibbs	25	lbw b Sobers	32
5 D. B. Close	b Griffith	0	c Solomon b Griffith	56
6 P. J. Sharpe	c Kanhai b Griffith	0	c Kanhai b Gibbs	13
7 J. M. Parks†	c Gibbs b Griffith	22	lbw b Gibbs	57
8 F. J. Titmus	lbw b Gibbs	33	st Murray b Gibbs	5
9 F. S. Trueman	c Hall b Gibbs	4	c Griffith b Gibbs	5
10 G. A. R. Lock	b Griffith	53	c Murray b Griffith	1
11 D. Shackleton	not out	1	not out	1
Extras (B 4, LB 6, NB 2)		12	(B 3, LB 5)	8
Total		174		231

Bowling

	O	M	R	W	O	M	R	W
England								
Trueman	46	10	117	4	13	1	46	2
Shackleton	42	10	88	1	26	2	63	3
Dexter	23	4	68	1	2	0	15	0
Titmus	25	5	60	1	19	2	44	4
Lock	28.4	9	54	3	7.1	0	54	1
West Indies								
Hall	13	2	61	1	5	1	12	0
Griffith	21	5	36	6	18	5	45	3
Gibbs	14	2	50	3	37.4	12	76	4
Sobers	6	1	15	0	32	6	90	3

Fall of Wickets

	WI 1st	E 1st	WI 2nd	E 2nd
1st	28	13	1	0
2nd	42	19	20	23
3rd	71	32	85	82
4th	214	32	181	95
5th	287	34	186	130
6th	348	69	188	199
7th	355	87	196	221
8th	379	93	206	224
9th	389	172	212	225
10th	397	174	229	231

Umpires: J. G. Langridge and W. E. Phillipson Captain* Wicket-keeper†

England v West Indies 1963 (Fifth Test)

VENUE: Kennington Oval
DATE: 22, 23, 24, 26 August. England won the toss
RESULT: West Indies won by 8 wickets

Batted First: England

1 J. B. Bolus	c Murray b Sobers	33	c Gibbs b Sobers	15
2 J. H. Edrich	c Murray b Sobers	25	c Murray b Griffith	12
3 E. R. Dexter*	c and b Griffith	29	c Murray b Sobers	27
4 K. F. Barrington	c Sobers b Gibbs	16	b Griffith	28
5 D. B. Close	b Griffith	46	lbw b Sobers	4
6 P. J. Sharpe	c Murray b Griffith	63	c Murray b Hall	83
7 J. M. Parks†	c Kanhai b Griffith	19	lbw b Griffith	23
8 F. S. Trueman	b Griffith	19	c Sobers b Hall	5
9 G. A. R. Lock	hit wkt b Griffith	4	b Hall	0
10 J. B. Statham	b Hall	8	b Hall	14
11 D. Shackleton	not out	0	not out	0
Extras (B 4, LB 2, NB 7)		13	(B 5, LB 3, NB 4)	12
Total		275		223

Batted Second: West Indies

1 C. C. Hunte	c Parks b Shackleton	80	not out	108
2 W. V. Rodriguez	c Lock b Statham	5	c Lock b Dexter	28
3 R. B. Kanhai	b Lock	30	c Bolus b Lock	77
4 B. F. Butcher	run out	53	not out	31
5 G. St. A. Sobers	run out	26		
6 J. S. Solomon	c Trueman b Statham	16		
7 F. M. Worrell*	b Statham	9		
8 D. L. Murray†	c Lock b Trueman	5		
9 W. W. Hall	b Trueman	2		
10 C. C. Griffith	not out	13		
11 L. R. Gibbs	b Trueman	4		
Extras (LB 3)		3	(B 4, LB 7)	11
Total		246	(2 wkts)	255

Bowling

	O	M	R	W	O	M	R	W
West Indies								
Hall	22.2	2	71	1	16	3	39	4
Griffith	27	4	71	6	23	7	66	3
Sobers	21	4	44	2	33	6	77	3
Gibbs	27	7	50	1	9	1	29	0
Worrell	5	0	26	0				
England								
Trueman	26.1	2	65	3	1	1	0	0
Statham	22	3	68	3	22	2	54	0
Shackleton	21	5	37	1	32	7	68	0
Lock	29	6	65	1	25	8	52	1
Dexter	6	1	8	0	9	1	34	1
Close					6	0	36	0

Fall of Wickets

	E 1st	WI 1st	E 2nd	WI 2nd
1st	59	10	29	78
2nd	64	72	31	191
3rd	103	152	64	
4th	115	185	69	
5th	216	198	121	
6th	224	214	173	
7th	254	221	196	
8th	258	225	196	
9th	275	233	218	
10th	275	246	223	

Umpires: J. S. Buller and A. E. G. Rhodes Captain* Wicket-keeper†

Appendix 4 **1966**

Tests: Played 5, Won 3, Drawn 1, Lost 1

First-class Matches: Played 27, Won 8, Drawn 15, Lost 4

All Matches: Played 34, Won 13, Drawn 16, Lost 5

Won: England (3), Duke of Norfolk's XI, Cambridge University, Derbyshire, Minor Counties, Kent, Surrey, Warwickshire (2), Leicestershire, Rest of the World.

Drawn: England, Worcestershire, Oxford University, Nottinghamshire, MCC, Lancashire, Yorkshire, Gloucestershire, Essex, Middlesex, Somerset, President of MCC's XI, Glamorgan, Scotland, Hampshire, A. E. R. Gilligan's XI.

Lost: England, Sussex, Northamptonshire, T. N. Pearce's XI, An England XI.

First-class Averages

Batting

	M	I	NO	R	HS	Av	100	Ct	St
G. St A. Sobers	18	25	3	1349	174	61.31	4	23	—
B. F. Butcher	19	25	2	1105	209*	48.04	3	8	—
S. M. Nurse	19	26	1	1105	155	44.20	3	17	—
R. B. Kanhai	19	28	1	1028	192*	38.07	3	13	—
D. A. J. Holford	19	26	6	759	107*	37.95	2	12	—
C. C. Hunte	19	27	0	970	206	35.92	2	9	—
J. S. Solomon	17	21	4	585	104*	34.41	1	6	—
P. D. Lashley	18	24	2	647	78	29.40	—	15	—
E. D. McMorris	17	25	3	634	157*	28.81	2	2	—
M. C. Carew	18	29	1	720	132	25.71	1	9	—
C. C. Griffith	16	20	6	297	63*	21.21	—	4	—
R. C. Brancker	16	19	1	329	37	18.27	—	10	—
D. W. Allan	14	15	2	209	56	16.07	—	27	8
W. W. Hall	19	21	5	246	34*	15.37	—	6	—
J. L. Hendriks	14	16	5	144	20	13.09	—	24	10
R. A. Cohen	18	15	8	72	32	10.28	—	9	—
L. R. Gibbs	17	18	8	98	19	9.80	—	9	—

Bowling

	O	M	R	W	Av
C. C. Griffith	357	86	998	49	20.36
G. St A. Sobers	557.2	158	1235	60	20.58
R. A. Cohen	283.3	59	969	40	24.22
L. R. Gibbs	608.4	207	1190	47	25.31
R. C. Brancker	330.4	81	861	33	26.09
D. A. J. Holford	507	117	1459	51	28.60
P. D. Lashley	162.2	40	407	14	29.07
M. C. Carew	233	78	531	17	31.23
W. W. Hall	439	104	1280	39	32.82

Also bowled: R. B. Kanhai 5.1–0–47–1; C. C. Hunte 32–8–93–1; J. S. Solomon 54–10–204–1; B. F. Butcher 2–0–7–0; S. M. Nurse 2–0–3–0.

Test Averages

England Batting

	M	I	NO	R	HS	Av
T. W. Graveney	4	7	1	459	165	76.50
C. Milburn	4	8	2	316	126*	52.66
B. L. D'Oliveira	4	6	0	256	88	42.66
R. W. Barber	2	3	0	97	55	32.33
M. C. Cowdrey	4	8	0	252	96	31.50
G. Boycott	4	7	0	186	71	26.57
J. M. Parks	4	8	0	181	91	22.62
J. A. Snow	3	5	2	62	59*	20.66
K. Higgs	5	8	0	147	63	18.37
W. E. Russell	2	4	0	61	26	15.25
K. F. Barrington	2	4	0	59	30	14.75
F. J. Titmus	3	5	0	61	22	12.20
D. L. Underwood	2	4	2	22	12*	11.00
R. Illingworth	2	3	0	7	4	2.33
I. J. Jones	2	3	3	0	0*	—

Also batted: J. T. Murray 112; D. A. Allen 37, 1; J. H. Edrich 35; D. J. Brown 14, 10; D. L. Amiss 17; M. J. K. Smith 5, 6; B. R. Knight 6; D. B. Close 4.

England Bowling

	O	M	R	W	Av
K. Higgs	236.4	49	611	24	25.45
R. W. Barber	51.1	7	182	6	30.33
J. A. Snow	138.5	29	451	12	37.58
F. J. Titmus	81	20	190	5	38.00
B. L. D'Oliveira	160	48	329	8	41.12
R. Illingworth	63	24	165	4	41.25
B. R. Knight	51	3	169	4	42.25

Also bowled: D. A. Allen 31.1–8–104–2; D. B. Close 12–3–28–1; D. J. Brown 28–4–84–0; D. L. Underwood 69–25–172–1; I. J. Jones 74–11–259–1.

West Indies Batting

	M	I	NO	R	HS	Av
G. St A. Sobers	5	8	1	722	174	103.14
S. M. Nurse	5	8	0	501	137	62.62
B. F. Butcher	5	8	1	420	209*	60.00
R. B. Kanhai	5	8	0	324	104	40.50
D. A. J. Holford	5	8	2	227	105*	37.83
C. C. Hunte	5	8	0	243	135	30.37
P. D. Lashley	2	3	0	81	49	27.00
W. W. Hall	5	6	2	69	30*	17.25
C. C. Griffith	5	6	1	82	30	16.40
E. D. McMorris	2	3	0	26	14	8.66
L. R. Gibbs	5	6	3	22	12	7.33
D. W. Allan	2	2	0	14	13	7.00
J. L. Hendriks	3	4	1	11	9*	3.66

Also batted: M. C. Carew 2, 0.

West Indies Bowling

	O	M	R	W	Av
L. R. Gibbs	273.4	103	520	21	24.76
G. St A. Sobers	269.4	78	545	20	27.25
W. W. Hall	175.3	35	555	18	30.83
C. C. Griffith	144.3	27	438	14	31.28
D. A. J. Holford	90.5	13	302	5	60.40

Also bowled: P. D. Lashley 3–2–1–1; M. C. Carew 3–0–11–1; C. C. Hunte 13–2–41–0.

England v West Indies 1966 (First Test)

VENUE: Old Trafford, Manchester
DATE: 2, 3, 4 June. West Indies won the toss
RESULT: West Indies won by an innings and 40 runs

Batted First: West Indies

1 C. C. Hunte	c Smith b Higgs	135
2 E. D. McMorris	c Russell b Higgs	11
3 R. B. Kanhai	b Higgs	0
4 B. F. Butcher	c Parks b Titmus	44
5 S. M. Nurse	b Titmus	49
6 G. St A. Sobers*	c Cowdrey b Titmus	161
7 D. A. J. Holford	c Smith b Allen	32
8 D. W. Allan†	lbw b Titmus	1
9 C. C. Griffith	lbw b Titmus	30
10 W. W. Hall	b Allen	1
11 L. R. Gibbs	not out	1
Extras (B 8, LB 10, NB 1)		19
Total		484

Batted Second: England

1 C. Milburn	run out	0	b Gibbs	94
2 W. E. Russell	c Sobers b Gibbs	26	b Griffith	20
3 K. F. Barrington	c and b Griffith	5	c Nurse b Holford	30
4 M. C. Cowdrey	c and b Gibbs	12	c Butcher b Sobers	69
5 M. J. K. Smith*	c Butcher b Gibbs	5	b Gibbs	6
6 J. M. Parks†	c Nurse b Holford	43	c and b Sobers	11
7 F. J. Titmus	b Holford	15	c Butcher b Sobers	12
8 D. A. Allen	c Sobers b Gibbs	37	c Allan b Gibbs	1
9 D. J. Brown	b Gibbs	14	c Sobers b Gibbs	10
10 K. Higgs	c Sobers b Holford	1	st Allan b Gibbs	5
11 I. J. Jones	not out	0	not out	0
Extras (B 1, LB 4, NB 4)		9	(B 11, LB 1, NB 7)	19
Total		167		277

Bowling

	O	M	R	W	O	M	R	W
England								
Jones	28	6	100	0				
Brown	28	4	84	0				
Higgs	31	5	94	3				
Allen	31.1	8	104	2				
Titmus	35	10	83	5				
West Indies								
Hall	14	6	43	0	5	0	28	0
Griffith	10	3	28	1	6	1	25	1
Sobers	7	1	16	0	42	11	87	3
Gibbs	28.1	13	37	5	41	16	69	5
Holford	15	4	34	3	14	2	49	1

Fall of Wickets

	WI 1st	E 1st	E 2nd
1st	38	11	53
2nd	42	24	142
3rd	116	42	166
4th	215	48	184
5th	283	65	203
6th	410	85	217
7th	411	143	218
8th	471	153	268
9th	482	163	276
10th	484	167	277

Umpires: J. S. Buller and C. S. Elliott Captain* Wicket-keeper†

England v West Indies 1966 (Second Test)

VENUE: Lord's

DATE: 16, 17, 18, 20, 21 June. West Indies won the toss

RESULT: Match Drawn

Batted First: West Indies

1	C. C. Hunte	c Parks b Higgs	18	c Milburn b Knight	13
2	M. C. Carew	c Parks b Higgs	2	c Knight b Higgs	0
3	R. B. Kanhai	c Titmus b Higgs	25	c Parks b Knight	40
4	B. F. Butcher	c Milburn b Knight	49	lbw b Higgs	3
5	S. M. Nurse	b D'Oliveira	64	c Parks b D'Oliveira	35
6	G. St A. Sobers*	lbw b Knight	46	not out	163
7	D. A. J. Holford	b Jones	26	not out	105
8	D. W. Allan†	c Titmus b Higgs	13		
9	C. C. Griffith	lbw b Higgs	5		
10	W. W. Hall	not out	8		
11	L. R. Gibbs	c Parks b Higgs	4		
	Extras (B 2, LB 7)		9	(LB 8, NB 2)	10
	Total		269	(5 wkts dec.)	369

Batted Second: England

1	G. Boycott	c Griffith b Gibbs	60	c Allan b Griffith	25
2	C. Milburn	lbw b Hall	6	not out	126
3	T. W. Graveney	c Allan b Hall	96	(6) not out	30
4	K. F. Barrington	b Sobers	19	(3) b Griffith	5
5	M. C. Cowdrey*	c Gibbs b Hall	9	(4) c Allan b Hall	5
6	J. M. Parks†	lbw b Carew	91	(5) b Hall	0
7	B. L. D'Oliveira	run out	27		
8	B. R. Knight	b Griffith	6		
9	F. J. Titmus	c Allan b Hall	6		
10	K. Higgs	c Holford b Gibbs	13		
11	I. J. Jones	not out	0		
	Extras (B 7, LB 10, NB 5)		22	(B 4, LB 2,)	6
	Total		355	(4 wkts)	197

Bowling

	O	M	R	W	O	M	R	W
England								
Jones	21	3	64	1	25	2	95	0
Higgs	33	9	91	6	34	5	82	2
Knight	21	0	63	2	30	3	106	2
Titmus	5	0	18	0	19	3	30	0
D'Oliveria	14	5	24	1	25	7	46	1
West Indies								
Sobers	39	12	89	1	8	4	8	0
Hall	36	2	106	4	14	1	65	2
Griffith	28	4	79	1	11	2	43	2
Gibbs	37.3	18	48	2	13	4	40	0
Carew	3	0	11	1				
Holford					9	1	35	0

Fall of Wickets

	WI 1st	E 1st	WI 2nd	E 2nd
1st	8	8	2	37
2nd	42	123	22	43
3rd	53	164	25	67
4th	119	198	91	67
5th	205	203	95	
6th	213	251		
7th	252	266		
8th	252	296		
9th	261	355		
10th	269	355		

Umpires: J. S. Buller and W. F. F. Price Captain* Wicket-keeper†

England v West Indies 1966 (Third Test)

VENUE: Trent Bridge
DATE: 30 June, 1, 2, 4, 5 July. West Indies won the toss
RESULT: West Indies won by 139 runs

Batted First: West Indies

1 C. C. Hunte	lbw b Higgs 9	c Graveney b D'Oliveira 12
2 P. D. Lashley	c Parks b Snow 49	lbw b D'Oliveira 23
3 R. B. Kanhai	c Underwood b Higgs 32	c Cowdrey b Higgs 63
4 B. F. Butcher	b Snow 5	not out 209
5 S. M. Nurse	c Illingworth b Snow 93	lbw b Higgs 53
6 G. St A. Sobers*	c Parks b Snow 3	c Underwood b Higgs 94
7 D. A. J. Holford	lbw b D'Oliveira 11	not out 17
8 J. L. Hendriks†	b D'Oliveira 2	
9 C. C. Griffith	c Cowdrey b Higgs 14	
10 W. W. Hall	b Higgs 12	
11 L. R. Gibbs	not out 0	
Extras (B 3, LB 2)	5	(LB 6, W 5) 11
Total	235	(5 wkts dec.) 482

Batted Second: England

1 G. Boycott	lbw b Sobers 0	c Sobers b Griffith 71
2 C. Milburn	c Sobers b Hall 7	c Griffith b Hall 12
3 W. E. Russell	b Hall 4	c Sobers b Gibbs 11
4 T. W. Graveney	c Holford b Sobers 109	c Hendriks b Griffith 32
5 M. C. Cowdrey*	c Hendriks b Griffith 96	c Sobers b Gibbs 32
6 J. M. Parks†	c Butcher b Sobers 11	c Lashley b Hall 7
7 B. L. D'Oliveira	b Hall 76	lbw b Griffith 54
8 R. Illingworth	c Lashley b Griffith 0	c Lashley b Sobers 4
9 K. Higgs	c Lashley b Sobers 5	c Sobers b Gibbs 4
10 J. A. Snow	b Hall 0	b Griffith 3
11 D. L. Underwood	not out 12	not out 10
Extras (LB 2, NB 3)	5	(B 8, LB 2, NB 3) 13
Total	325	253

Bowling

	O	M	R	W	O	M	R	W
England								
Snow	25	7	82	4	38	10	117	0
Higgs	25.4	3	71	4	38	6	109	3
D'Oliveira	30	14	51	2	34	8	77	2
Underwood	2	1	5	0	43	15	86	0
Illingworth	8	1	21	0	25	7	82	0
West Indies								
Sobers	49	12	90	4	31	6	71	1
Hall	34.3	8	105	4	16	3	52	2
Griffith	20	5	62	2	13.3	3	34	4
Gibbs	23	9	40	0	48	16	83	3
Holford	8	2	23	0				

Fall of Wickets

	WI 1st	E 1st	WI 2nd	E 2nd
1st	19	0	29	32
2nd	68	10	65	71
3rd	80	13	175	125
4th	140	182	282	132
5th	144	221	455	142
6th	180	238		176
7th	190	247		181
8th	215	255		222
9th	228	260		240
10th	235	325		253

Umpires: C. S. Elliott and A. Jepson Captain* Wicket-keeper†

England v West Indies 1966 (Fourth Test)

VENUE: Headingley
DATE: 4, 5, 6, 8 August. West Indies won the toss
RESULT: West Indies won by an innings and 55 runs

Batted First: West Indies

1 C. C. Hunte	lbw b Snow	48
2 P. D. Lashley	b Higgs	9
3 R. B. Kanhai	c Graveney b Underwood	45
4 B. F. Butcher	c Parks b Higgs	38
5 S. M. Nurse	c Titmus b Snow	137
6 G. St. A. Sobers*	b Barber	174
7 D. A. J. Holford	b Higgs	24
8 C. C. Griffith	b Higgs	0
9 J. L. Hendriks†	not out	9
10 W. W. Hall	b Snow	1
11 L. R. Gibbs	not out	2
Extras (B 1, LB 12)		13
Total	(9 wkts dec.)	500

Batted Second: England

1 G. Boycott	c Holford b Hall	12	c Hendriks b Lashley	14
2 R. W. Barber	c Hendriks b Griffith	6	b Sobers	55
3 C. Milburn	not out	29	(7) b Gibbs	42
4 T. W. Graveney	b Hall	8	b Gibbs	19
5 M. C. Cowdrey*	b Hall	17	lbw b Gibbs	12
6 B. L. D'Oliveira	c Hall b Griffith	88	(3) c Butcher b Sobers	7
7 J. M. Parks†	lbw b Sobers	2	(6) c Nurse b Gibbs	16
8 F. J. Titmus	c Hendriks b Sobers	6	b Gibbs	22
9 K. Higgs	c Nurse b Sobers	49	c Hunte b Sobers	7
10 D. L. Underwood	c Gibbs b Sobers	0	c Kanhai b Gibbs	0
11 J. A. Snow	c Holford b Sobers	0	not out	0
Extras (B 12, LB 11)		23	(B 8, LB 1, NB 2)	11
Total		240		205

Bowling

	O	M	R	W	O	M	R	W
England								
Snow	42	6	146	3				
Higgs	43	11	94	4				
D'Oliveira	19	3	52	0				
Titmus	22	7	59	0				
Underwood	24	9	81	1				
Barber	14	2	55	1				
West Indies								
Hall	17	5	47	3	8	2	24	0
Griffith	12	2	37	2	12	0	52	0
Sobers	19.3	4	41	5	20.1	5	39	3
Gibbs	20	5	49	0	19	6	39	6
Holford	10	3	43	0	9	0	39	0
Lashley					3	2	1	1

Fall of Wickets

	WI 1st	E 1st	E 2nd
1st	37	10	28
2nd	102	18	70
3rd	122	42	84
4th	154	49	109
5th	419	63	128
6th	467	83	133
7th	467	179	184
8th	489	238	205
9th	491	240	205
10th		240	205

Umpires: J. S. Buller and C. S. Elliott Captain* Wicket-keeper†

England v West Indies 1966 (Fifth Test)

VENUE: Kennington Oval
DATE: 18, 19, 20, 22 August. West Indies won the toss
RESULT: England won by an innings and 34 runs

Batted First: West Indies

1	C. C. Hunte	b Higgs	1	c Murray b Snow	7
2	E. D. McMorris	b Snow	14	c Murray b Snow	1
3	R. B. Kanhai	c Graveney b Illingworth	104	b D'Oliveira	15
4	B. F. Butcher	c Illingworth b Close	12	c Barber b Illingworth	60
5	S. M. Nurse	c Graveney b D'Oliveira	0	c Edrich b Barber	70
6	G. St A. Sobers*	c Graveney b Barber	81	(7) c Close b Snow	0
7	D. A. J. Holford	c D'Oliveira b Illingworth	5	(6) run out	7
8	J. L. Hendriks†	b Barber	0	b Higgs	0
9	C. C. Griffith	c Higgs b Barber	4	not out	29
10	W. W. Hall	not out	30	c D'Oliveira b Illi'worth	17
11	L. R. Gibbs	c Murray b Snow	12	c and b Barber	3
	Extras	(B 1, LB 3, NB 1)	5	(B 1, LB 14, NB 1)	16
	Total		268		225

Batted Second: England

1	G. Boycott	b Hall	4
2	R. W. Barber	c Nurse b Sobers	36
3	J. H. Edrich	c Hendriks b Sobers	35
4	T. W. Graveney	run out	165
5	D. L. Amiss	lbw b Hall	17
6	B. L. D'Oliveira	b Hall	4
7	D. B. Close*	run out	4
8	R. Illingworth	c Hendriks b Griffith	3
9	J. T. Murray†	lbw b Sobers	112
10	K. Higgs	c and b Holford	63
11	J. A. Snow	not out	59
	Extras	(B 8, LB 14, NB 3)	25
	Total		527

Bowling

	O	M	R	W	O	M	R	W
England								
Snow	20.5	1	66	2	13	5	40	3
Higgs	17	4	52	1	15	6	18	1
D'Oliveira	21	7	35	1	17	4	44	1
Close	9	2	21	1	3	1	7	0
Barber	15	3	49	3	22.1	2	78	2
Illingworth	15	7	40	2	15	9	22	2
West Indies								
Hall	31	8	85	3				
Griffith	32	7	78	1				
Sobers	54	23	104	3				
Holford	25.5	1	79	1				
Gibbs	44	16	115	0				
Hunte	13	2	41	0				

Fall of Wickets

	WI 1st	E 1st	WI 2nd
1st	1	6	5
2nd	56	72	12
3rd	73	85	50
4th	74	126	107
5th	196	130	137
6th	218	150	137
7th	218	166	142
8th	223	383	168
9th	223	399	204
10th	268	527	225

Umpires: J. S. Buller and C. S. Elliott Captain* Wicket-keeper†

Appendix 5 **1969**

Tests: Played 3, Drawn 1, Lost 2

First-class Matches: Played 19, Won 2, Drawn 14, Lost 3, Abandoned 1

All Matches: Played 22, Won 3, Drawn 15, Lost 4, Abandoned 1

Won: Somerset, Hampshire, Duke of Norfolk's XI.

Drawn: England, D. H. Robins's XI, Worcestershire, Lancashire, Oxford/Cambridge XI, Kent, Gloucestershire, Yorkshire, MCC, Minor Counties, Nottinghamshire, Surrey, Ireland, Glamorgan, Leicestershire.

Lost: England (2), Northamptonshire, Ireland.

Abandoned: Warwickshire

First-class Averages

Batting

	M	I	NO	R	HS	Av	100	Ct	St
B. F. Butcher	15	20	4	984	151	61.50	3	2	—
C. H. Lloyd	16	21	5	904	201*	56.50	2	6	—
R. C. Fredericks	18	29	4	1132	168*	45.28	3	14	—
M. C. Carew	12	18	3	677	172*	45.13	3	8	—
C. A. Davis	16	25	5	848	106*	42.40	2	3	—
G. St A. Sobers	12	15	2	432	81	33.23	—	12	—
G. S. Camacho	16	25	1	746	101	31.08	1	10	—
M. L. C. Foster	14	19	4	396	87*	26.40	—	2	—
J. L. Hendriks	10	8	2	106	69*	17.66	—	11	3
P. Roberts	11	9	3	104	35*	17.33	—	2	—
J. N. Shepherd	13	16	2	186	32	13.28	—	6	—
V. A. Holder	13	11	2	104	35	11.55	—	2	—
T. M. Findlay	10	14	0	134	23	9.44	—	25	—
L. R. Gibbs	13	11	5	47	18*	7.83	—	8	—
G. C. Shillingford	11	8	1	32	10	4.57	—	1	—
P. S. Blair	9	5	3	4	4*	2.00	—	2	—

Bowling

	O	M	R	W	Av
B. F. Butcher	37	6	103	6	17.16
G. C. Shillingford	221.2	41	669	36	18.58
J. N. Shepherd	329.3	100	803	29	27.68
G. St Sobers	267.1	78	623	22	28.31
V. A. Holder	367.5	112	907	30	30.23
M. L. C. Foster	88.4	25	248	7	35.42
P. D. Blair	130.1	16	509	14	36.35
M. C. Carew	76.4	16	261	7	37.28
L. R. Gibbs	352.1	109	720	19	37.89
P. Roberts	279	84	744	16	46.50
C. H. Lloyd	37.5	9	106	2	53.00
C. A. Davis	182.2	39	479	7	69.83

Also bowled: G. S. Camacho 13–2–31–1; R. C. Fredericks 4–0–16–0.

Test Averages

England Batting

	M	I	NO	R	HS	Av
G. Boycott	3	6	1	270	125	54.00
R. Illingworth	3	5	1	163	113	40.75
J. H. Edrich	3	6	1	169	79	33.80
J. H. Hampshire	2	4	0	135	107	33.75
B. L. D'Oliveira	3	5	0	162	57	32.40
A. P. E. Knott	3	5	0	139	53	27.80
J. A. Snow	3	4	3	25	15*	25.00
P. J. Sharpe	3	5	0	120	86	24.00
B. R. Knight	3	5	1	66	31	16.50
D. J. Brown	3	4	0	62	34	15.50
D. L. Underwood	2	3	1	31	16	15.50

Also batted: P. H. Parfitt 4, 39; T. W. Graveney 75.

England Bowling

	O	M	R	W	Av
D. L. Underwood	53	29	101	6	16.83
D. J. Brown	110.3	25	288	14	20.57
B. R. Knight	120.1	29	279	11	25.36
J. A. Snow	139.3	26	406	15	27.06
B. L. D'Oliveira	75	25	169	4	42.25
R. Illingworth	93	32	218	5	43.60

Also bowled: P. H. Parfitt 1–0–8–0.

West Indies Batting

	M	I	NO	R	HS	Av
G. S. Camacho	2	4	0	187	71	46.75
B. F. Butcher	3	6	0	238	91	39.66
C. A. Davis	3	6	0	208	103	34.66
R. C. Fredericks	3	6	0	204	64	34.00
C. H. Lloyd	3	6	0	183	70	30.50
G. St A. Sobers	3	6	1	150	50*	30.00
V. A. Holder	3	6	0	80	35	13.33
J. N. Shepherd	3	5	0	65	32	13.00
T. M. Findlay	2	4	0	51	23	12.75
L. R. Gibbs	3	6	3	34	18*	11.33
G. C. Shillingford	2	3	1	11	5	5.50

Also batted: M. C. Carew 1, 44; M. L. C. Foster 4, 3; J. L. Hendriks 1, 5.

West Indies Bowling

	O	M	R	W	Av
J. N. Shepherd	137.5	44	266	12	22.16
G. C. Shillingford	59.4	12	160	6	26.66
G. St A. Sobers	145	47	318	11	28.90
V. A. Holder	148.5	52	335	9	37.22
L. R. Gibbs	168.4	57	317	6	52.83

Also bowled: B. F. Butcher 3–1–6–0; M. L. C. Foster 2–0–7–0; M. C. Carew 11–3–19–0; C. A. Davis 20–8–32–1.

England v West Indies 1969 (First Test)

VENUE: Old Trafford
DATE: 12, 13, 14, 16, 17 June. England won the toss
RESULT: England won by 10 wickets

Batted First: England

1 G. Boycott	lbw b Shepherd	128	not out 1
2 J. H. Edrich	run out	58	not out 9
3 P. J. Sharpe	b Gibbs	2	
4 T. W. Graveney	b Holder	75	
5 B. L. D'Oliveira	c Hendriks b Shepherd	57	
6 A. P. E. Knott†	c Gibbs b Shepherd	0	
7 R. Illingworth*	c and b Gibbs	21	
8 B. R. Knight	lbw b Shepherd	31	
9 D. J. Brown	b Sobers	15	
10 D. L. Underwood	not out	11	
11 J. A. Snow	b Shepherd	0	
Extras (B 5, LB 9, W 1)		15	(LB 1, NB 1) 2
Total		413	(no wkt) 12

Batted Second: West Indies

1 R. C. Fredericks	c Graveney b Snow	0	c Ill'worth b Underwood	64
2 M. C. Carew	b Brown	1	c Sharpe b D'Oliveira	44
3 B. F. Butcher	lbw b Snow	31	lbw b Knight	48
4 C. A. Davis	c D'Oliveira b Brown	34	c Underwood b Ill'worth	24
5 G. St A. Sobers*	c Edrich b Brown	10	c Sharpe b Knight	48
6 C. H. Lloyd	b Snow	32	c Knott b Brown	13
7 M. L. C. Foster	st Knott b Underwood	4	lbw b Brown	3
8 J. N. Shepherd	c Illingworth b Snow	9	lbw b Snow	13
9 J. L. Hendriks†	c Edrich b Brown	1	not out	5
10 V. A. Holder	run out	19	lbw b Brown	0
11 L. R. Gibbs	run out	1	b Snow	0
Extras (LB 3, NB 2)		5	(B 4, LB 8, NB 1)	13
Total		147		275

Bowling

	O	M	R	W	O	M	R	W
West Indies								
Sobers	27	7	78	1	2	1	1	0
Holder	38	11	93	1	2.5	1	9	0
Shepherd	58.5	19	104	5				
Gibbs	60	22	96	2				
Davis	1	0	1	0				
Carew	11	3	19	0				
Foster	2	0	7	0				
England								
Snow	15	2	54	4	22.3	4	76	2
Brown	13	1	39	4	22	3	59	3
Knight	2	0	11	0	12	3	15	2
Illingworth	6	2	23	0	30	12	52	1
Underwood	12	6	15	1	19	11	31	1
D'Oliveira					9	2	29	1

Fall of Wickets

	E	WI	WI
	1st	1st	2nd
1st	112	0	92
2nd	121	5	138
3rd	249	58	180
4th	307	72	202
5th	314	83	234
6th	343	92	256
7th	365	119	258
8th	390	126	273
9th	411	139	274
10th	413	147	275

Umpires: J. S. Buller and C. S. Elliott Captain* Wicket-keeper†

England v West Indies 1969 (Second Test)

VENUE: Lord's

DATE: 26, 27, 28, 30 June, 1 July. West Indies won the toss

RESULT: Match Drawn

Batted First: West Indies

1 R. C. Fredericks	c Hampshire b Knight	63	c Hampshire b Illi'worth	60
2 G. S. Camacho	c Sharpe b Snow	67	b D'Oliveira	45
3 C. A. Davis	c Knott b Brown	103	c Illingworth b D'Oliveira	0
4 B. F. Butcher	c Hampshire b Brown	9	b Illingworth	24
5 G. St A. Sobers*	run out	29	(7) not out	50
6 C. H. Lloyd	c Illingworth b Brown	18	(5) c Knott b Snow	70
7 J. N. Shepherd	c Edrich b Snow	32	(6) c Sharpe b Illingworth	11
8 T. M. Findlay†	b Snow	23	c Sharpe b Knight	11
9 V. A. Holder	lbw b Snow	6	run out	7
10 L. R. Gibbs	not out	18	b Knight	5
11 G. C. Shillingford	c Knott b Snow	3		
Extras (B 5, LB 4)		9	(B 4, LB 7, NB 1)	12
Total		380	(9 wkts dec.)	295

Batted Second: England

1 G. Boycott	c Findlay b Shepherd	23	c Butcher b Shilli'ford	106
2 J. H. Edrich	c Fredericks b Holder	7	c Camacho b Holder	1
3 P. H. Parfitt	c Davis b Sobers	4	c Findlay b Shepherd	39
4 B. L. D'Oliveira	c Shepherd b Sobers	0	c Fredericks b Gibbs	18
5 P. J. Sharpe	b Holder	11	c Davis b Sobers	86
6 J. H. Hampshire	lbw b Shepherd	107	run out	5
7 A. P. E. Knott†	b Shillingford	53	(8) b Shillingford	11
8 R. Illingworth*	c and b Gibbs	113	(7) not out	9
9 B. R. Knight	lbw b Shillingford	0	not out	1
10 D. J. Brown	c Findlay b Shepherd	1		
11 J. A. Snow	not out	9		
Extras (B 1, LB 5, NB 10)		16	(B 9, LB 5, NB 5)	19
Total		344	(7 wkts)	295

Bowling

	O	M	R	W	O	M	R	W
England								
Snow	39	5	114	5	22	4	69	1
Brown	38	8	99	3	9	3	25	0
Knight	38	11	65	1	27.5	6	78	2
D'Oliveira	26	10	46	0	15	2	45	2
Illingworth	16	4	39	0	27	9	66	3
Parfitt	1	0	8	0				
West Indies								
Sobers	26	12	57	2	29	8	72	1
Holder	38	16	83	2	11	4	36	1
Shilli'ford	19	4	53	2	13	4	30	2
Shepherd	43	14	74	3	12	3	45	1
Gibbs	27.4	9	53	1	41	14	93	1
Davis	1	0	2	0				
Butcher	3	1	6	0				

Fall of Wickets

	WI 1st	E 1st	WI 2nd	E 2nd
1st	106	19	73	1
2nd	151	37	73	94
3rd	167	37	128	137
4th	217	37	135	263
5th	247	61	191	271
6th	324	189	232	272
7th	336	249	263	292
8th	343	250	280	
9th	376	261	295	
10th	380	344		

Umpires: J. S. Buller and A. E. Fagg Captain* Wicket-keeper†

England v West Indies 1969 (Third Test)

VENUE: Headingley

DATE: 10, 11, 12, 14, 15 July. England won the toss

RESULT: England won by 30 runs

Batted First: England

1 G. Boycott	lbw b Sobers	12	c Findlay b Sobers	0
2 J. H. Edrich	lbw b Shepherd	79	lbw b Sobers	15
3 P. J. Sharpe	c Findlay b Holder	6	lbw b Sobers	15
4 J. H. Hampshire	c Findlay b Holder	1	lbw b Shillingford	22
5 B. L. D'Oliveira	c Sobers b Shepherd	48	c Sobers b Davis	39
6 A. P. E. Knott†	c Findlay b Sobers	44	c Findlay b Sobers	31
7 R. Illingworth*	b Shepherd	1	c Lloyd b Holder	19
8 B. R. Knight	c Fredericks b Gibbs	7	c Holder b Gibbs	27
9 D. L. Underwood	c Findlay b Holder	4	b Sobers	16
10 D. J. Brown	b Holder	12	b Shillingford	34
11 J. A. Snow	not out	1	not out	15
Extras (B 4, LB 3, NB 1)		8	(LB 5, W 1, NB 1)	7
Total		223		240

Batted Second: West Indies

1 R. C. Fredericks	lbw b Knight	11	c Sharpe b Snow	6
2 G. S. Camacho	c Knott b Knight	4	c Hampshire b U'wood	71
3 C. A. Davis	c Underwood b Knight	18	c and b Underwood	29
4 B. F. Butcher	b Snow	35	c Knott b Underwood	91
5 G. St A. Sobers*	c Sharpe b Knight	13	(6) b Knight	0
6 C. H. Lloyd	c Snow b Brown	27	(5) c Knott b Illingworth	23
7 T. M. Findlay†	lbw b D'Oliveira	1	lbw b Knight	16
8 V. A. Holder	b Snow	35	(9) c Sharpe b Brown	13
9 L. R. Gibbs	not out	6	(10) c Knott b Brown	4
10 G. C. Shillingford	c Knott b Brown	3	(11) not out	5
11 J. N. Shepherd	absent hurt		(8) c Knott b Underwood	0
Extras (LB 7, NB 1)		8	(LB 11, NB 3)	14
Total		161		272

Bowling

	O	M	R	W	O	M	R	W
West Indies								
Sobers	21	1	68	2	40	18	42	5
Holder	26	7	48	4	33	13	66	1
Shilli'ford	7	0	21	0	20.4	4	56	2
Gibbs	19	6	33	1	21	6	42	1
Shepherd	24	8	43	3				
Davis	1	0	2	0	17	8	27	1
England								
Snow	20	4	50	2	21	7	43	1
Brown	7.3	2	13	2	21	8	53	2
Knight	22	5	63	4	18.2	4	47	2
D'Oliveira	15	8	27	1	10	3	22	0
Illingworth					14	5	38	1
Underwood					22	12	55	4

Fall of Wickets

	E 1st	WI 1st	E 2nd	WI 2nd
1st	30	17	0	8
2nd	52	37	23	69
3rd	64	46	42	177
4th	140	80	58	219
5th	165	88	102	224
6th	167	91	147	228
7th	182	151	147	228
8th	199	153	171	251
9th	217	161	203	255
10th	223		240	272

Umpires: C. S. Elliott and A. E. Fagg Captain* Wicket-keeper†

Appendix 6 **1973**

Tests: Played 3, Won 2, Drawn 1

First-class Matches: Played 18, Won 7, Drawn 10, Lost 1

All Matches: Played 23, Won 10, Drawn 11, Lost 2

Won: England (3), Hampshire, Nottinghamshire, Glamorgan (2), Combined Services, Derbyshire, T. N. Pearce's XI.

Drawn: England, Essex, Middlesex, Sussex, Kent, Young England, Minor Counties, Gloucestershire, Yorkshire, T. N. Pearce's XI, Yorkshire League XI.

Lost: D. H. Robins's XI, England.

First-class Averages

Batting

	M	I	NO	R	HS	Av	100	Ct	St
G. St A.Sobers	3	5	1	306	150*	76.50	1	7	—
M. L. C. Foster	15	20	7	828	127	63.69	1	4	—
C. H. Lloyd	15	23	4	1128	174	59.36	3	7	—
R. B. Kanhai	12	16	3	653	157	50.23	2	6	—
R. C. Fredericks	14	25	2	1091	150	47.43	3	7	—
A. I. Kallicharran	13	20	1	889	135	46.78	3	13	—
B. D. Julien	11	13	0	521	127	40.07	3	6	—
D. A. Murray	10	13	5	285	107*	35.62	1	28	8
G. S. Camacho	2	4	1	97	63	32.33	—	—	—
E. T. Willett	11	9	5	115	56	28.75	—	8	—
L. G. Rowe	8	13	1	344	84	28.66	—	6	—
K. D. Boyce	11	13	1	312	87	26.00	—	5	—
R. G. A. Headley	7	13	0	292	62	22.46	—	5	—
D. L. Murray	12	15	3	260	53*	21.66	—	26	5
G. C. Shillingford	11	8	5	65	35*	21.66	—	1	—
Inshan Ali	11	8	1	123	63	17.57	—	5	—
V. A. Holder	11	11	1	111	23*	11.10	—	5	—
L. R. Gibbs	10	7	5	14	4*	7.00	—	6	—

Bowling

	O	M	R	W	Av
C. H. Lloyd	56	12	133	6	22.16
K. D. Boyce	294	52	921	41	22.46
E. T. Willett	251.4	77	694	30	23.13
V. A. Holder	318	87	724	28	28.85
B. D. Julien	253	52	722	27	26.74
Inshan Ali	352.2	87	1020	38	26.84
M. L. C. Foster	84	28	191	7	27.28
L. R. Gibbs	332.4	105	676	24	28.16
G. St A Sobers	82.1	24	169	6	28.16
G. C. Shillingford	224.5	46	720	22	32.72

Also bowled: R. C. Fredericks 25–2–120–1; R. B. Kanhai 13.3–1–58–1; D. A. Murray 1–0–10–0.

Test Averages

England Batting

	M	I	NO	R	HS	Av
K. W. R. Fletcher	3	6	2	266	86*	66.50
G. Boycott	3	5	1	202	97	50.50
D. L. Amiss	3	6	1	231	86*	46.20
F. C. Hayes	3	6	1	159	106*	31.80
A. W. Greig	3	5	0	122	44	24.40
R. Illingworth	3	5	0	107	40	21.40
B. W. Luckhurst	2	4	0	67	42	16.75
A. P. E. Knott	3	5	1	35	21	8.75
G. G. Arnold	3	5	0	38	24	7.60
D. L. Underwood	3	5	0	35	14	7.00

Also batted: C. M. Old 0; G. R. J. Roope 9, 31; J. A. Snow 0, 1; R. G. D. Willis 5*, 0.

England Bowling

	O	M	R	W	Av
G. G. Arnold	149.1	37	390	15	26.00
R. G. D. Willis	35	3	118	4	29.50
C. M. Old	44	3	151	4	37.75
D. L. Underwood	133	38	330	8	41.25
J. A. Snow	49	12	133	3	44.38
R. Illingworth	128.4	39	311	6	51.83
A. W. Greig	105.1	12	402	7	57.42

Also bowled: B. W. Luckhurst 4–2–12–0; G. R. J. Roope 6–1–26–0.

West Indies Batting

	M	I	NO	R	HS	Av
G. St A. Sobers	3	5	1	306	150*	76.50
C. H. Lloyd	3	5	0	318	132	63.60
R. C. Fredericks	3	5	0	251	150	50.20
R. B. Kanhai	3	5	0	223	157	44.60
B. D. Julien	3	5	0	220	121	44.00
A. I. Kallicharran	3	5	0	212	80	42.40
K. D. Boyce	3	5	0	129	72	25.80
V. A. Holder	2	3	1	39	23*	19.50
R. G. A. Headley	2	4	0	62	42	15.50
D. L. Murray	3	5	0	76	28	15.20
L. R. Gibbs	3	4	3	8	3*	8.00

Also batted: Inshan Ali 15, 5*; M. L. C. Foster 9.

West Indies Bowling

	O	M	R	W	Av
K. D. Boyce	98.1	22	294	19	15.47
V. A. Holder	80	24	174	7	24.85
L. R. Gibbs	135.1	46	227	9	25.22
G. St A. Sobers	82.1	24	169	6	28.16
B. D. Julien	110	27	266	7	38.00

Also bowled: Inshan Ali 34–9–101–1; M. L. C. Foster 1–0–2–0; R. C. Fredericks 4–0–23–0; R. B. Kanhai 7–1–21–0; C. H. Lloyd 14–3–31–2.

England v West Indies 1973 (First Test)

VENUE: Kennington Oval
DATE: 26, 27, 28, 30, 31 July. West Indies won the toss
RESULT: West Indies won by 158 runs

Batted First: West Indies

1	R. C. Fredericks	lbw b Arnold	35	c Hayes b Arnold	3
2	R. G. A. Headley	lbw b Greig	8	b Arnold	42
3	R. B. Kanhai*	b Greig	10	c Knott b Snow	0
4	C. H. Lloyd	lbw b Arnold	132	c Greig b Snow	14
5	A. I. Kallicharran	c Knott b Arnold	80	b Illingworth	80
6	D. L. Murray†	c Roope b Arnold	28	(7) c Roope b Underwood	4
7	G. St A. Sobers	run out	10	(6) c Underwood b Snow	51
8	B. D. Julien	lbw b Arnold	11	b Illingworth	23
9	K. D. Boyce	b Underwood	72	b Illingworth	9
10	Inshan Ali	c Boycott b Underwood	15	not out	5
11	L. R. Gibbs	not out	1	c Knott b Arnold	3
	Extras	(B 1, LB 2, NB 10)	13	(B 2, LB 13, NB 6)	21
	Total		415		255

Batted Second: England

1	G. Boycott	c Murray b Julien	97	c and b Gibbs	30
2	D. L. Amiss	b Boyce	29	c Kanhai b Boyce	15
3	G. R. J. Roope	b Boyce	9	c and b Gibbs	31
4	F. C. Hayes	c Lloyd b Sobers	16	not out	106
5	K. W. R. Fletcher	c Lloyd b Julien	11	c Kallicharran b Gibbs	5
6	A. W. Greig	c Sobers b Boyce	38	c Gibbs b Ali	0
7	R. Illingworth*	lbw b Sobers	27	(8) b Boyce	40
8	A. P. E. Knott†	not out	4	(9) lbw b Boyce	5
9	J. A. Snow	b Boyce	0	(11) b Boyce	1
10	G. G. Arnold	c Kallicharran b Boyce	4	c Headley b Boyce	4
11	D. L. Underwood	c Headley b Sobers	0	(7) lbw b Boyce	7
	Extras	(B 2, LB 7, W 2, NB 11)	22	(LB 5, W 1, NB 5)	11
	Total		257		255

Bowling

	O	M	R	W	O	M	R	W
England								
Snow	31	8	71	0	18	4	62	3
Arnold	39	10	113	5	18.1	7	49	3
Greig	30.3	6	81	2	8	1	22	0
Roope	6	1	26	0				
Underwood	23.3	8	68	2	19	5	51	1
Illingworth	15	3	43	0	24	8	50	3
West Indies								
Sobers	22.1	13	27	3	11	3	22	0
Boyce	22	4	70	5	21.1	4	77	6
Julien	20	6	49	2	17	4	35	0
Gibbs	23	8	37	0	33	9	61	3
Ali	11	3	52	0	23	6	49	1

Fall of Wickets

	WI 1st	E 1st	WI 2nd	E 2nd
1st	33	50	9	36
2nd	47	95	31	66
3rd	64	134	52	91
4th	272	163	117	97
5th	275	185	177	107
6th	297	247	184	136
7th	309	247	215	229
8th	346	247	232	239
9th	405	257	252	253
10th	415	257	255	255

Umpires: D. J. Constant and T. W. Spencer Captain* Wicket-keeper†

England v West Indies 1973 (Second Test)

VENUE: Edgbaston
DATE: 9, 10, 11, 13, 14 August. West Indies won the toss
RESULT: Match Drawn

Batted First: West Indies

1	R. C. Fredericks	c Amiss b Underwood	150	c Knott b Arnold	12
2	R. G. A. Headley	b Old	1	c Knott b Old	11
3	R. B. Kanhai*	c Greig b Arnold	2	c Arnold b Illingworth	54
4	C. H. Lloyd	lbw b Old	15	c Knott b Underwood	94
5	A. I. Kallicharran	c Hayes b Arnold	34	b Underwood	4
6	G. St A. Sobers	b Old	21	b Arnold	74
7	D. L. Murray†	b Underwood	25	hit wkt b Arnold	15
8	B. D. Julien	c Greig b Arnold	54	b Greig	11
9	K. D. Boyce	lbw b Illingworth	12	c Knott b Arnold	0
10	V. A. Holder	c Boycott b Underwood	6	c Luckhurst b Greig	10
11	L. R. Gibbs	not out	1	not out	3
	Extras (LB 2, W 1, NB 3)		6	(LB 10, NB 4)	14
	Total		327		302

Batted Second: England

1	G. Boycott	not out	56		
2	D. L. Amiss	c Murray b Julien	56	not out	86
3	B. W. Luckhurst	lbw b Sobers	12	(1) c Murray b Lloyd	42
4	F. C. Hayes	c Kallicharran b Holder	29	(3) lbw b Lloyd	0
5	A. W. Greig	c Fredericks b Julien	27		
6	A. P. E. Knott†	b Holder	0		
7	K. W. R. Fletcher	c Holder b Sobers	52	(4) not out	44
8	R. Illingworth*	lbw b Holder	27		
9	C. M. Old	run out	0		
10	G. G. Arnold	c Kallicharran b Sobers	24		
11	D. L. Underwood	c Murray b Gibbs	2		
	Extras (B 4, LB 1, NB 15)		20	(B 8, NB 2)	10
	Total		305	(2 wkts)	182

Bowling

	O	M	R	W	O	M	R	W
England								
Arnold	37	13	74	3	20	1	43	4
Old	30	3	86	3	14	0	65	1
Greig	36	3	84	0	7.4	0	35	2
Illingworth	32	19	37	1	26	6	67	1
Underwood	24.3	10	40	3	32	9	66	2
Luckhurst					4	2	12	0
West Indies								
Holder	44	16	83	3	7	1	17	0
Sobers	30	6	62	3	7	1	21	0
Boyce	19	2	48	0				
Julien	26	8	55	2	18	3	32	0
Gibbs	35.4	21	32	1	12	2	32	0
Lloyd	2	0	5	0	12	3	26	2
Fredericks					4	0	23	0
Kanhai					7	1	21	0

Fall of Wickets

	WI 1st	E 1st	WI 2nd	E 2nd
1st	14	119	24	96
2nd	17	139	42	100
3rd	39	191	136	
4th	93	191	152	
5th	128	197	197	
6th	242	249	247	
7th	280	249	283	
8th	302	299	283	
9th	325	302	293	
10th	327	305	302	

Umpires: H. D. Bird and A. E. Fagg Captain* Wicket-keeper†

England v West Indies 1973 (Third Test)

VENUE: Lord's

DATE: 23, 24, 25, 27 August. West Indies won the toss

RESULT: West Indies won by an innings and 226 runs

Batted First: West Indies

1 R. C. Fredericks	c Underwood b Willis	51
2 D. L. Murray†	b Willis	4
3 R. B. Kanhai*	c Greig b Willis	157
4 C. H. Lloyd	c and b Willis	63
5 A. I. Kallicharran	c Arnold b Illingworth	14
6 G. St. A. Sobers	not out	150
7 M. L. C. Foster	c Willis b Greig	9
8 B. D. Julien	c and b Greig	121
9 K. D. Boyce	c Amiss b Greig	36
10 V. A. Holder	not out	23
11 L. R. Gibbs	did not bat	
Extras (B 1, LB 14, W 1, NB 8)		24
Total	(8 wkts dec.)	652

Batted Second: England

1 G. Boycott	c Kanhai b Holder	4	c Kallicharran b Boyce	15
2 D. L. Amiss	c Sobers b Holder	35	c Sobers b Boyce	10
3 B. W. Luckhurst	c Murray b Boyce	1	(4) c Sobers b Julien	12
4 F. C. Hayes	c Fredericks b Holder	8	(5) c Holder b Boyce	0
5 K. W. R. Fletcher	c Sobers b Gibbs	68	(6) not out	86
6 A. W. Greig	c Sobers b Boyce	44	(7) lbw b Julien	13
7 R. Illingworth*	c Sobers b Gibbs	0	(8) c Kanhai b Gibbs	13
8 A. P. E. Knott†	c Murray b Boyce	21	(3) c Murray b Boyce	5
9 G. G. Arnold	c Murray b Boyce	5	c Fredericks b Gibbs	1
10 R. G. D. Willis	not out	5	c Fredericks b Julien	0
11 D. L. Underwood	c Gibbs b Holder	12	b Gibbs	14
Extras (B 6, LB 4, W 3, NB 17)		30	(B 9, W 1, NB 14)	24
Total		233		193

Bowling

	O	M	R	W	O	M	R	W
England								
Arnold	35	6	111	0				
Willis	35	3	118	4				
Greig	33	2	180	3				
Underwood	34	6	105	0				
Illingworth	31.4	3	114	1				
West Indies								
Holder	15	3	56	4	14	4	18	0
Boyce	20	7	50	4	16	5	49	4
Julien	11	4	26	0	18	2	69	3
Gibbs	18	3	39	2	13.3	3	26	3
Sobers	8	0	30	0	4	1	7	0
Foster	1	0	2	0				

Fall of Wickets

	WI 1st	E 1st	E 2nd
1st	8	5	32
2nd	87	7	38
3rd	225	29	42
4th	256	97	49
5th	339	176	63
6th	373	176	87
7th	604	187	132
8th	610	205	143
9th		213	146
10th		233	193

Umpires: H. D. Bird and C. S. Elliott Captain* Wicket-keeper†

Appendix 7 **1976**

Tests: Played 5, Won 3, Drawn 2

First-class Matches: Played 26, Won 18, Drawn 6, Lost 2

All Matches: Played 35, Won 26, Drawn 7, Lost 2

Won: England (6), Hampshire, Kent, MCC, Somerset, Oxford/Cambridge XI, Lancashire, Northamptonshire, Leicestershire, Yorkshire, Derbyshire, Essex, Minor Counties, Glamorgan, Worcestershire, Nottinghamshire, Lavinia Duchess of Norfolk's XI, Ireland, Glamorgan, T. N. Pearce's XI, Northern League's XI.

Drawn: England (2), Surrey, Sussex, Warwickshire, Gloucestershire, NCA XI.

Lost: Middlesex, T. N. Pearce's XI.

First-class Averages

Batting

	M	I	NO	R	HS	Av	100	Ct	St
I. V. A. Richards	16	25	1	1724	291	71.83	7	17	1
C. H. Lloyd	19	26	4	1363	201*	61.95	3	23	—
C. G. Greenidge	20	38	3	1952	134	55.77	9	28	—
C. L. King	21	34	10	1320	163	55.00	6	27	—
H. A. Gomes	21	35	6	1393	190	48.03	5	5	—
L. G. Rowe	17	27	1	971	152	37.34	3	11	—
R. C. Fredericks	21	38	3	1250	138	35.71	3	19	—
A. I. Kallicharran	12	21	2	678	104	35.68	1	5	—
D. L. Murray	18	25	9	397	55	24.81	—	37	1
B. D. Julien	18	26	3	549	89	23.86	—	9	—
V. A. Holder	13	14	6	173	42*	21.62	—	2	—
T. M. Findlay	18	21	7	276	51*	19.71	—	36	8
A. M. E. Roberts	12	10	2	135	56*	16.87	—	5	—
M. A. Holding	12	13	1	152	42	12.66	—	5	—
A. L. Padmore	16	16	6	99	26*	9.90	—	4	—
W. W. Daniel	15	10	3	62	30	8.85	—	5	—
R. R. Jumadeen	17	12	4	49	21	6.12	—	14	—

Bowling

	O	M	R	W	Av
M. A. Holding	339.3	111	791	55	14.38
V. A. Holder	387.1	109	1004	52	19.30
W. W. Daniel	371.3	88	1106	52	21.26
A. L. Padmore	497.3	128	1381	59	23.40
A. M. E. Roberts	411.1	109	1089	44	24.75
B. D. Julien	468.4	126	1339	51	26.25
R. R. Jumadeen	584	140	1740	58	30.00
H. A. Gomes	157.3	41	434	14	31.00
R. C. Fredericks	124.4	26	401	12	33.41
C. L. King	384.4	91	928	27	34.37

Also bowled: C. H. Lloyd 39–13–90–3; I. V. A. Richards 31–12–56–1; D. L. Murray 5–2–12–0; A. I. Kallicharran 10–3–18–0.

Test Averages

England Batting

	M	I	NO	R	HS	Av
J. H. Edrich	2	4	1	145	76*	48.33
D. B. Close	3	6	1	166	60	33.20
D. S. Steele	5	10	0	308	106	30.80
A. W. Greig	5	9	1	243	116	30.37
A. P. E. Knott	5	9	0	270	116	30.00
P. Willey	2	4	0	115	45	28.75
R. A. Woolmer	5	9	0	245	82	27.22
C. M. Old	2	3	0	65	33	21.66
J. A. Snow	3	5	2	54	20*	18.00
J. M. Brearley	2	4	0	70	40	17.50
J. C. Balderstone	2	4	0	39	35	9.75
F. C. Hayes	2	4	0	25	18	6.25
M. W. W. Selvey	2	4	2	10	4*	5.00
D. L. Underwood	5	9	0	40	31	4.44
P. I. Pocock	2	4	1	13	7	4.33
M. Hendrick	2	3	1	5	5	2.50
R. G. D. Willis	2	4	2	5	5*	2.50

Also batted: D. L. Amiss 203, 16; G. Miller 36, 24; A. Ward 0, 0; B. Wood 6, 30.

England Bowling

	O	M	R	W	Av
R. G. D. Willis	57.3	11	234	9	26.00
J. A. Snow	106.4	16	423	15	28.20
A. Ward	24	2	128	4	32.00
D. L. Underwood	224	59	631	17	37.11
C. M. Old	68.3	11	248	6	41.33
P. I. Pocock	61	15	173	4	43.25
M. W. W. Selvey	67	8	263	6	43.83
M. Hendrick	69	14	192	4	48.00
A. W. Greig	98	15	336	5	67.20

Also bowled: J. C. Balderstone 16–0–80–1; G. Miller 27–4–106–1; D. S. Steele 3–0–18–0; P. Willey 4–0–15–0; R. A. Woolmer 40–2–194–1.

West Indies Batting

	M	I	NO	R	HS	Av
I. V. A. Richards	4	7	0	829	291	118.42
C. G. Greenidge	5	10	1	592	134	65.77
R. C. Fredericks	5	10	1	517	138	57.44
L. G. Rowe	2	3	0	126	70	42.00
C. L. King	3	5	1	167	63	41.75
A. I. Kallicharran	3	6	1	180	97	36.00
C. H. Lloyd	5	9	0	296	84	32.88
D. L. Murray	5	8	2	123	36	20.50
V. A. Holder	4	6	3	50	19*	16.66
B. D. Julien	2	4	0	38	21	9.50
A. M. E. Roberts	5	5	0	45	19	9.00
W. W. Daniel	4	4	2	18	10	9.00
M. A. Holding	4	5	0	41	32	8.20
H. A. Gomes	2	3	0	11	11	3.66

Also batted: R. R. Jumadeen 0*; A. L. Padmore 8*.

West Indies Bowling

	O	M	R	W	Av
M. A. Holding	159.3	54	356	28	12.71
A. M. E. Roberts	221.4	69	537	28	19.17
W. W. Daniel	108	28	317	13	24.38
V. A. Holder	158	48	367	15	24.46

Also bowled: R. C. Fredericks 43.4–11–119–1; H. A. Gomes 13–2–26–0; R. R. Jumadeen 28–8–64–1; B. D. Julien 86–28–168–2; A. I. Kallicharran 10–3–18–0; C. L. King 39–11–95–2; C. H. Lloyd 7–3–9–0; A. L. Padmore 3–2–1–0; I. V. A. Richards 31–12–56–1.

England v West Indies 1976 (First Test)

VENUE: Trent Bridge, Nottingham
DATE: 3, 4, 5, 7, 8 June. West Indies won the toss
RESULT: Match Drawn

Batted First: West Indies

	First innings		Second innings	
1 R. C. Fredericks	c Hendrick b Greig	42	b Snow	15
2 C. G. Greenidge	c Edrich b Hendrick	22	c and b Old	23
3 I. V. A. Richards	c Greig b Underwood	232	lbw b Snow	63
4 A. I. Kallicharran	c Steele b Underwood	97	(6) not out	29
5 C. H. Lloyd*	c Hendrick b Underwood	16	(4) c Brearley b Snow	21
6 B. D. Julien	c Knott b Old	21	(5) c Hendrick b Snow	13
7 H. A. Gomes	c Close b Underwood	0		
8 D. L. Murray†	c Close b Snow	19		
9 V. A. Holder	not out	19		
10 A. M. E. Roberts	b Old	1		
11 W. W. Daniel	c Knott b Old	4		
Extras (LB 12, W 1, NB 8)		21	(LB 6, W 2, NB 4)	12
Total		494	(5 wkts dec.)	176

Batted Second: England

	First innings		Second innings	
1 J. H. Edrich	c Murray b Daniel	37	not out	76
2 J. M. Brearley	c Richards b Julien	0	c Murray b Holder	17
3 D. S. Steele	c Roberts b Daniel	106	c Julien b Roberts	6
4 D. B. Close	c Murray b Daniel	2	not out	36
5 R. A. Woolmer	lbw b Julien	82		
6 A. W. Greig*	b Roberts	0		
7 A. P. E. Knott†	c sub b Holder	9		
8 C. M. Old	b Daniel	33		
9 J. A. Snow	not out	20		
10 D. L. Underwood	c Murray b Holder	0		
11 M. Hendrick	c Daniel b Fredericks	5		
Extras (B 5, LB 1, W 3, NB 29)		38	(B 9, W 2, NB 10)	21
Total		332	(2 wkts)	156

Bowling

	O	M	R	W	O	M	R	W
England								
Snow	31	5	123	1	11	2	53	4
Hendrick	24	7	59	1	7	2	22	0
Old	34.3	7	80	3	10	0	64	1
Greig	27	4	82	1	1	0	16	0
Woolmer	10	2	47	0				
Underwood	27	8	82	4	7	3	9	0
West Indies								
Roberts	34	15	53	1	9	3	20	1
Julien	34	9	75	2	16	8	19	0
Holder	25	5	66	2	12	6	12	1
Daniel	23	8	53	4	10	2	20	0
Fredericks	8.4	2	24	1	9	1	21	0
Richards	3	1	8	0	3	1	7	0
Gomes	4	1	8	0	9	1	18	0
Lloyd	3	1	7	0				
Kallicharran					10	3	18	0

Fall of Wickets

	WI 1st	E 1st	WI 2nd	E 2nd
1st	36	0	33	38
2nd	105	98	77	55
3rd	408	105	109	
4th	423	226	124	
5th	432	229	176	
6th	432	255		
7th	458	278		
8th	481	279		
9th	488	318		
10th	494	332		

Umpires: H. D. Bird and T. W. Spencer Captain* Wicket-keeper†

England v West Indies 1976 (Second Test)

VENUE: Lord's
DATE: 17, 18, 19, 21, 22 June. England won the toss
RESULT: Match Drawn

Batted First: England

	1st innings		2nd innings	
1 B. Wood	c Murray b Roberts	6	c Murray b Holding	30
2 J. M. Brearley	b Roberts	40	b Holding	13
3 D. S. Steele	lbw b Roberts	7	(4) c Jumadeen b Roberts	64
4 D. B. Close	c Holder b Jumadeen	60	(5) c and b Holder	46
5 R. A. Woolmer	c Murray b Holding	38	(6) c Murray b Roberts	29
6 A. W. Greig*	c Lloyd b Roberts	6	(7) c Gomes b Holder	20
7 A. P. E. Knott†	b Holder	17	(8) lbw b Roberts	4
8 C. M. Old	b Holder	19	(9) run out	13
9 J. A. Snow	b Roberts	0	(10) not out	6
10 D. L. Underwood	b Holder	31	(11) b Roberts	2
11 P. I. Pocock	not out	0	(3) c Jumadeen b Roberts	3
Extras	(B 7, LB 5, W 5, NB 9)	26	(B 7, LB 7, NB 10)	24
Total		250		254

Batted Second: West Indies

	1st innings		2nd innings	
1 R. C. Fredericks	c Snow b Old	0	c Greig b Old	138
2 C. G. Greenidge	c Snow b Underwood	84	c Close b Pocock	22
3 H. A. Gomes	c Woolmer b Snow	11	(7) b Underwood	0
4 A. I. Kallicharran	c Old b Snow	0	(3) b Greig	34
5 C. H. Lloyd*	c Knott b Underwood	50	(4) b Greig	33
6 D. L. Murray†	b Snow	2	not out	7
7 B. D. Julien	lbw b Snow	3	(5) b Underwood	1
8 M. A. Holding	b Underwood	0		
9 V. A. Holder	c Woolmer b Underwood	12	(8) not out	0
10 A. M. E. Roberts	b Underwood	16		
11 R. R. Jumadeen	not out	0		
Extras	(B 2, NB 2)	4	(B 3, LB 2, NB 1)	6
Total		182	(6 wkts)	241

Bowling

	O	M	R	W	O	M	R	W
West Indies								
Roberts	23	6	60	5	29.5	10	63	5
Holding	19	4	52	1	27	10	56	2
Julien	23	6	54	0	13	5	20	0
Holder	18.4	7	35	3	19	2	50	2
Jumadeen	12	4	23	1	16	4	41	0
England								
Old	10	0	58	1	14	4	46	1
Snow	19	3	68	4	7	2	22	0
Underwood	18.4	7	39	5	24.3	8	73	2
Pocock	3	0	13	0	27	9	52	1
Greig					14	3	42	2

Fall of Wickets

	E 1st	WI 1st	E 2nd	WI 2nd
1st	15	0	29	41
2nd	31	28	29	154
3rd	115	40	112	230
4th	153	139	169	233
5th	161	141	186	238
6th	188	145	207	238
7th	196	146	215	
8th	197	153	245	
9th	249	178	249	
10th	250	182	254	

Umpires: H. D. Bird and D. J. Constant Captain* Wicket-keeper†

England v West Indies 1976 (Third Test)

VENUE: Old Trafford
DATE: 8, 9, 10, 12, 13 July. West Indies won the toss
RESULT: West Indies won by 425 runs

Batted First: West Indies

1	R. C. Fredericks	c Underwood b Selvey 0	hit wicket b Hendrick 50
2	C. G. Greenidge	b Underwood 134	b Selvey 101
3	I. V. A. Richards	b Selvey 4	lbw b Pocock 135
4	A. I. Kallicharran	b Selvey 0	(5) c Close b Pocock 20
5	C. H. Lloyd*	c Hayes b Hendrick 2	(4) c Underwood b Selvey 43
6	C. L. King	c Greig b Underwood 32	not out 14
7	D. L. Murray†	c Greig b Hendrick 1	not out 7
8	M. A. Holding	b Selvey 3	
9	A. M. E. Roberts	c Steele b Pocock 6	
10	A. L. Padmore	not out 8	
11	W. W. Daniel	lbw b Underwood 10	
	Extras (LB 8, NB 3)	11	(B 5, LB 30, W 1, NB 5) 41
	Total	211	(5 wkts dec.) 411

Batted Second: England

1	J. H. Edrich	c Murray b Roberts 8	b Daniel 24
2	D. B. Close	lbw b Daniel 2	b Roberts 20
3	D. S. Steele	lbw b Roberts 20	c Roberts b Holding 15
4	P. I. Pocock	c Kallicharran b Holding 7	(10) c King b Daniel 3
5	R. A. Woolmer	c Murray b Holding 3	(4) lbw b Roberts 0
6	F. C. Hayes	c Lloyd b Roberts 0	(5) c Greenidge b Roberts 18
7	A. W. Greig*	b Daniel 9	(6) b Holding 3
8	A. P. E. Knott†	c Greenidge b Holding 1	(7) c Fredericks b Roberts 14
9	D. L. Underwood	b Holding 0	(8) c King b Roberts 0
10	M. W. W. Selvey	not out 2	(9) c Greenidge b Roberts 4
11	M. Hendrick	b Holding 0	not out 0
	Extras (B 8, NB 11)	19	(B 4, LB 1, NB 20) 25
	Total	71	126

Bowling

	O	M	R	W	O	M	R	W
England								
Hendrick	14	1	48	2	24	4	63	1
Selvey	17	4	41	4	26	3	111	2
Greig	8	1	24	0	2	0	8	0
Woolmer	3	0	22	0				
Underwood	24	5	55	3	35	9	90	0
Pocock	4	2	10	1	27	4	98	2
West Indies								
Roberts	12	4	22	3	20.5	8	37	6
Holding	14.5	7	17	5	23	15	24	2
Daniel	6	2	13	2	17	8	39	2
Padmore					3	2	1	0

Fall of Wickets

	WI 1st	E 1st	WI 2nd	E 2nd
1st	1	9	116	54
2nd	15	36	224	60
3rd	19	46	356	60
4th	26	48	385	80
5th	137	48	388	94
6th	154	65		112
7th	167	66		112
8th	193	67		118
9th	193	71		124
10th	211	71		126

Umpires: W. E. Alley and W. L. Budd Captain* Wicket-keeper†

England v West Indies 1976 (Fourth Test)

VENUE: Headingley
DATE: 22, 23, 24, 26, 27 July. West Indies won the toss
RESULT: West Indies won by 55 runs

Batted First: West Indies

1 R. C. Fredericks	b Willis	109	b Snow	6
2 C. G. Greenidge	c Ward b Snow	115	lbw b Ward	6
3 I. V. A. Richards	c Knott b Willis	66	b Willis	38
4 L. G. Rowe	c Greig b Woolmer	50	run out	6
5 C. H. Lloyd*	c Steele b Ward	18	b Ward	29
6 C. L. King	c Hayes b Ward	0	c Greig b Snow	58
7 D. L. Murray†	c Willis b Snow	33	b Willis	18
8 M. A. Holding	b Snow	2	(9) lbw b Willis	4
9 V. A. Holder	c Hayes b Willis	1	(8) b Willis	5
10 A. M. E. Roberts	b Snow	19	b Willis	3
11 W. W. Daniel	not out	4	not out	0
Extras	(B 1, LB 15, W 2, NB 15)	33	(B 4, LB 6, W 1, NB 12)	23
Total		450		196

Batted Second: England

1 R. A. Woolmer	c Greenidge b Holder	18	lbw b Holder	37
2 D. S. Steele	b Holding	4	c Murray b Roberts	0
3 F. C. Hayes	c Murray b Daniel	7	c Richards b Roberts	0
4 J. C. Balderstone	c Murray b Roberts	35	c Murray b Roberts	4
5 P. Willey	lbw b Roberts	36	c Roberts b Holding	45
6 A. W. Greig*	c Lloyd b Daniel	116	not out	76
7 A. P. E. Knott†	c Daniel b Holder	116	(8) c Murray b Daniel	2
8 J. A. Snow	c Fredericks b Holder	20	(9) c Greenidge b Daniel	8
9 D. L. Underwood	c Lloyd b King	1	(7) c Murray b Daniel	0
10 A. Ward	lbw b Roberts	0	c Murray b Holding	0
11 R. G. D. Willis	not out	0	lbw b Holding	0
Extras	(B 2, LB 7, W 2, NB 23)	34	(B 12, LB 5, W 7, NB 8)	32
Total		387		204

Bowling

	O	M	R	W	O	M	R	W
England								
Willis	20	2	71	3	15.3	6	42	5
Snow	18.4	3	77	4	20	1	80	2
Underwood	18	2	80	0				
Ward	15	0	103	2	9	2	25	2
Greig	10	2	57	0				
Woolmer	6	0	25	1	7	0	26	0
Willey	1	0	4	0				
West Indies								
Roberts	35	7	102	3	18	8	41	3
Holding	8	2	14	1	14	1	44	3
Daniel	29	7	102	2	13	0	60	3
Holder	30.3	13	73	3	11	3	27	1
King	26	6	56	1				
Fredericks	3	1	5	0				
Lloyd	2	1	1	0				

Fall of Wickets

	WI 1st	E 1st	WI 2nd	E 2nd
1st	192	4	13	5
2nd	287	24	23	12
3rd	330	32	60	23
4th	370	80	72	80
5th	370	169	121	140
6th	413	321	178	148
7th	421	364	184	150
8th	423	367	188	158
9th	433	379	193	204
10th	450	387	196	204

Umpires: D. J. Constant and T.W. Spencer Captain* Wicket-keeper†

England v West Indies 1976 (Fifth Test)

VENUE: Kennington Oval
DATE: 12, 13, 14, 16, 17 August. West Indies won the toss
RESULT: West Indies won by 231 runs

Batted First: West Indies

1	R. C. Fredericks	c Balderstone b Miller	71	not out	86
2	C. G. Greenidge	lbw b Willis	0	not out	85
3	I. V. A. Richards	b Greig	291		
4	L. G. Rowe	st Knott b Underwood	70		
5	C. H. Lloyd*	c Knott b Greig	84		
6	C. L. King	c Selvey b Balderstone	63		
7	D. L. Murray†	c and b Underwood	36		
8	V. A. Holder	not out	13		
9	M. A. Holding	b Underwood	32		
10	A. M. E. Roberts				
11	W. W. Daniel				
	Extras	(B 1, LB 17, NB 9)	27	(B 4, LB 1, W 1, NB 5)	11
	Total	(8 wkts dec.)	687	(no wkt dec.)	182

Batted Second: England

1	R. A. Woolmer	lbw b Holding	8	c Murray b Holding	30
2	D. L. Amiss	b Holding	203	c Greenidge b Holding	16
3	D. S. Steele	lbw b Holding	44	c Murray b Holder	42
4	J. C. Balderstone	b Holding	0	b Holding	0
5	P. Willey	c Fredericks b King	33	c Greenidge b Holder	1
6	A. W. Greig*	b Holding	12	b Holding	1
7	D. L. Underwood	b Holding	4	(9) c Lloyd b Roberts	2
8	A. P. E. Knott†	b Holding	50	(7) b Holding	57
9	G. Miller	c sub b Holder	36	(8) b Richards	24
10	M. W. W. Selvey	b Holding	0	not out	4
11	R. G. D. Willis	not out	5	lbw b Holding	0
	Extras	(B 8, LB 11, NB 21)	40	(B 15, LB 3, W 8)	26
	Total		435		203

Bowling

	O	M	R	W	O	M	R	W
England								
Willis	15	3	73	1	7	0	48	0
Selvey	15	0	67	0	9	1	44	0
Underwood	60.5	15	165	3	9	2	38	0
Woolmer	9	0	44	0	5	0	30	0
Miller	27	4	106	1				
Balderstone	16	0	80	1				
Greig	34	5	96	2	2	0	11	0
Willey	3	0	11	0				
Steele	3	0	18	0				
West Indies								
Roberts	27	4	102	0	13	4	37	1
Holding	33	9	92	8	20.4	6	57	6
Holder	27.5	7	75	1	14	5	29	2
Daniel	10	1	30	0				
Fredericks	11	2	36	0	12	5	33	0
Richards	14	4	30	0	11	6	11	1
King	7	3	30	1	6	2	9	0
Lloyd					2	1	1	0

Fall of Wickets

	WI	E	E
	1st	1st	2nd
1st	5	47	49
2nd	159	147	54
3rd	350	151	64
4th	524	279	77
5th	547	303	78
6th	640	323	148
7th	642	342	196
9th		411	202
10th		435	203

Umpires: W. E. Alley and H. D. Bird Captain* Wicket-keeper†

Appendix 8 **1980**

Tests: Played 5, Won 1, Drawn 4

First-class Matches: Played 16, Won 8, Drawn 8

All Matches: Played 28, Won 16, Drawn 10, Lost 2

Won: England (2), Derbyshire, Gloucestershire, Kent, Leicestershire, Northamptonshire, Worcestershire, Yorkshire, Essex, Glamorgan, Ireland, Lavinia Duchess of Norfolk's XI, Middlesex, Oxford/Cambridge XI, Scotland.

Drawn: England (4), Glamorgan, Somerset, Sussex, Warwickshire, Ireland, Minor Counties.

Lost: England, Essex.

First-class Averages

Batting

	M	I	NO	R	HS	Av	100	Ct	St
I. V. A. Richards	13	17	1	911	145	56.93	5	13	—
C. H. Lloyd	12	12	2	487	116	48.70	3	7	—
D. L. Haynes	14	22	3	874	184	46.00	1	2	—
A. I. Kallicharran	15	19	1	653	90	36.27	—	14	—
C. C. Greenidge	13	18	2	577	165	36.06	1	6	—
S. F. A. Bacchus	15	23	2	710	164*	33.80	2	14	—
D. A. Murray	6	8	2	161	49	26.83	—	16	1
D. L. Murray	12	14	2	315	64	26.25	—	33	2
M. D. Marshall	12	12	2	211	52	21.10	—	2	—
J. Garner	11	10	0	206	104	20.60	1	8	—
D. R. Parry	11	13	8	103	26*	20.60	—	2	—
M. A. Holding	11	11	6	99	35	19.80	—	2	—
A. M. E. Roberts	9	10	1	114	31*	12.66	—	—	—
C. L. King	9	11	2	86	26*	9.55	—	4	—
C. E. H. Croft	9	4	3	8	7*	8.00	—	—	—
L. G. Rowe	3	2	0	13	13	6.50	—	2	—

Also batted: Timur Mohamed 2,45

Bowling

	O	M	R	W	Av
J. Garner	351	123	683	49	13.93
M. D. Marshall	336.3	86	864	49	17.63
D. R. Parry	303.1	93	800	40	20.00
A. M. E. Roberts	234.2	57	657	27	24.33
M. A. Holding	392.1	96	1096	44	24.90
C. E. H. Croft	230.3	54	690	25	27.60
C. L. King	98	24	301	7	43.00

Also bowled: S. F. A. Bacchus 2–0–11–0; C. G. Greenidge 6–3–6–0; D. L. Haynes 1–0–2–0; A. I. Kallicharran 15–3–55–2; C. H. Lloyd 1–0–1–0; D. A. Murray 1–0–1–0; I. V. A. Richards 68–21–177–1.

Test Averages

England Batting

	M	I	NO	R	HS	Av
B. C. Rose	3	6	1	243	70	48.60
G. Boycott	5	10	1	368	86	40.88
G. A. Gooch	5	10	0	394	123	39.40
P. Willey	5	9	2	262	100*	37.42
R. A. Woolmer	2	4	1	109	46	36.33
M. W. Gatting	4	7	0	172	56	24.57
J. E. Emburey	3	5	2	70	28*	23.33
R. G. D. Willis	4	6	3	61	24*	20.33
M. Hendrick	2	3	3	19	10*	19.00
I. T. Botham	5	9	0	169	57	18.77
C. J. Tavaré	2	4	0	65	42	16.25
W. Larkins	3	6	0	90	33	15.00
A. P. E. Knott	4	7	0	36	9	5.14
G. R. Dilley	3	4	0	2	1	0.50

Also batted: D. L. Bairstow 40, 9*; D. I. Gower 20, 1; J. K. Lever 15, 4; C. M. Old 6; D. L. Underwood 3.

England Bowling

	O	M	R	W	Av
J. E. Emburey	39.3	13	83	6	13.83
G. R. Dilley	74	19	183	11	16.63
G. A. Gooch	25	7	59	3	19.66
R. G. D. Willis	110.1	27	407	14	29.07
I. T. Botham	131	41	185	13	29.61

Also bowled: G. Boycott 7–2–11–0; M. Hendrick 44–11–141–2; J. K. Lever 28–4–101–1; C. M. Old 28.5–9–64–2; D. L. Underwood 29.2–7–108–1; P. Willey 43–16–111–2.

West Indies Batting

	M	I	NO	R	HS	Av
I. V. A. Richards	5	6	0	379	145	63.16
D. L. Haynes	5	6	0	308	184	51.33
C. H. Lloyd	4	4	0	169	101	42.25
M. A. Holding	5	6	4	61	35	30.50
A. M. E. Roberts	3	4	1	78	24	26.00
D. L. Murray	5	6	0	145	64	24.16
C. G. Greenidge	5	6	0	124	53	20.66
S. F. A. Bacchus	5	6	0	121	61	20.16
M. D. Marshall	4	5	0	90	45	18.00
A. I. Kallicharran	5	6	0	102	37	17.00
J. Garner	5	5	0	63	46	12.60
C. E. H. Croft	3	3	2	1	1*	1.00

Also batted: C. L. King 12.

West Indies Bowling

	O	M	R	W	Av
J. Garner	212.4	73	371	26	14.26
A. M. E. Roberts	105.2	24	262	11	23.81
M. D. Marshall	172.3	42	436	15	29.06
M. A. Holding	230.5	56	632	20	31.60
C. E. H. Croft	104	25	306	9	34.00

Also bowled: S. F. A. Bacchus 1–0–3–0; C. G. Greenidge 3–2–4–0; D. L. Haynes 1–0–2–0; A. I. Kallicharran 7–1–24–0; C. L. King 12–3–32–0; C. H. Lloyd 1–0–1–0; I. V. A. Richards 36–12–85–0.

England v West Indies 1980 (First Test)

VENUE: Trent Bridge
DATE: 5, 6, 7, 9, 10 June England won the toss
RESULT: West Indies won by 2 wickets

Batted First: England

1 G. A. Gooch	c Murray b Roberts	17	run out	27
2 G. Boycott	c Murray b Garner	36	b Roberts	75
3 C. J. Tavaré	b Garner	13	c Richards b Garner	4
4 R. A. Woolmer	c Murray b Roberts	46	c Murray b Roberts	29
5 D. I. Gower	c Greenidge b Roberts	20	lbw b Garner	1
6 I. T. Botham*	c Richards b Garner	57	c Richards b Roberts	4
7 P. Willey	b Marshall	13	b Marshall	38
8 A. P. E. Knott†	lbw b Roberts	6	lbw b Marshall	7
9 J. K. Lever	c Richards b Holding	15	c Murray b Garner	4
10 R. G. D. Willis	b Roberts	8	b Garner	9
11 M. Hendrick	not out	7	not out	2
Extras (B 7, LB 11, W 3, NB 4)		25	(B 19, LB 13, W 10, NB 10)	52
Total		263		252

Batted Second: West Indies

1 C. G. Greenidge	c Knott b Hendrick	53	c Knott b Willis	6
2 D. L. Haynes	c Gower b Willis	12	run out	62
3 I. V. A. Richards	c Knott b Willis	64	lbw b Botham	48
4 S. F. A. Bacchus	c Botham b Willis	30	c Knott b Hendrick	19
5 A. I. Kallicharran	b Botham	17	c Knott b Willis	9
6 D. L. Murray†	b Willis	64	(7) c Hendrick b Willis	16
7 C. H. Lloyd*	c Knott b Lever	9	(6) lbw b Willis	3
8 M. D. Marshall	c Tavaré b Gooch	20	b Willis	7
9 A. M. E. Roberts	lbw b Botham	21	not out	22
10 J. Garner	c Lever b Botham	2		
11 M. A. Holding	not out	0	(10) not out	0
Extras (B 1, LB 9, W 2, NB 4)		16	(LB 8, NB 9)	17
Total		308	(8 wkts)	209

Bowling

	O	M	R	W	O	M	R	W
West Indies								
Roberts	25	7	72	5	24	6	57	3
Holding	23.5	7	61	1	26	5	65	0
Marshall	19	3	52	1	24	8	44	2
Richards	1	0	9	0				
Garner	23	9	44	3	34.1	20	30	4
Greenidge					3	2	4	0
England								
Willis	20.1	5	82	4	26	4	65	5
Lever	20	2	76	1	8	2	25	0
Hendrick	19	4	69	1	14	5	40	1
Willey	5	3	4	0	2	0	12	0
Botham	20	6	50	3	16.4	6	48	1
Gooch	7	2	11	1	2	1	2	0

Fall of Wickets

	E 1st	WI 1st	E 2nd	WI 2nd
1st	27	19	46	11
2nd	72	107	68	69
3rd	74	151	174	109
4th	114	165	175	125
5th	204	208	180	129
6th	208	227	183	165
7th	228	265	218	180
8th	246	306	237	205
9th	254	308	248	
10th	263	308	252	

Umpires: D. J. Constant and D. O. Oslear Captain* Wicket-keeper†

England v West Indies 1980 (Second Test)

VENUE: Lord's
DATE: 19, 20, 21, 23, 24 June. England won the toss
RESULT: Match Drawn

Batted First: England

1 G. A. Gooch	lbw b Holding	123	b Garner	47
2 G. Boycott	c Murray b Holding	8	not out	49
3 C. J. Tavaré	c Greenidge b Holding	42	lbw b Garner	6
4 R. A. Woolmer	c Kallicharran b Garner	15	not out	19
5 M. W. Gatting	b Holding	18		
6 I. T. Botham*	lbw b Garner	8		
7 D. L. Underwood	lbw b Garner	3		
8 P. Willey	b Holding	4		
9 A. P. E. Knott†	c Garner b Holding	9		
10 R. G. D. Willis	b Garner	14		
11 M. Hendrick	not out	10		
Extras (B 4, LB 1, W 4, NB 6)		15	(LB 1, NB 11)	12
Total		269	(2 wkts)	133

Batted Second: West Indies

1 C. G. Greenidge	lbw b Botham	25
2 D. L. Haynes	lbw b Botham	184
3 I. V. A. Richards	c sub b Willey	145
4 C. E. H. Croft	run out	0
5 A. I. Kallicharran	c Knott b Willis	15
6 S. F. A. F. Bacchus	c Gooch b Willis	0
7 C. H. Lloyd*	b Willey	56
8 D. L. Murray†	c Tavaré b Botham	34
9 A. M. E. Roberts	b Underwood	24
10 J. Garner	c Gooch b Willis	15
11 M. A. Holding	not out	0
Extras (B 1, LB 9, W 1, NB 9)		20
Total		518

Bowling

	O	M	R	W	O	M	R	W
West Indies								
Roberts	18	3	50	0	13	3	24	0
Holding	28	11	67	6	15	5	51	0
Garner	24.3	8	36	4	15	6	21	2
Croft	20	3	77	0	8	2	24	0
Richards	5	1	24	0	1	0	1	0
England								
Willis	31	12	103	3				
Botham	37	7	145	3				
Underwood	29.2	7	108	1				
Hendrick	11	2	32	0				
Gooch	7	1	26	0				
Willey	25	8	73	2				
Boycott	7	2	11	0				

Fall of Wickets

	E	WI	E
	1st	1st	2nd
1st	20	37	71
2nd	165	260	96
3rd	190	275	
4th	219	326	
5th	220	330	
6th	231	437	
7th	232	469	
8th	244	486	
9th	245	518	
10th	269	518	

Umpires: W. E. Alley and B. J. Meyer Captain* Wicket-keeper†

England v West Indies 1980 (Third Test)

VENUE: Old Trafford
DATE: 10, 11, 12, 14, 15 July. West Indies won the toss
RESULT: Match Drawn

Batted First: England

1 G. A. Gooch	lbw b Roberts	2	c Murray b Marshall	26
2 G. Boycott	c Garner b Roberts	5	lbw b Holding	86
3 B. C. Rose	b Marshall	70	c Kall'arran b Holding	32
4 W. Larkins	lbw b Garner	11	c Murray b Marshall	33
5 M. W. Gatting	c Richards b Marshall	33	c Kallicharran b Garner	56
6 I. T. Botham*	c Murray b Garner	8	lbw b Holding	35
7 P. Willey	b Marshall	0	not out	62
8 A. P. E. Knott†	run out	2	c and b Garner	6
9 J. E. Emburey	c Murray b Roberts	3	not out	28
10 G. R. Dilley	b Garner	0		
11 R. G. D. Willis	not out	5		
Extras	(LB 4, W 3, NB 4)	11	(B 5, LB 8, W 1, NB 13)	27
Total		150	(7 wkts)	391

Batted Second: West Indies

1 C. G. Greenidge	c Larkins b Dilley	0
2 D. L. Haynes	c Knott b Willis	1
3 I. V. A. Richards	b Botham	65
4 S. F. A. F. Bacchus	c Botham b Dilley	0
5 A. I. Kallicharran	c Knott b Botham	13
6 C. H. Lloyd*	c Gooch b Emburey	101
7 D. L. Murray†	b Botham	17
8 M. D. Marshall	c Gooch b Dilley	18
9 A. M. E. Roberts	c Knott b Emburey	11
10 J. Garner	lbw b Emburey	0
11 M. A. Holding	not out	4
Extras	(B 2, LB 13, W 3, NB 12)	30
Total		260

Bowling

	O	M	R	W	O	M	R	W
West Indies								
Roberts	11.2	3	23	3	14	2	36	0
Holding	14	2	46	0	34	8	100	3
Garner	11	2	34	3	40	11	73	2
Marshall	12	5	36	3	35	5	116	2
Richards					16	6	31	0
Lloyd					1	0	1	0
Bacchus					1	0	3	0
Haynes					1	0	2	0
Kallicharran					1	0	2	0
England								
Willis	14	1	99	1				
Dilley	28	7	47	3				
Botham	20	6	64	3				
Emburey	10.3	1	20	3				

Fall of Wickets

	E 1st	WI 1st	E 2nd
1st	3	4	32
2nd	18	25	86
3rd	35	25	181
4th	126	67	217
5th	131	100	290
6th	132	154	290
7th	142	209	309
8th	142	250	
9th	142	250	
10th	150	260	

Umpires: H. D. Bird and K. E. Palmer Captain* Wicket-keeper†

England v West Indies 1980 (Fourth Test)

VENUE: Kennington Oval
DATE: 24, 25, 26, 28, 29 July. England won the toss
RESULT: Match Drawn

Batted First: England

1 G. A. Gooch	lbw b Holding	83	lbw b Holding	0
2 G. Boycott	run out	53	c Murray b Croft	5
3 B. C. Rose	b Croft	50	lbw b Garner	41
4 W. Larkins	lbw b Garner	7	b Holding	0
5 M. W. Gatting	b Croft	48	(6) c Murray b Garner	15
6 P. Willey	c Lloyd b Holding	34	(8) not out	100
7 A. P. E. Knott†	c Lloyd b Marshall	3	(9) lbw b Holding	3
8 I. T. Botham*	lbw b Croft	9	(7) c Greenidge b Garner	4
9 J. E. Emburey	c Holding b Marshall	24	(5) c Bacchus b Croft	2
10 G. R. Dilley	b Garner	1	c sub b Holding	1
11 R. G. D. Willis	not out	1	not out	24
Extras (B 7, LB 21, W 10, NB 19)		57	(LB 6, W 1, NB 7)	14
Total		370	(9 wkts dec.)	209

Batted Second: West Indies

1 C. G. Greenidge	lbw b Willis	6
2 D. L. Haynes	c Gooch b Dilley	7
3 I. V. A. Richards	c Willey b Botham	26
4 S. F. A. Bacchus	c Knott b Emburey	61
5 A. I. Kallicharran	c Rose b Dilley	11
6 D. L. Murray†	hit wkt b Dilley	0
7 M. D. Marshall	c Rose b Emburey	45
8 J. Garner	c Gatting b Botham	46
9 M. A. Holding	lbw b Dilley	22
10 C. E. H. Croft	not out	0
11 C. H. Lloyd*	absent hurt	
Extras (LB 12, W 1, NB 28)		41
Total		265

Bowling

	O	M	R	W	O	M	R	W
West Indies								
Holding	28	5	67	2	29	7	79	4
Croft	35	9	97	3	10	6	8	2
Marshall	29.3	6	77	2	23	7	47	0
Garner	33	8	67	2	17	5	24	3
Richards	3	1	5	0	9	3	15	0
Kallicharran					6	1	22	0
England								
Willis	19	5	58	1				
Dilley	23	6	57	4				
Botham	18.2	8	47	2				
Emburey	23	12	38	2				
Gooch	1	0	2	0				
Willey	11	5	22	0				

Fall of Wickets

	E	WI	E
	1st	1st	2nd
1st	155	15	2
2nd	157	34	10
3rd	182	72	13
4th	269	99	18
5th	303	105	63
6th	312	187	67
7th	336	197	73
8th	343	261	84
9th	368	265	92
10th	370		

Umpires: B. J. Meyer and D. O. Oslear Captain* Wicket-keeper†

England v West Indies 1980 (Fifth Test)

VENUE: Headingley
DATE: 7, 8, 9, 11, 12 August. West Indies won the toss
RESULT: Match Drawn

Batted First: England

1	G. A. Gooch	c Marshall b Garner	14	lbw b Marshall	55
2	G. Boycott	c Kallicharran b Holding	4	c Kallicharran b Croft	47
3	B. C. Rose	b Croft	7	(5) not out	43
4	W. Larkins	c Kallicharran b Garner	9	(3) lbw b Marshall	30
5	M. W. Gatting	c Marshall b Croft	1	(4) lbw b Holding	1
6	I. T. Botham*	c Richards b Holding	37	lbw b Marshall	7
7	P. Willey	c Murray b Croft	1	c Murray b Holding	10
8	D. L. Bairstow†	lbw b Marshall	40	not out	9
9	J. E. Emburey	not out	13		
10	C. M. Old	c Garner b Marshall	6		
11	G. R. Dilley	b Garner	0		
	Extras (B 3, LB 3, W 1, NB 4)		11	(B 5, LB 11, W 2, NB 7)	25
	Total		143	(6 wkts dec.)	227

Batted Second: West Indies

1	C. G. Greenidge	lbw b Botham	34
2	D. L. Haynes	b Emburey	42
3	I. V. A. Richards*	b Old	31
4	S. F. A. Bacchus	c and b Dilley	11
5	A. I. Kallicharran	c Larkins b Dilley	37
6	C. L. King	c Bairstow b Gooch	12
7	D. L. Murray†	c Emburey b Dilley	14
8	M. D. Marshall	c Bairstow b Dilley	0
9	M. A. Holding	b Old	35
10	J. Garner	c Emburey b Gooch	0
11	C. E. H. Croft	not out	1
	Extras (B 2, LB 9, W 3, NB 14)		28
	Total		245

Bowling

	O	M	R	W	O	M	R	W
West Indies								
Holding	10	4	34	2	23	2	62	2
Croft	12	3	35	3	19	2	65	1
Garner	14	4	41	3	1	0	1	0
Marshall	11	3	22	2	19	5	42	3
King					12	3	32	0
Richards					1	1	0	0
England								
Dilley	23	6	79	4				
Old	28.5	9	64	2				
Botham	19	8	31	1				
Emburey	6	0	25	1				
Gooch	8	3	18	2				

Fall of Wickets

	E 1st	WI 1st	E 2nd
1st	9	83	95
2nd	27	105	126
3rd	28	133	129
4th	34	142	162
5th	52	170	174
6th	59	198	203
7th	89	198	
8th	131	207	
9th	140	207	
10th	143	245	

Umpires: W. E. Alley and K. E. Palmer Captain* Wicket-keeper†

Appendix 9 **1984**

Tests: Played 5, Won 5

First-class Matches: Played 14, Won 8, Drawn 6

All Matches: Played 23, Won 12, Drawn 10, Lost 1

Won: England (7), Derbyshire, Glamorgan, Somerset, Lancashire, Lavinia Duchess of Norfolk's XI.

Drawn: Essex, Leicestershire, Middlesex, Northamptonshire, Nottinghamshire, Worcestershire, Oxford/Cambridge XI, Ireland, League Cricket Conference, Minor Counties.

Lost: England.

First-class Averages

Batting

	M	I	NO	R	HS	Av	100	Ct	St
C. G. Greenidge	11	16	3	1069	223	82.23	4	5	—
A. L. Logie	8	10	2	585	141	73.12	2	3	—
H. A. Gomes	12	17	5	841	143	70.08	4	2	—
C. H. Lloyd	9	9	2	364	72	52.00	—	12	—
I. V. A. Richards	12	15	1	625	170	44.64	2	12	—
P. J. L. Dujon	12	15	2	558	107	42.92	2	27	—
D. L. Haynes	12	17	1	632	125	39.50	1	9	—
T. R. O. Payne	7	8	3	191	44	38.20	—	4	1
W. W. Davis	4	4	1	112	77	37.33	—	1	—
R. B. Richardson	8	10	0	335	111	33.50	1	3	—
R. A. Harper	13	12	2	328	73	32.80	—	14	—
M. A. Holding	7	7	0	189	69	27.00	—	3	—
E. A. E. Baptiste	10	9	1	196	87*	24.50	—	1	—
M. D. Marshall	8	9	0	103	34	11.44	—	3	—
J. Garner	8	8	1	61	29	8.71	—	4	—
M. A. Small	5	3	2	6	3*	6.00	—	1	—

Also batted: C. A. Walsh 2*, 0, 0, 0*, 0.

Bowling

	O	M	R	W	Av
W. W. Davis	66	13	199	14	14.21
J. Garner	270.5	81	624	39	16.00
M. D. Marshall	260.4	75	646	40	16.15
R. A. Harper	302.1	106	632	37	17.08
M. A. Holding	178.5	42	486	21	23.14
M. A. Small	100	17	321	13	24.69
E. A. E. Baptiste	221.2	64	517	19	27.21
C. A. Walsh	156.1	32	557	14	39.79

Also bowled: C. G. Greenidge 9–6–11–1; H. A. Gomes 44–15–81–2; I. V. A. Richards 74–20–183–3.

Test Averages

England Batting

	M	I	NO	R	HS	Av
A. J. Lamb	5	10	1	386	110	42.88
I. T. Botham	5	10	0	347	81	34.70
G. Fowler	5	10	0	260	106	26.00
B. C. Broad	4	8	0	195	55	24.37
P. R. Downton	5	10	1	210	56	23.33
R. G. D. Willis	3	5	3	43	22	21.50
D. I. Gower	5	10	1	171	57*	19.00
D. R. Pringle	3	6	1	81	46*	16.20
P. J. W. Allott	3	6	0	67	26	11.16
G. Miller	2	4	0	42	22	10.50
V. P. Terry	2	3	0	16	8	5.33
N. G. B. Cook	3	6	0	25	13	4.16
P. I. Pocock	2	4	0	0	0	0.00

Also batted: J. P. Agnew 5, 2*; N. G. Cowans 0, 14; R. M. Ellison 20*, 13; N. A. Foster 6, 9*; M. W. Gatting 1, 29; T. A. Lloyd 10*; D. W. Randall 0, 1; C. J. Tavaré 16, 49.

England Bowling

	O	M	R	W	Av
R. M. Ellison	44	10	94	5	18.80
P. J. W. Allott	104.5	26	282	14	20.14
I. T. Botham	163.2	30	667	19	35.10
P. I. Pocock	53.3	17	145	4	36.25
D. R. Pringle	71.3	10	257	5	51.40
N. G. B. Cook	95	15	297	5	59.40
R. G. D. Willis	85	15	367	6	61.16

Also bowled: J. P. Agnew 26–4–97–2; N. G. Cowans 19–2–46–0; N. A. Foster 18–2–82–0; G. Miller 28–1–142–1.

West Indies Batting

	M	I	NO	R	HS	Av
C. G. Greenidge	5	8	1	572	223	81.71
H. A. Gomes	5	8	3	400	143	80.00
C. H. Lloyd	5	6	1	255	71	51.00
I. V. A. Richards	5	7	1	250	117	41.66
P. J. L. Dujon	5	6	0	210	101	35.00
E. A. E. Baptiste	5	6	1	174	87*	34.80
M. A. Holding	4	5	0	158	69	31.60
D. L. Haynes	5	8	0	235	125	29.37
R. A. Harper	5	6	1	96	39*	19.20
M. D. Marshall	4	5	0	47	29	9.40
J. Garner	5	6	1	29	10*	5.80

Also batted: W. W. Davis 77; M. A. Small 3*.

West Indies Bowling

	O	M	R	W	Av
M. D. Marshall	167.4	50	437	24	18.20
J. Garner	217.5	60	540	29	18.62
R. A. Harper	128.4	47	276	13	21.23
M. A. Holding	122.2	24	343	15	22.87
E. A. E. Baptiste	125	39	265	8	33.12

Also bowled: W. W. Davis 23–3–77–2; I. V. A. Richards 1–0–2–0; M. A. Small 21–2–78–3.

England v West Indies 1984 (First Test)

VENUE: Edgbaston
DATE: 14, 15, 16, 18 June. England won the toss
RESULT: West Indies won by an innings and 180 runs

Batted First: England

1	G. Fowler	c Dujon b Garner 0	lbw b Garner 7
2	T. A. Lloyd	retired hurt 10	absent hurt
3	D. W. Randall	b Garner 0	c Lloyd b Garner 1
4	D. I. Gower*	c Harper b Holding 10	c Dujon b Garner 12
5	A. J. Lamb	c Lloyd b Baptiste 15	c Richards b Marshall 13
6	I. T. Botham	c Garner b Harper 64	lbw b Garner 38
7	G. Miller	c Dujon b Garner 22	c Harper b Marshall 11
8	D. R. Pringle	c Dujon b Holding 4	not out 46
9	P. R. Downton†	lbw b Garner 33	(2) c Greenidge b Harper 56
10	N. G. B. Cook	c Lloyd b Marshall 2	(9) run out 9
11	R. G. D. Willis	not out 10	(10) c Dujon b Garner 22
	Extras (B 8, LB 5, NB 8)	 21	(B 1, LB 5, W 4, NB 10) 20
	Total	 191	235

Batted Second: West Indies

1	C. G. Greenidge	lbw b Willis 19
2	D. L. Haynes	lbw b Willis 8
3	H. A. Gomes	c Miller b Pringle 143
4	I. V. A. Richards	c Randall b Cook 117
5	P. J. L. Dujon†	c Gower b Miller 23
6	C. H. Lloyd*	c Pringle b Botham 71
7	M. D. Marshall	lbw b Pringle 2
8	R. A. Harper	b Pringle 14
9	E. A. E. Baptiste	not out 87
10	M. A. Holding	c Willis b Pringle 69
11	J. Garner	c Lamb b Pringle 0
	Extras (B 6, LB 17, W 2, NB 28)	 53
	Total	 606

Bowling

	O	M	R	W	O	M	R	W
West Indies								
Marshall	14	4	37	1	23	7	65	2
Garner	14.3	2	53	4	23.5	7	55	5
Holding	16	4	44	2	12	3	29	0
Baptiste	11	3	28	1	5	1	18	0
Harper	4	1	8	1	13	3	48	1
England								
Willis	25	3	108	2				
Botham	34	7	127	1				
Pringle	31	5	108	5				
Cook	38	6	127	1				
Miller	15	1	83	1				

Fall of Wickets

	E	WI	E
	1st	1st	2nd
1st	1	34	17
2nd	5	35	21
3rd	45	241	37
4th	49	294	65
5th	89	418	127
6th	103	418	138
7th	168	421	181
8th	173	455	193
9th	191	605	235
10th		606	

Umpires: H. D. Bird and B. J. Meyer Captain* Wicket-keeper†

England v West Indies 1984 (Second Test)

VENUE: Lord's
DATE: 28, 29, 30 June, 2, 3 July. West Indies won the toss
RESULT: West Indies won by 9 wickets

Batted First: England

1 G. Fowler	c Harper b Baptiste	106	lbw b Small	11
2 B. C. Broad	c Dujon b Marshall	55	c Harper b Garner	0
3 D. I. Gower*	lbw b Marshall	3	c Lloyd b Small	21
4 A. J. Lamb	lbw b Marshall	23	c Dujon b Marshall	110
5 M. W. Gatting	lbw b Marshall	1	lbw b Marshall	29
6 I. T. Botham	c Richards b Baptiste	30	lbw b Garner	81
7 P. R. Downton†	not out	23	lbw b Small	4
8 G. Miller	run out	0	b Harper	9
9 D. R. Pringle	lbw b Garner	2	lbw b Garner	8
10 N. A. Foster	c Harper b Marshall	6	not out	9
11 R. G. D. Willis	b Marshall	2		
Extras	(B 4, LB 14, W 2, NB 15)	35	(B 4, LB 7, W 1, NB 6)	18
Total		286	(9 wkts dec.)	300

Batted Second: West Indies

1 C. G. Greenidge	c Miller b Botham	1	not out	214
2 D. L. Haynes	lbw b Botham	12	run out	17
3 H. A. Gomes	c Gatting b Botham	10	not out	92
4 I. V. A. Richards	lbw b Botham	72		
5 C. H. Lloyd*	lbw b Botham	39		
6 P. J. L. Dujon†	c Fowler b Botham	8		
7 M. D. Marshall	c Pringle b Willis	29		
8 E. A. E. Baptiste	c Downton b Willis	44		
9 R. A. Harper	c Gatting b Botham	8		
10 J. Garner	c Downton b Botham	6		
11 M. A. Small	not out	3		
Extras	(LB 5, W 1, NB 7)	13	(B 4, LB 4, NB 13)	21
Total		245	(1 wkt)	344

Bowling

	O	M	R	W	O	M	R	W
West Indies								
Garner	32	10	67	1	30.3	3	91	3
Small	9	0	38	0	12	2	40	3
Marshall	36.5	10	85	6	22	6	85	2
Baptiste	20	6	36	2	26	8	48	0
Harper	8	0	25	0	8	1	18	1
England								
Willis	19	5	48	2	15	5	48	0
Botham	27.4	6	103	8	20.1	2	117	0
Pringle	11	0	54	0	8	0	44	0
Foster	6	2	13	0	12	0	69	0
Miller	2	0	14	0	11	0	45	0

Fall of Wickets

	E 1st	WI 1st	E 2nd	WI 2nd
1st	101	1	5	57
2nd	106	18	33	
3rd	183	35	36	
4th	185	138	88	
5th	243	147	216	
6th	248	173	230	
7th	251	213	273	
8th	255	231	290	
9th	264	241	300	
10th	286	245		

Umpires: D. G. L. Evans and B. J. Meyer Captain* Wicket-keeper†

England v West Indies 1984 (Third Test)

VENUE: Headingley
DATE: 12, 13, 14, 16 July. England won the toss
RESULT: West Indies won by 8 wickets

Batted First: England

1 G. Fowler	lbw b Garner	10	c and b Marshall	50
2 B. C. Broad	c Lloyd b Harper	32	c Baptiste b Marshall	2
3 V. P. Terry	c Harper b Holding	8	lbw b Garner	1
4 D. I. Gower*	lbw b Garner	2	c Dujon b Harper	43
5 A. J. Lamb	b Harper	100	lbw b Marshall	3
6 I. T. Botham	c Dujon b Baptiste	45	c Dujon b Garner	14
7 P. R. Downton†	c Lloyd b Harper	17	c Dujon b Marshall	27
8 D. R. Pringle	c Haynes b Holding	19	(9) lbw b Marshall	2
9 P. J. W. Allott	b Holding	3	(10) lbw b Marshall	4
10 N. G. B. Cook	b Holding	1	(8) c Lloyd b Marshall	0
11 R. G. D. Willis	not out	4	not out	5
Extras (B 4, LB 7, NB 18)		29	(LB 6, NB 2)	8
Total		270		159

Batted Second: West Indies

1 C. G. Greenidge	c Botham b Willis	10	c Terry b Cook	49
2 D. L. Haynes	b Allott	18	c Fowler b Cook	43
3 H. A. Gomes	not out	104	not out	2
4 I. V. A. Richards	c Pringle b Allott	15	not out	22
5 C. H. Lloyd*	c Gower b Cook	48		
6 P. J. L. Dujon†	lbw b Allott	26		
7 E. A. E. Baptiste	c Broad b Allott	0		
8 R. A. Harper	c Downton b Allott	0		
9 M. A. Holding	c Allott b Willis	59		
10 J. Garner	run out	0		
11 M. D. Marshall	c Botham b Allott	4		
Extras (LB 3, NB 15)		18	(LB 2, NB 13)	15
Total		302	(2 wkts)	131

Bowling

	O	M	R	W	O	M	R	W
West Indies								
Garner	30	11	73	2	16	7	37	2
Marshall	6	4	6	0	26	9	53	7
Holding	29.2	8	70	4	7	1	31	0
Baptiste	13	1	45	1				
Harper	19	6	47	3	16	8	30	1
England								
Willis	18	1	123	2	8	1	40	0
Allott	26.5	7	61	6	7	2	24	0
Botham	7	0	45	0				
Pringle	13	3	26	0	8.3	2	25	0
Cook	9	1	29	1	9	2	27	2

Fall of Wickets

	E 1st	WI 1st	E 2nd	WI 2nd
1st	13	16	10	106
2nd	43	43	13	108
3rd	53	78	104	
4th	87	148	106	
5th	172	201	107	
6th	236	206	135	
7th	237	206	138	
8th	244	288	140	
9th	254	290	146	
10th	270	302	159	

Umpires: D. J. Constant and D. G. L. Evans Captain* Wicket-keeper†

England v West Indies 1984 (Fourth Test)

VENUE: Old Trafford

DATE: 26, 27, 28, 30, 31 July. West Indies won the toss

RESULT: West Indies won by an innings and 64 runs

Batted First: West Indies

1 C. G. Greenidge	c Downton b Pocock	223
2 D. L. Haynes	c Cowans b Botham	2
3 H. A. Gomes	c Botham b Allott	30
4 I. V. A. Richards	c Cook b Allott	1
5 C. H. Lloyd*	c Downton b Allott	1
6 P. J. L. Dujon†	c Downton b Botham	101
7 W. W. Davis	b Pocock	77
8 E. A. E. Baptiste	b Pocock	6
9 R. A. Harper	not out	39
10 M. A. Holding	b Cook	0
11 J. Garner	c Terry b Pocock	7
Extras (B 4, LB 6, W 2, NB 1)		13
Total		500

Batted Second: England

1 G. Fowler	b Baptiste	38	b Holding	0
2 B. C. Broad	c Harper b Davis	42	lbw b Harper	21
3 V. P. Terry	b Garner	7	absent hurt	
4 D. I. Gower*	c Dujon b Baptiste	4	not out	57
5 A. J. Lamb	not out	100	b Harper	9
6 I. T. Botham	c Garner b Baptiste	6	c Haynes b Harper	1
7 P. R. Downton†	c Harper b Garner	0	(3) b Harper	24
8 P. J. W. Allott	c Gomes b Davis	26	(7) b Garner	14
9 N. G. B. Cook	b Holding	13	(8) c Dujon b Garner	0
10 P. I. Pocock	b Garner	0	(9) c Garner b Harper	0
11 N. G. Cowans	b Garner	0	(10) b Harper	14
Extras (B 5, LB 21, NB 18)		44	(B 9, LB 3, NB 3)	16
Total		280		156

Bowling

	O	M	R	W	O	M	R	W
England								
Botham	29	5	100	2				
Cowans	19	2	76	0				
Allott	28	9	76	3				
Cook	39	6	114	1				
Pocock	45.3	14	121	4				
West Indies								
Garner	22.2	7	51	4	12	4	25	2
Davis	20	2	71	2	3	1	6	0
Harper	23	10	33	0	28.4	12	57	6
Holding	21	2	50	1	11	2	21	1
Baptiste	19	8	31	3	11	5	29	0
Richards					1	0	2	0

Fall of Wickets

	WI 1st	E 1st	E 2nd
1st	11	90	0
2nd	60	112	39
3rd	62	117	77
4th	70	138	99
5th	267	147	101
6th	437	228	125
7th	443	257	127
8th	470	278	128
9th	471	278	156
10th	500	280	

Umpires: H. D. Bird and D. O. Oslear Captain* Wicket-keeper†

England v West Indies 1984 (Fifth Test)

VENUE: Kennington Oval
DATE: 9, 10, 11, 13, 14 August. West Indies won the toss
RESULT: West Indies won by 172 runs

Batted First: West Indies

1	C. G. Greenidge	lbw b Botham	22	c Botham b Agnew	34
2	D. L. Haynes	b Allott	10	b Botham	125
3	H. A. Gomes	c Botham b Ellison	18	c Tavaré b Ellison	1
4	I. V. A. Richards	c Allott b Botham	8	lbw b Agnew	15
5	P. J. L. Dujon†	c Tavaré b Botham	3	(6) c Lamb b Ellison	49
6	C. H. Lloyd*	not out	60	(5) c Downton b Ellison	36
7	M. D. Marshall	c Gower b Ellison	0	(8) c Lamb b Botham	12
8	E. A. E. Baptiste	c Fowler b Allott	32	(7) c Downton b Allott	5
9	R. A. Harper	b Botham	18	c Downton b Allott	17
10	M. A. Holding	lbw b Botham	0	lbw b Botham	30
11	J. Garner	c Downton b Allott	6	not out	10
	Extras (B 1, LB 4, W 7, NB 1)		13	(LB 12)	12
	Total		190		346

Batted Second: England

1	G. Fowler	c Richards b Baptiste	31	c Richards b Marshall	7
2	B. C. Broad	b Garner	4	c Greenidge b Holding	39
3	P. I. Pocock	c Greenidge b Marshall	0	(10) c and b Holding	0
4	C. J. Tavaré	c Dujon b Holding	16	(3) c Richards b Garner	49
5	D. I. Gower*	c Dujon b Holding	12	(4) lbw b Holding	7
6	A. J. Lamb	lbw b Marshall	12	(5) c Haynes b Holding	1
7	I. T. Botham	c Dujon b Marshall	14	(6) c Marshall b Garner	54
8	P. R. Downton†	c Lloyd b Garner	16	(7) lbw b Garner	10
9	R. M. Ellison	not out	20	(8) c Holding b Garner	13
10	P. J. W. Allott	b Marshall	16	(9) c Lloyd b Holding	4
11	J. P. Agnew	b Marshall	5	not out	2
	Extras (B 2, LB 4, NB 10)		16	(LB 2, W 1, NB 13)	16
	Total		162		202

Bowling

	O	M	R	W	O	M	R	W
England								
Agnew	12	3	46	0	14	1	51	2
Allott	17	7	25	3	26	1	96	2
Botham	23	8	72	5	22.3	2	103	3
Ellison	18	3	34	2	26	7	60	3
Pocock					8	3	24	0
West Indies								
Garner	18	6	37	2	18.4	3	51	4
Marshall	17.5	5	35	5	22	5	71	1
Holding	13	2	55	2	13	2	43	5
Baptiste	12	4	19	1	8	3	11	0
Harper	1	1	0	0	8	5	10	0

Fall of Wickets

	WI 1st	E 1st	WI 2nd	E 2nd
1st	19	10	51	15
2nd	45	22	52	75
3rd	64	45	69	88
4th	64	64	132	90
5th	67	83	214	135
6th	70	84	237	181
7th	124	116	264	186
8th	154	133	293	200
9th	154	156	329	200
10th	190	162	346	202

Umpires: D. J. Constant and B. J. Meyer Captain* Wicket-keeper†

Appendix 10 **1988**

Tests: Played 5, Won 4, Drawn 1

First-class Matches: Played 16, Won 6, Drawn 10

All Matches: Played 23, Won 9, Drawn 11, Lost 3

Won: England (4), Kent, Somerset, Hampshire, Lavinia Duchess of Norfolk's XI, Oxford/Cambridge XI.

Drawn: England, Essex, Glamorgan, Gloucestershire, Lancashire, Leicestershire, Northamptonshire, Nottinghamshire, Sussex, Worcestershire, Minor Counties.

Lost: England (3).

First-class Averages

Batting

	M	I	NO	R	HS	Av	100	Ct	St
R. A. Harper	12	13	5	622	217*	77.75	1	22	—
C. G. Greenidge	11	16	1	762	111	50.80	3	6	—
P. J. L. Dujon	12	16	4	601	141	50.08	1	31	—
K. L. T. Arthurton	10	13	3	499	121	49.90	2	8	—
D. L. Haynes	14	23	4	903	158	47.52	1	6	—
A. L. Logie	13	18	4	586	95*	41.85	—	9	—
I. V. A. Richards	13	16	1	624	128	41.60	1	9	—
C. L. Hooper	14	20	1	625	87	32.89	—	9	—
M. D. Marshall	9	10	1	289	76	32.11	—	3	—
C. E. L. Ambrose	13	15	3	278	59	23.16	—	1	—
D. Williams	8	10	1	182	51	20.22	—	11	1
R. B. Richardson	10	14	0	279	82	19.92	—	9	—
W. K. M. Benjamin	10	10	4	102	21*	17.00	—	6	—
I. R. Bishop	8	6	2	56	23	14.00	—	1	—
B. P. Patterson	9	7	2	60	23*	12.00	—	1	—
C. A. Walsh	9	7	3	31	9*	7.75	—	—	—

Also batted: P. V. Simmons 53*.

Bowling

	O	M	R	W	Av
M. D. Marshall	254.4	56	553	42	13.16
W. K. M. Benjamin	183.1	43	467	33	14.15
I. R. Bishop	142	30	406	21	19.33
C. E. L. Ambrose	329.1	86	733	35	20.94
R. A. Harper	227.3	70	521	21	24.80
B. P. Patterson	196	33	632	25	25.28
C. L. Hooper	106.1	16	303	9	33.66
C. A. Walsh	232.2	55	622	18	34.55

Also bowled: K. L. T. Arthurton 27.1–8–80–3; I. V. A. Richards 45.4–10–122–3; R. B. Richardson 4–0–22–0.

Test Averages

England Batting

	M	I	NO	R	HS	Av
G. A. Gooch	5	10	0	459	146	45.90
A. J. Lamb	4	8	2	254	113	42.33
D. I. Gower	4	8	1	211	88*	30.14
R. A. Smith	2	4	0	106	57	26.50
P. R. Downton	3	5	1	84	27	21.00
P. W. Jarvis	2	3	1	42	29*	21.00
B. C. Broad	2	4	0	71	54	17.75
T. S. Curtis	2	4	0	69	30	17.25
N. A. Foster	2	4	1	49	34	16.33
M. D. Moxon	2	4	0	55	26	13.75
G. R. Dilley	4	7	1	58	28	9.66
M. W. Gatting	2	4	0	38	29	9.50
J. E. Emburey	3	5	0	46	30	9.20
D. R. Pringle	4	7	0	52	39	7.42
D. J. Capel	2	4	0	29	16	7.25
P. A. J. DeFreitas	3	5	0	36	18	7.20
C. J. Richards	2	4	0	13	8	3.25
J. H. Childs	2	4	4	2	2*	–

Also batted: C. J. W. Athey 16, 11; R. J. Bailey 43, 3; C. S. Cowdrey 0, 5; M. P. Maynard 3, 10; G. C. Small 5*, 7.

England Bowling

	O	M	R	W	Av
G. R. Dilley	136.1	26	403	15	26.86
N. A. Foster	73.2	12	250	9	27.77
D. R. Pringle	119	33	326	11	29.63
G. C. Small	37.5	6	140	4	35.00
P. W. Jarvis	57.1	6	217	6	36.16
J. H. Childs	86	29	183	3	61.00
J. E. Emburey	62	14	228	3	76.00
P. A. J. DeFreitas	92	16	253	3	84.33

Also bowled: D. J. Capel 22–2–79–1; C. S. Cowdrey 5.3–0–21–0.

West Indies Batting

	M	I	NO	R	HS	Av
A. L. Logie	5	7	2	364	95*	72.80
P. J. L. Dujon	5	7	1	305	67	50.83
R. A. Harper	3	3	0	147	74	49.00
C. G. Greenidge	4	6	0	282	103	47.00
D. L. Haynes	4	7	2	235	77*	47.00
I. V. A. Richards	5	6	0	223	80	37.16
M. D. Marshall	5	6	1	135	72	27.00
C. L. Hooper	5	7	0	166	84	23.71
C. E. L. Ambrose	5	6	2	75	43	18.75
R. B. Richardson	3	4	0	71	26	17.75
C. A. Walsh	5	5	3	26	9*	13.00
W. K. M. Benjamin	3	2	0	9	9	4.50
B. P. Patterson	2	2	0	2	2	1.00

Also batted: K. L. T. Arthurton 27.

West Indies Bowling

	O	M	R	W	Av
W. K. M. Benjamin	67	17	151	12	12.58
R. A. Harper	29	111	63	5	12.60
M. D. Marshall	203.1	49	443	35	12.65
C. E. L. Ambrose	203.1	56	445	22	20.22
C. A. Walsh	157.2	40	412	12	34.33
B. P. Patterson	74.5	13	270	4	67.50

Also bowled: C. L. Hooper 24–3–57–0; I. V. A. Richards 10–1–28–0.

England v West Indies 1988 (First Test)

VENUE: Trent Bridge
DATE: 2, 3, 4, 6, 7 June. England won the toss
RESULT: Match Drawn

Batted First: England

1	G. A. Gooch	b Marshall	73	c Dujon b Patterson 146
2	B. C. Broad	b Marshall	54	c Dujon b Ambrose 16
3	M. W. Gatting*	c Logie b Marshall	5	b Marshall 29
4	D. I. Gower	c Dujon b Ambrose	18	not out 88
5	A. J. Lamb	lbw b Marshall	0	not out 6
6	D. R. Pringle	b Marshall	39	
7	P. R. Downton†	not out	16	
8	J. E. Emburey	c Dujon b Marshall	0	
9	P. A. J. DeFreitas	b Ambrose	3	
10	P. W. Jarvis	b Ambrose	6	
11	G. R. Dilley	b Ambrose	2	
	Extras (LB 13, W 5, NB 11)		29	(LB 10, NB 6) 16
	Total		245	(3 wkts) 301

Batted Second: West Indies

1	C. G. Greenidge	c Downton b Jarvis	25
2	D. L. Haynes	c Downton b Jarvis	60
3	R. B. Richardson	c Gatting b Emburey	17
4	I. V. A. Richards*	c Gooch b DeFreitas	80
5	C. L. Hooper	c Downton b DeFreitas	84
6	A. L. Logie	c Gooch b Pringle	20
7	P. J. L. Dujon†	c and b Dilley	16
8	M. D. Marshall	b Emburey	72
9	C. E. L. Ambrose	run out	43
10	C. A. Walsh	not out	3
11	B. P. Patterson		
	Extras (B 6, LB 8, NB 14)		28
	Total	(9 wkts dec.)	448

Bowling

	O	M	R	W	O	M	R	W
West Indies								
Marshall	30	4	69	6	13	4	23	1
Patterson	16	2	49	0	24	6	69	1
Ambrose	26	10	53	4	23	4	56	1
Walsh	20	4	39	0	25	5	84	0
Hooper	8	1	20	0	14	1	33	0
Richards	1	0	2	0	9	1	26	0
England								
Dilley	34	5	101	1				
DeFreitas	27	5	93	2				
Jarvis	18.1	1	63	2				
Pringle	34	11	82	1				
Emburey	16	4	95	2				

Fall of Wickets

	E 1st	WI 1st	E 2nd
1st	125	54	39
2nd	141	84	116
3rd	161	159	277
4th	161	231	
5th	186	271	
6th	223	309	
7th	223	334	
8th	235	425	
9th	243	448	
10th	245		

Umpires: H. D. Bird and J. Birkenshaw   Captain*   Wicket-keeper†

England v West Indies 1988 (Second Test)

VENUE: Lord's
DATE: 16, 17, 18, 20, 21 June. West Indies won the toss
RESULT: West Indies won by 134 runs

Batted First: West Indies

1 C. G. Greenidge	c Downton b Dilley 22	c Emburey b Dilley 103
2 D. L. Haynes	c Moxon b Dilley 12	c Downton b Dilley 5
3 R. B. Richardson	c Emburey b Dilley 5	lbw b Pringle 26
4 I. V. A. Richards*	c Downton b Dilley 6	b Pringle 72
5 C. L. Hooper	c Downton b Small 3	c Downton b Jarvis 11
6 A. L. Logie	c Emburey b Small 81	not out 95
7 P. J. L. Dujon†	b Emburey 53	b Jarvis 52
8 M. D. Marshall	c Gooch b Dilley 11	b Jarvis 6
9 C. E. L. Ambrose	c Gower b Small 0	b Dilley 0
10 C. A. Walsh	not out 9	b Dilley 0
11 B. P. Patterson	b Small 0	c Downton b Jarvis 2
Extras (LB 6, NB 1)	 7	(LB 19, W 1, NB 5) 25
Total	 209	397

Batted Second: England

1 G. A. Gooch	b Marshall 44	lbw b Marshall 16
2 B. C. Broad	lbw b Marshall 0	c Dujon b Marshall 1
3 M. D. Moxon	c Richards b Ambrose 26	run out 14
4 D. I. Gower	c sub b Walsh 46	c Richardson b Patterson 1
5 A. J. Lamb	lbw b Marshall 10	run out 113
6 D. R. Pringle	c Dujon b Walsh 1	lbw b Walsh 0
7 P. R. Downton†	lbw b Marshall 11	lbw b Marshall 27
8 J. E. Emburey*	b Patterson 7	b Ambrose 30
9 G. C. Small	not out 5	c Richards b Marshall 7
10 P. W. Jarvis	c Haynes b Marshall 7	not out 29
11 G. R. Dilley	b Marshall 0	c Rich'son b Patterson 28
Extras (LB 6, NB 2)	 8	(B 5, LB 20, W 2, NB 14) 41
Total	 165	307

Bowling

	O	M	R	W	O	M	R	W
England								
Dilley	23	6	55	5	27	6	73	4
Jarvis	13	2	47	0	26	3	107	4
Small	18.5	5	64	4	19	1	76	0
Pringle	7	3	20	0	21	4	60	2
Emburey	6	2	17	1	15	1	62	0
West Indies								
Marshall	18	5	32	6	25	5	60	4
Patterson	13	3	52	1	21.5	2	100	2
Ambrose	12	1	39	1	20	4	47	1
Walsh	16	6	36	2	20	1	75	1

Fall of Wickets

	WI 1st	E 1st	WI 2nd	E 2nd
1st	21	13	32	27
2nd	40	58	115	29
3rd	47	112	198	31
4th	50	129	226	104
5th	54	134	240	105
6th	184	140	371	161
7th	199	153	379	212
8th	199	157	380	232
9th	199	165	384	254
10th	209	165	397	307

Umpires: K. E. Palmer and D. R. Shepherd   Captain*   Wicket-keeper†

England v West Indies 1988 (Third Test)

VENUE: Old Trafford

DATE: 30 June, 1, 2, 4, 5 July. England won the toss

RESULT: West Indies won by an innings and 156 runs

Batted First: England

		1st innings		2nd innings	
1	G. A. Gooch	c Dujon b Benjamin	27	lbw b Marshall	1
2	M. D. Moxon	b Marshall	0	c Richards b Benjamin	15
3	M. W. Gatting	lbw b Marshall	0	c Richardson b Marshall	4
4	D. I. Gower	c Harper b Walsh	9	c Richardson b Marshall	34
5	A. J. Lamb	c Greenidge b Ambrose	33	c Logie b Ambrose	9
6	D. J. Capel	b Benjamin	1	c sub b Marshall	0
7	P. R. Downton†	c Greenidge b Walsh	24	c Harper b Marshall	6
8	J. E. Emburey*	c Dujon b Walsh	1	c Logie b Ambrose	8
9	P. A. J. DeFreitas	c Greenidge b Ambrose	15	c Harper b Marshall	0
10	G. R. Dilley	c Harper b Walsh	14	b Marshall	4
11	J. H. Childs	not out	2	not out	0
	Extras (LB 4, NB 5)		9	(B 1, LB 10, NB 1)	12
	Total		135		93

Batted Second: West Indies

1	C. G. Greenidge	lbw b DeFreitas	45
2	R. B. Richardson	b Dilley	23
3	C. L. Hooper	lbw b Childs	15
4	I. V. A. Richards*	b Capel	47
5	A. L. Logie	lbw b Dilley	39
6	P. J. L. Dujon†	c Capel b Dilley	67
7	R. A. Harper	b Dilley	74
8	M. D. Marshall	not out	43
9	C. E. L. Ambrose	not out	7
10	W. K. M. Benjamin		
11	C. A. Walsh		
	Extras (LB 21, NB 3)		24
	Total	(7 wkts dec.)	384

Bowling

	O	M	R	W	O	M	R	W
West Indies								
Marshall	12	5	19	2	15.4	5	22	7
Ambrose	17	5	35	2	16	4	36	2
Walsh	18.2	4	46	4	4	1	10	0
Benjamin	13	4	31	2	4	1	6	1
Harper					2	1	4	0
Hooper					1	0	4	0
England								
Dilley	28.1	4	99	4				
Emburey	25	7	54	0				
DeFreitas	35	5	81	1				
Capel	12	2	38	1				
Childs	40	12	91	1				

Fall of Wickets

	E 1st	WI 1st	E 2nd
1st	12	35	6
2nd	14	77	22
3rd	33	101	36
4th	55	175	73
5th	61	187	73
6th	94	281	73
7th	98	373	87
8th	113		87
9th	123		93
10th	135		93

Umpires: D. J. Constant and N. T. Plews Captain* Wicket-keeper†

England v West Indies 1988 (Fourth Test)

VENUE: Headingley
DATE: 21, 22, 23, 25, 26 July. West Indies won the toss
RESULT: West Indies won by 10 wickets

Batted First: England

1 G. A. Gooch	c Dujon b Marshall	9	c Hooper b Walsh	50
2 T. S. Curtis	lbw b Benjamin	12	b Ambrose	12
3 C. W. J. Athey	lbw b Ambrose	16	c Dujon b Walsh	11
4 D. I. Gower	c Dujon b Benjamin	13	c Dujon b Marshall	2
5 A. J. Lamb	retired hurt	64	(8) c Dujon b Ambrose	19
6 R. A. Smith	c Dujon b Ambrose	38	(5) lbw b Marshall	11
7 C. S. Cowdrey*	lbw b Marshall	0	(6) b Walsh	5
8 C. J. Richards†	b Ambrose	2	(7) b Ambrose	8
9 D. R. Pringle	c Dujon b Marshall	0	b Benjamin	3
10 N. A. Foster	not out	8	c Hooper b Benjamin	0
11 G. R. Dilley	c Hooper b Ambrose	8	not out	2
Extras (B 1, LB 18, W 6, NB 6)		31	(B 3, LB 8, NB 4)	15
Total		201		138

Batted Second: West Indies

1 D. L. Haynes	lbw b Pringle	54	not out	25
2 P. J. L. Dujon†	c Smith b Dilley	13	not out	40
3 C. L. Hooper	lbw b Foster	19		
4 I. V. A. Richards*	c Curtis b Foster	18		
5 A. L. Logie	c Foster b Pringle	44		
6 K. L. T. Arthurton	c Richards b Pringle	27		
7 R. A. Harper	c Gower b Foster	56		
8 M. D. Marshall	c Gooch b Pringle	3		
9 C. E. L. Ambrose	lbw b Pringle	8		
10 W. K. M. Benjamin	run out	9		
11 C. A. Walsh	not out	9		
Extras (LB 15)		15	(LB 2)	2
Total		275	(no wkt)	67

Bowling

	O	M	R	W	O	M	R	W
West Indies								
Marshall	23	8	55	3	17	4	47	2
Ambrose	25.1	8	58	4	19.5	4	40	3
Benjamin	9	2	27	2	5	4	2	2
Walsh	12	4	42	0	20	9	38	3
England								
Dilley	20	5	59	1	4	0	16	0
Foster	32.2	6	98	3	7	1	36	0
Pringle	27	7	95	5				
Cowdrey	2	0	8	0	3.3	0	13	0

Fall of Wickets

	E	WI	E
	1st	1st	2nd
1st	14	15	56
2nd	43	61	80
3rd	58	97	85
4th	80	137	85
5th	183	156	105
6th	183	194	105
7th	185	210	127
8th	185	222	132
9th	201	245	132
10th		275	138

Umpires: H. D. Bird and D. R. Shepherd Captain* Wicket-keeper†

England v West Indies 1988 (Fifth Test)

VENUE: Kennington Oval
DATE: 4, 5, 6, 8 August. England won the toss
RESULT: West Indies won by 8 wickets

Batted First: England

1 G. A. Gooch*	c Logie b Ambrose	9	c Greenidge b Ambrose	84
2 T. S. Curtis	c Dujon b Benjamin	30	lbw b Marshall	15
3 R. J. Bailey	c Dujon b Ambrose	43	b Benjamin	3
4 R. A. Smith	c Harper b Marshall	57	lbw b Benjamin	0
5 M. P. Maynard	c Dujon b Ambrose	3	(6) c and b Benjamin	10
6 D. J. Capel	c Marshall b Harper	16	(7) lbw b Walsh	12
7 C. J. Richards†	c Logie b Harper	0	(8) c Dujon b Walsh	3
8 D. R. Pringle	c Dujon b Marshall	1	(9) b Harper	8
9 P. A. J. DeFreitas	c Haynes b Harper	18	(10) c Haynes b Harper	0
10 N. A. Foster	c sub b Marshall	7	(5) c Logie b Benjamin	34
11 J. H. Childs	not out	0	not out	0
Extras (LB 6, NB 15)		21	(B 3, LB 15, NB 15)	33
Total		205		202

Batted Second: West Indies

1 C. G. Greenidge	c DeFreitas b Foster	10	c Richards b Childs	77
2 D. L. Haynes	c Richards b Foster	2	not out	77
3 C. L. Hooper	c Gooch b Foster	11	b Foster	23
4 I. V. A. Richards*	c Curtis b Foster	0		
5 A. L. Logie	c Gooch b Foster	47	(4) not out	38
6 P. J. L. Dujon†	lbw b Pringle	64		
7 R. A. Harper	run out	17		
8 M. D. Marshall	c and b Childs	0		
9 C. E. L. Ambrose	not out	17		
10 W. K. M. Benjamin	b Pringle	0		
11 C. A. Walsh	c DeFreitas b Pringle	5		
Extras (LB 7, W 1, NB 2)		10	(B 2, LB 3, NB 6)	11
Total		183	(2 wkts)	226

Bowling

	O	M	R	W	O	M	R	W
West Indies								
Marshall	24.3	3	64	3	25	6	52	1
Ambrose	20	6	31	3	24.1	10	50	1
Walsh	10	1	21	0	12	5	21	2
Benjamin	14	2	33	1	22	4	52	4
Harper	21	7	50	3	6	3	9	2
Hooper	1	1	0	0				
England								
Foster	16	2	64	5	18	3	52	1
DeFreitas	13	4	33	0	17	2	46	0
Pringle	17	4	45	3	13	4	24	0
Capel	7	0	21	0	3	0	20	0
Childs	6	1	13	1	40	16	79	1

Fall of Wickets

	E	WI	E	WI
	1st	1st	2nd	2nd
1st	12	9	50	131
2nd	77	16	55	162
3rd	116	16	55	
4th	121	57	108	
5th	160	126	125	
6th	160	155	139	
7th	165	156	157	
8th	196	167	175	
9th	198	168	177	
10th	205	183	202	

Umpires: H. D. Bird and K. E. Palmer Captain* Wicket-keeper†